Super Sundays

I–XVI

LOU SAHADI

Super

Contemporary Books, Inc.
Chicago

Sundays
I–XVI

Library of Congress Cataloging in Publication Data

Sahadi, Lou.
    Super Sundays I–XVI.

    1. Super Bowl Game (Football)—History.
I. Title.   II. Title: Super Sundays 1–16.
GV956.2.S8S23   1982   796.332′7   82-45436
ISBN 0-8092-5623-1   AACR2

Published by Contemporary Books, Inc.
180 North Michigan Avenue, Chicago, Illinois 60601
Manufactured in the United States of America
Library of Congress Catalog Card Number: 82-45436
International Standard Book Number: 0-8092-5623-1

Published simultaneously in Canada by
Beaverbooks, Ltd.
150 Lesmill Road
Don Mills, Ontario M3B 2T5
Canada

Dedication

For Mickey Palmer, who not only attended all sixteen Super Bowls, but without whose color shots this book would have been difficult to produce.

Contents

FOREWORD   IX

SUPER BOWL **I**   KANSAS CITY-GREEN BAY   XIV

SUPER BOWL **II**   GREEN BAY-OAKLAND   10

SUPER BOWL **III** NEW YORK-BALTIMORE   22

SUPER BOWL **IV**   MINNESOTA-KANSAS CITY   34

SUPER BOWL **V**   BALTIMORE-DALLAS   46

SUPER BOWL **VI**   DALLAS-MIAMI   60

SUPER BOWL **VII** MIAMI-WASHINGTON   76

SUPER BOWL **VIII** MINNESOTA-MIAMI   88

SUPER BOWL **IX**   PITTSBURGH-MINNESOTA   98

SUPER BOWL **X**   DALLAS-PITTSBURGH   108

SUPER BOWL **XI**   OAKLAND-MINNESOTA   118

SUPER BOWL **XII**   DALLAS-DENVER   128

SUPER BOWL **XIII**   PITTSBURGH-DALLAS   138

SUPER BOWL **XIV**   PITTSBURGH-LOS ANGELES   150

SUPER BOWL **XV**   OAKLAND-PHILADELPHIA   164

SUPER BOWL **XVI**   SAN FRANCISCO-CINCINNATI   174

INDEX   187

Foreword

Super Bowl I was a very memorable occasion for the Kansas City Chiefs and the American Football League. It provided us with the opportunity to compete in the first Super Bowl, a game we sincerely thought we could win. It was an emotional day because of the strong feeling we had for our league. The fact that Lamar Hunt, our owner, was the founder of the American Football League made it even more meaningful. We played the game for ourselves, naturally; for Kansas City—but also for all the players, coaches, owners, and organizations in the entire history of the league.

We were a very explosive team offensively and felt we could score on Green Bay. We were, however, concerned about our ability to stop the Packers. Our only chance was to outscore them. Our plan was to throw inside and in front of the Packer secondary and to run right at the defense and also feature our play-action passes.

The plan was effective in the first half; only the pinpoint passing of Bart Starr and the incredible catches of Max McGee were the difference in the 14-10 halftime score.

An interception in the third quarter by Willie Wood blew the game open. The Packers, with no concern about our running and play-action passes, controlled the game and won it 35-10. It was a bitter disappointment, but it strongly pointed out our weakness and helped us develop and grow as a team. We got the players we needed and went on to be the winningest team during the ten-year history of the American Football League—and eventually we were winners of Super Bowl IV.

In his book, Lou Sahadi, through astute observation of fact and his close association with coaches and players in the NFL, captures the emotional and competitive climate of all sixteen Super Bowls and gives us an insight that only he could give.

Hank Stram

Acknowledgments

The author wishes to express his thanks to the following, who assisted in the completion of this book: Fran Connors, National Football League; Marge Blatt, Baltimore Colts; Joe Gordon, Pittsburgh Steelers; Frank Ramos, New York Jets; Al Locasale, Oakland Raiders.

Super Sundays

I-XVI

Super Bowl I

Kansas City (AFL)	0	10	0	0	—	10
Green Bay (NFL)	7	7	14	7	—	35

xiv

It was the realization of a dream. A six-year one. It wasn't exactly a peaceful dream. Rather, it was one filled with anxieties, disappointments, hopes, and fears. Yet, it was a typical American dream, one that held fulfillment and joy. And in the waking moments of a warm, California Sunday in the middle of January, the dream was realized. Historians will log the date as January 15, 1967. That was the start of it all. The first Super Bowl—in Roman numeral terminology, Super Bowl I. That's where it was for the American Football League. It had taken six long years to become recognized, to be accepted. They were now members of the lodge. The crusty National Football League opened its hallowed halls to the new kid on the block.

Yet, perhaps because of disbelief or lack of interest, the football public didn't exactly storm the gates of the Los Angeles Coliseum. When the Kansas City Chiefs of the AFL met the fabled Green Bay Packers of the NFL on that golden afternoon, only 63,036 of the 93,000 seats had somebody in them. That meant that one-third of the arena was empty. It could have been that the sophisticated football denizens of Los Angeles were not warmed by the prospect of the mighty legions of Green Bay girding themselves against the weak minions of Kansas City. They were definitely in no mood for the anticipated carnage of the lions devouring the Christians according to ancient scripture.

Modern scripture had established the Packers as solid 13-point favorites. That was how it was listed on the books in Las Vegas. There were very few who found it convenient to argue with the oddsmakers. After all, the Packers were already being enshrined in pro football's Hall of Fame as one of the greatest teams of all time. They

had won championships in four of the last six years under the coaching genius of Vince Lombardi, who, because of his ancestral lineage, had been likened to a Roman general. No other coach dominated professional football like Lombardi. He was the epitome of excellence and indeed a disciple of discipline who demanded the ultimate sacrifice from his players. It was only fitting that his team should represent the NFL in its first encounter with the AFL.

And, too, it was only fitting that the Chiefs should play in a game of such magnitude against the NFL champions. It was the Chiefs' owner, Lamar Hunt, who first envisioned a second professional football league in 1959. A year later, Hunt and seven other enterprising owners launched the American Football League to the drum beat of a million skeptics who looked upon their adventure as pure folly. They labored under the banner of the "Foolish Club," while experts scoffed at their league as nothing more than a collection of NFL discards and inferior college players who were below NFL standards.

Symbolically, it was Hunt who coined the name Super Bowl, only not by design. A quiet, reserved individual who plans and analyzes such business matters as the start of another league, Hunt came upon the name quite accidentally. He was sitting around his home one day observing his children playing.

"My kids have this ball; maybe you've seen it advertised on television," he said. "It's about the size of a handball, but it bounces ten times higher than a normal ball. They call it a Super Ball. My kids kept talking about it so much the name stuck in my mind. It just popped out when we started meetings to arrange the championship game."

Winning coach Vince Lombardi
of the Green Bay Packers.

Hunt's coach, Hank Stram, was a study in contrast to Lombardi. Stram was a gregarious, effervescent individual. Image-conscious, he had a keen awareness of the press, was friendly with writers and broadcasters, often calling them by their first names. He portrayed an image of always being cheerful in sharp contrast to the stern, rigid appearance of Lombardi. Stram was recognized as an innovator with such football strategy as the full-house backfield, the two-back I, the power I, and the moving pocket on offense, and the triple stack on defense. Among his peers in the older NFL, Stram was looked upon as a rebel with his innovative strategies.

"When you prepare for Kansas City, you work overtime, lots of overtime," confessed Buffalo Bills coach Joe Collier. Even then, it wasn't enough. In the AFL championship two weeks before, the Chiefs scalped the Bills, 31-7, displaying a great deal of Stram's offensive hardware.

"We wanted to shrink their reaction time," explained Stram quite simply afterward.

So elated were the Chiefs after the Buffalo victory that they had marked the occasion with the most raucous celebration in the team's seven-year history. Although the league had issued a dictum prohibiting champagne in the dressing room, the Chiefs had about five cases of the bubbly beverage hidden in the shower. That's how confident they were of victory. They wanted to play in the first Super Bowl with the passion they were feeling at that particular moment for champagne.

Clad only in a hat, middle linebacker Sherrill Headrick sat on a trunk and drank straight out of the bottle. The players escorted Stram into the shower, liberally pouring champagne over his head and over Hunt's. For their over-enthusiastic display of joy, the Chiefs were fined $2,000 by AFL commissioner Milt Woodard. He probably decided on that course of action later that evening at the team's victory celebration at a Buffalo hotel. E. J. Holub, the tall outside linebacker, displayed a surgeon's skill by cutting Woodard's tie below the knot. For all their wild endeavors, the Chiefs would have gladly paid $20,000.

Especially the team's quarterback, Len Dawson. He had languished on the bench for five years in the NFL, first at Pittsburgh

and later at Cleveland. He was a special reclamation project of Stram, who had been an assistant coach at Purdue in the years when Dawson starred. A picture quarterback, Dawson had led the AFL in passing for the third time in five years.

"When you're not winning, people always want to change the quarterback," explained Dawson. "That's added pressure to the tension that naturally goes with the position. I was going through a couple of frustrating years. Actually, I was having excellent seasons statistically, but I found out then that statistics didn't mean anything except one thing—winning. Since we weren't winning championships, the fans were not satisfied.

"After the Buffalo game, we went back to the hotel to watch the Green Bay-Dallas game for the NFL championship. The sentiment of most of the players was with Dallas. They wanted to play Dallas because of the past association of when we were the Dallas Texans. Personally, I didn't look at it that way. I didn't much care who won the game. I was just happy at that particular time that we were going to be at least half of the representatives in the game. Green Bay had been dominating the NFL the past few years and justifiably so because they had excellent personnel and a winning tradition, which was really important. They always believed that they would win, and this was evident in the game with Dallas. They came up with a great goal line stand to stop the Cowboys on the two-yard line in the closing minutes of play. The final score was 34-27, and thus they earned the right to represent the NFL.

"We were all elated after the Green Bay-Dallas game; and everybody's feeling was that we were finally going to get an opportunity to prove that we could compete against the NFL, showing that we were as good as they were. The younger players were anxious to play because they had made the choice to sign with the AFL instead of the NFL before the merger, and they had been downgraded ever since. This would also be a big event for me after having spent five years in the NFL, sitting on the bench watching all the time. I was quite anxious to play in the game, although I knew that it would be a really rough one because Green Bay was a great football team."

Although the game wasn't until January

Kansas City running back Mike Garrett moves through a small hole.

15, Stram took the Chiefs out to the West Coast on January 4. They were camped in Long Beach, and Stram wanted to have a relaxed atmosphere. Instead of imposing a strict nightly curfew, he placed his players on an honor system that would enable them to be in their rooms by midnight. The only time he would enforce an 11 P.M. rule would be the night before the game.

Then he made another change. Instead of having the players eat as a team every evening, he let them dine on their own. This was much the same routine the players were used to when they played a home game during the regular season. With this approach, Stram felt that a great deal of the pre-game tension would be alleviated. The game itself presented enough.

But the tranquility of the Chiefs' training grounds was disrupted a few days after the players were getting settled in their West Coast environs. Fred Williamson, their controversial cornerback, was making inflammatory statements about the Packers in general and some players in particular. Williamson himself had been a subject of discussion throughout the season for his rough style of play. He was a vicious tackler who would come around with his right arm, fist clenched, taking aim at his opponent's head while making a tackle. Because of the brutish nature of the maneuver, he was known as "The Hammer."

"I haven't seen anything in the films that offers much of a threat to me," boasted Williamson. "I'll be able to cover either Boyd Dowler or Carroll Dale. I don't see any Lance Alworths, Charlie Hennigans, or Elbert Dubenions in their films. Dale and Dowler don't have the speed or the combination moves of our own Otis Taylor. Did you notice the deep passes they were catching on Dallas? I guarantee you they won't beat me on a deep pattern. Dale has moves like Art Graham of Boston, and Dowler is like Glenn Bass of Buffalo. And Graham and Bass are not among the top receivers in our league.

"Dowler is so big he can shield the defensive back off the ball. On the curls and hitches, I'll have to play him; but on the deep passes, I'll be able to play the ball. The way he shields the ball, I won't be able to gamble. I can't go around him and play the ball if I'm not sure where it is.

"I got some experience covering a tall receiver when Reg Carolan was at split end and I worked against him in practice. I'll just dump Dowler when he leaves the line of scrimmage. If he catches the ball, I'll drop the hammer on him. Two hammers on Dowler and one on Dale should be enough. Bart Starr? Who's he, anyway?"

It was only the beginning. A week before the game, *Life* magazine had carried a story on the Chiefs. Naturally, the outspoken

3

Williamson was quoted most prominently. He openly boasted of how much damage he was prepared to inflict on Green Bay. While Williamson was generating publicity, most of his teammates were upset at what was going on. In fact, one evening as Williamson was walking through the lobby of the hotel, some of his teammates saw him and turned away. They didn't want any part of him.

"I feel as a football player representing a team and a city we should present an image of modesty and class," pointed out safety Johnny Robinson. "Under the circumstances, I felt we were made to look as if we were in a comic strip. As a player, I don't want someone like that representing me. I'm not perfect; but I try to project an image of being a half-decent guy, of someone who is dedicated to the game.

"I think this guy put me in a bad light by saying the things he did. In that vein I think he was wrong. You also have the psychological factor. If anyone says he's going to beat your brains out, this has to give you added incentive. I just don't like it."

Neither did Dawson, or Stram for that matter.

"It didn't sit too well with everybody on the club because we knew that Green Bay was going to be tough enough without getting them too fired up," remarked Dawson. "Stram thought it wouldn't be psychologically sound to say or do anything that would rile them up. You don't win wars and battles with words. One way or another you have to go out and do the job."

Stram was riled by Williamson's remarks. He strongly believed that it was a bad reflection on the Chiefs. Then, he was concerned that the Packers would certainly make use of Williamson's statements as a weapon in the psychological warfare that at times exists before a game of this importance.

The coach's immediate reaction was not only to inflict a fine on Williamson but to suspend him from playing in the game. But upon reflecting further, he felt a suspension would create a wave of dissension in the club, especially among the black players. Instead, Stram sternly warned Williamson not to make any more damaging statements.

Buck Buchanan, the Chiefs' big defensive tackle, had defended Williamson, which was a good reason why Stram did not sus-

pend the cornerback from playing. The Chiefs would have definitely been split.

"My thoughts are that a person says what he wants to say," remarked Buchanan. "It has all got to be proved by the way you play the game. That was Fred's personality. He had a lot of confidence. They always talked about a lot of the guys not liking Freddy, but I have always liked him. He has been great as far as I am concerned.

"It's his personality to talk a lot. He got a lot of publicity. Most of the white guys were upset about it, but I wasn't upset. I don't think the blacks were upset about it at all. He was just doing his thing. It's just like when people talk about Joe Namath and Daryle Lamonica. They are doing what they think is right, and that's how it is as far as I'm concerned."

The tension of the game was building. Perhaps the Chiefs felt it more than the Packers. Kansas City was a younger team and wasn't exposed to the pressure of big games as much as Green Bay. Three days before the game, Dawson himself felt his emotional strings tighten considerably.

"It got to be murder the last few days, getting ready for the game," Dawson confessed. "My wife and two children came down and were staying at the same motel, but they didn't dare come near me because I was so high-strung waiting to play.

"It was the same with most of the other players. They couldn't eat. They just couldn't hold any food down. Two weeks before the game is much too long a time.

"In watching Green Bay on film for two weeks, I could see that they were a solid team. Checking their defensive alignments and moves, I could see that they didn't make any mistakes. Not that they were superhuman, but they played exceedingly well as a team. They had a fine defensive rush from end Willie Davis and tackle Henry Jordan. They came at you all the time. And their linebackers—Ray Nitschke, who was having a great year, Dave Robinson and Leroy Caffey—constituted a real fine trio. We hadn't faced any better group of linebackers all year.

"Their secondary, featuring Herb Adderley and Bob Jeter at cornerback and Willie Wood and Tom Brown at the safeties, was a tightly knit unit. The Packers didn't display a number of variations as far as defense was concerned, such as we encountered in our

4

league. It was basically a four-man front with three linebackers, and they played man-to-man coverage in the secondary.

"The films revealed that Green Bay's pursuit was excellent. We were going to have a tough job containing them if we counted on throwing the ball. We were going to have to run it. In order to make a passing game effective, we were going to have to establish a ground game.

"Generally, prior to a game, the tension builds on the shoulders of a quarterback. He is the one everybody is watching because he handles the ball most of the time. My case was no exception. I felt like a pressure cooker. I was hoping we could get a couple of breaks and have a solid chance to play our type of game. We had to make the

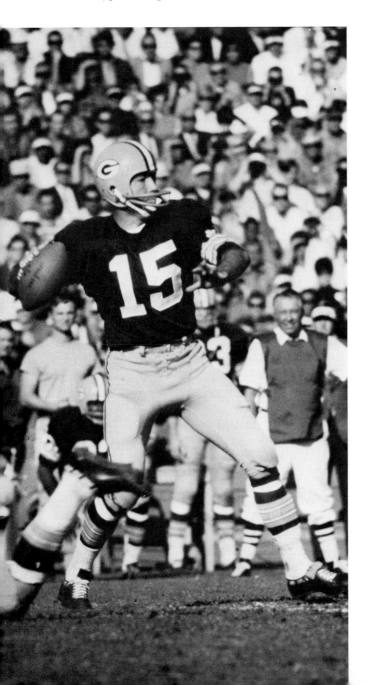

Green Bay quarterback Bart Starr has plenty of time to line up a receiver.

Packers do what we wanted them to do when we were on the attack, not let their defense dictate to us the kind of offensive maneuvers we'd employ.

"What is amazing about a crucial, championship contest is that the actual playing is not the difficult part. Rather, it is the waiting and the getting ready. It is the 10 or 15 minutes prior to going on the field to be introduced after you have warmed up. That to me is the most miserable part you can spend. Here it is, almost game time but not quite. You have done everything you possibly can do to get ready, and you are hoping that you prepared correctly and that the execution will be there. You don't have to worry about the other people. You just hope you can do your job to the best of your ability."

Lombardi set up shop in Santa Barbara with a business-as-usual approach. He prepared his champions on a low-key scale. His veteran squad had been there before. They knew all too well the significance of a big game. A man of few words, Lombardi let his personality speak on the playing field itself. He did not believe in any innovations or trickery. Rather, his football philosophy was summarized in one word, execution. Lombardi tirelessly ran plays over and over again in practice. He would rather have had one play work to perfection than a couple that were mediocre. And, he made certain his players worked hard to achieve their maximum.

"Kansas City's shifting pocket for the quarterback is nothing new," claimed Lombardi. "A good number of college teams use it. Their odd spacing of the defense won't bother us, either. That's nothing new. When George Wilson was coaching the Lions in the 1950s, he used it against us. After all, we've been in the business a long time; and it's pretty hard to get anything new into football.

"Don't worry about us being up for this game. If my team is taking on Kansas City lightly and isn't up emotionally Sunday, I'll be the most disappointed man in the world. Winning is like a drug. It's a hard thing to kick. We're playing for the Green Bay Packers, not the NFL."

It was Lombardi's way of putting down

5

The Chiefs' star wide receiver Otis Taylor gets squeezed by Herb Adderley, on ground, and Willie Davis.

all the media syndrome of building the game as something of a war of the worlds, the NFL against the AFL. It was his simple approach of getting ready to play a game. It was in contrast to what Stram felt.

"There's been a battle of words on paper for the last six years over whether we can compete with an NFL team, and it'll be settled on the grass out there at the Coliseum," exclaimed Stram. "We're not playing this one for the Chiefs. We're playing for every owner, coach, player, official, and anyone else who has ever had anything to do with the American Football League. We're playing for the people who had faith in the AFL during those dark early years."

Lombardi's sentiments were largely echoed by his players. Their approach was merely an extension of the coach's personality. They weren't awed by the magnitude of what the game represented.

"This is a game like any other," pointed out star fullback Jim Taylor. "Sure, we're up for it; but we're not excited. This is a tough game. You go out; and if you're man enough, you win. You do what you have to do, and you don't make a mistake. You don't have to get excited. If you lose, the world goes on. It's not a matter of life or death."

Lombardi exemplified his basic approach to the first Super Bowl in his daily practices. Despite the fact that it was a post-season game, far from the regimen of training camp, Lombardi had his defensive linemen tackling the sled. The linemen accepted it.

"It's not the same as having a 'live' back to tackle, because the sled doesn't move," explained star defensive tackle Henry Jordan. "But it's a good chance to get the feel of wrapping our arms around an object and wrestling it to the ground.

"A lineman does most of his work with his arms in close to his body, but to tackle properly you have to be sure to get your arms out and around your target. We didn't have any tackling practice in Tulsa in preparation for the NFL title game in Dallas, and it may have affected our performance. You've got to be careful not to try to just slap at your man with your forearm. That just doesn't work.

"I remember when Dan Currie was with the Packers. I always considered him one of the best tacklers I ever saw. Well, he'd work on his technique every day in slow motion. That's why he was so good at it, among other things."

Why the Packers were so good on offense was because of quarterback Bart Starr. He was a dividend nobody expected. Starr was so lightly regarded that he was selected on the 17th round of the 1956 college player draft. He was the 199th player picked and only then because he was recommended by no less than Alabama basketball coach Johnny Dee.

"We knew the Chiefs were physically strong and very talented, but that was about all we knew," admitted Starr. "As we got ready to play, we didn't really know what to expect. But we had another very good game plan, one that could be exploited very well.

"Coach Lombardi had a theory that any time a team tried to play us with two or more linebackers inside of their defensive ends that we should throw the ball because they couldn't possibly get out to cover on outside patterns."

So, on a sunny, hazy Sunday, with the temperature at 72 degrees, players of the NFL and the AFL met and shook hands for the first time on a football field. It was a momentous occasion that was symbolized by the releasing of 4,000 pigeons. Peace now existed between the two leagues. Only a few mid-air collisions of the fleeing birds served as a reminder of the six-year war.

The Packers went on the offense first. Starr took command on the 25-yard line. But after producing one first down, he was jostled by the fired-up Kansas City defense. Twice he was dropped for a loss while attempting to pass.

However, the next time Green Bay got the ball, they scored. Starr was the reason. Beginning on the 20-yard line, he got the Packers on the board in just six plays. He completed all four of his passes, the payoff being a 37-yard strike to wide receiver Max McGee, who replaced the injured Boyd Dowler. McGee reached behind him and caught the ball with one hand. Don Chandler's conversion gave the Packers a 7-0 lead.

Kansas City tried to come back after the kickoff. Dawson moved the Chiefs from the 13-yard line to the Green Bay 33. However, on fourth down, Mike Mercer's 40-yard field goal attempt sailed wide to the right. The quarter ended less than two minutes later.

A Green Bay punt gave the Chiefs the ball back again on the 34-yard line. Dawson took charge when the second quarter began. In six plays he tied the score much to the surprise of the Coliseum crowd. He completed the three passes he threw, the final one a seven-yard toss to fullback Curtis McClinton for the game-tying touchdown.

Aroused, Green Bay struck back. They took the kickoff and methodically marched 73 yards for a touchdown. The drive consumed 13 plays with Taylor breaking loose on a 14-yard run. It was a picture play. Taylor ran around left end behind guards Jerry Kramer and Fuzzy Thurston on the famous Green Bay sweep.

But the Chiefs didn't quit. Dawson again was the key. Beginning on his own 26, he quickly directed the Chiefs' second scoring drive. It took only seven plays, four of them passes with Dawson completing every one. Then, with less than a minute remaining, Mercer kicked a 31-yard field goal to narrow Green Bay's edge to 14-10 as the first half came to a conclusion.

The close score of the first half had most of the Coliseum throng buzzing. Kansas City's performance certainly established them as a threat. The four-point Packer margin was by no means definitive. In fact, the Chiefs had outgained the Packers 181 yards to 164 and made 11 first downs to Green Bay's nine. The upstart AFL's hopes were bright indeed.

Taking the second half kickoff, Dawson had a mild drive going. After a first down, he was faced with a third and five on his own 49-yard line. A pass was obvious. Willie Wood anticipated it and stepped in front of tight end Fred Arbanas and intercepted on the Green Bay 45. He ran all the way to the Kansas City five-yard line before he was caught. It took Elijah Pitts just one play to

7

Kansas City quarterback Len Dawson fires a pass after rolling out to his left.

score and push Green Bay's advantage to 21-10.

With less than a minute remaining in the third period, the Packers scored again. It took Starr ten plays to complete a 56-yard drive. Once again reverting to the pass, he hit McGee again, this time with a 13-yard aerial for a 28-10 Packer bulge. When the quarter ended, it appeared that the Chiefs were doomed.

To make sure, Starr ignited another scoring drive midway through the final period. He negotiated the Packers 80 yards in just eight plays, with Pitts scoring from a yard out. The three passes Starr completed accounted for 69 of the 80 yards. The 35-10 Packer bulge remained when the game ended.

The Packers were relieved, and the Chiefs disappointed. Not only did the Packers win, but they succeeded in doing so by a decisive margin. Even Lombardi looked satisfied.

"Our best game?" pondered Lombardi. "No, I wouldn't say this was one of our better games. We were not aggressive enough at the start. Our defense was grabbing instead of tackling. Their stacked defense dictated why we passed so much. They do a lot of unusual things on defense, and it's difficult to run against them. But they can't get a very good rush on the passer out of the stack, and you can pass on them. The Kansas City secondary played very loose. They seemed to be daring us to throw against them. We were glad to accommodate them.

"We actually made very few adjustments in the second half. Our game plan was basically sound, and we stayed with it. The difference was that we played more aggressively in the second half. I told the players, 'Start tackling and stop grabbing.'

"In my opinion the Chiefs don't rate with the top teams in the National Football League. They're a good football team with fine speed, but I'll have to say NFL football is tougher. Dallas is better and so are several others. But I really don't want to get into this kind of comparison. Yet, I've said what you wanted me to say, didn't I?"

Starr was the obvious hero with his precision passing. He connected on 17 of 23 passes for 250 yards and two touchdowns. But the receiver who caught the touchdown passes, McGee, was an unlikely hero. During the regular season, the veteran 34-year-old flanker caught only four passes for 91 yards. Yet, against the Chiefs, he grabbed seven passes for 138 yards when he entered the game as a replacement for Boyd Dowler, the team's regular flanker.

McGee was sitting on the bench with the injured Paul Hornung. They were discussing, of all things, Hornung's wedding plans. Like McGee, Hornung had been one of the prime eligible bachelors in the NFL. The two were close, roommates on the road, running around together, many times after curfew hours.

"I almost fell off the bench when Lombardi called me," said McGee, smiling. "I thought he was going to fine me for not paying attention. I like to have fun, and Vince doesn't like you to have too much fun. It's cost me chunks of money in fines, but that's usually during training camp.

"Anyway, I like to run to the left side, and the cornerback Willie Mitchell gave me room underneath. They give you more room than NFL defenses do; and there's nobody who can cover man-to-man like that, not even an old man like me. I don't get there as fast as I used to, but I still get to the same place. I guess now we can play Alabama and get the whole thing settled."

On that one day, the argument of which was the better league was settled. But it was only the beginning . . .

9

Super Bowl II

Green Bay (NFL)	3	13	10	7	—	33
Oakland (AFL)	0	7	0	7	—	14

It was almost as if the game was secondary. Perhaps the previous year's relatively easy victory had something to do with it, or the mere fact that the Green Bay Packers were back again. Two Super Bowls. The mighty legions of coach Vince Lombardi were the first team to appear twice in the Super Bowl arena. It bordered on perfection. But then again, that was what the world of professional football had come to expect of Lombardi and the Packers. In the past six years, they had ruled the professional ranks. From 1961 through 1966, they had won five championships. And now they were back again in Super Bowl II to see if they could win again.

But for awhile, the interest did not really center on the game itself. The oddsmakers didn't help any. They established the Packers as solid 14-point favorites to defeat the Oakland Raiders. They still looked down their noses at the younger American Football League. But earlier in the week in Miami, there were strong rumors circulating that this was going to be Lombardi's last game as a coach. That was almost more momentous than the game itself. It was like Moses coming down from the mountain.

The game was Sunday. That would take care of itself. But Lombardi quitting, that was now. Nobody dared to ask him directly. No one did that to Lombardi. Maybe, just maybe, it could be hinted; and only then with great temerity. And when somebody did, Lombardi snarled. He was much too clever to be caught off guard, especially on the blind side, and could throw a well-executed block, the kind he demanded on a football field.

At this particular moment, Lombardi was telling his listeners about the electric wiring he had installed under Lambeau Field in Green Bay. Lombardi knew all too well how the field became frozen tundra in the cold days of a Wisconsin winter. Like the year before in the NFL championship game against the Dallas Cowboys when it reached 13 degrees below zero. It was so cold that some of the players walked off the field of that memorable game with frostbite.

"It'll be corrected, and it'll work all right next year," promised Lombardi.

"You mean you'll be back in Green Bay?" someone asked.

Lombardi paused, fully realizing the significance of the question.

"I'll be back in Green Bay," he snapped. "As coach?"

Oakland quarterbacks George Blanda, left, and Daryle Lamonica discuss strategy.

Miami's Orange Bowl was the setting for Super Bowl II.

Now he snarled. The trap play was being carried out all the way.

"I don't think this is the time to discuss that," he growled.

But the obvious was there. He didn't deny or confirm that he would return as coach. What he wanted to do now in the remaining few days was to concentrate on the game itself. He didn't want any distractions. He never did. Football was a 24-hour challenge to him just about 12 months a year.

The rumored heir apparent to Lombardi's coaching job was his long-time defensive aide, Phil Bengtson. He had been on Lombardi's staff for nine years, the only coach who remained with him the entire time Lombardi was at Green Bay. Others on Lombardi's staff, Norb Hecker, Tom Fears, and Bill Austin, moved on to head coaching jobs.

These were times of change in pro football, and Lombardi recognized it. Gone was his glorious running tandem of Jim Taylor and Paul Hornung. They retired after Super Bowl I. The game was also beginning to get more complex. Unions and player agents had brought another dimension to the sport, one that had practically required full-time attention. In executing the responsibilities of both general manager and head coach, Lombardi's time was being splintered. That bothered him. He believed in total dedication to one job. The presence of the players' union disturbed him.

"I want to tell you something about the players' union," said Lombardi. "Dave Robinson is our player rep; and he didn't attend any meeting, and he didn't cast any vote. Yet, they announced this decision to form a union as unanimous among the player reps. I don't know what the hell the players want anyway; they're making so much money now. Most of them are overpaid.

"If there is one thing wrong with football, it's the length of the season. It's too long. The regular season should never end as late as December 31. There are just too many games and not enough players. I'd like to see the roster limit raised from 40 players to 43 or even 45. We need more bodies. This is our twenty-third game of the season.

"Another thing, I don't think we should move the championship game away from the home city to a warm, neutral climate. But the Super Bowl would have to be played in the South. It's too late for anything else.

"A lot of people consider the AFL a junior league. But I don't think it makes a lot of difference whether a league is eight years old or forty. You can do a lot of maturing in eight years in this game."

Another story persisted that Lombardi would be leaving Green Bay entirely after the Super Bowl and not remain solely as general manager. Some insiders were positive he would be returning to New York to take over the troubled Jets. It was believable. Lombardi, a native New Yorker, had missed the city and his many friends during the nine years he had been at Green Bay. The Jet job would have offered him a glorious opportunity to return to his native town and some of his favorite haunts such

Oakland wide receiver Warren Wells looks on worriedly from the sidelines.

12

as Mike Manuche's and Toots Shor's.

"The rumors started during the summer," disclosed Bengtson, a quiet person the complete opposite of the fiery Lombardi. "Some of them were utterly ridiculous, not to mention unfounded. During the season, a Chicago columnist with a few inches of space to fill said that I would be the successor to Norm Van Brocklin as head coach of the Minnesota Vikings and that Van Brocklin would come to Green Bay as Lombardi's top assistant. But no team had contacted me for a couple of years. Everybody knew that it would have taken an extremely attractive offer to lure me away from the Packers. Lombardi squelched the rumor for once and for all, and I told the press that I intended to stay right where I was.

"But after that episode, I seemed to have developed an automatic identification in the press as 'Vince Lombardi's heir apparent, Phil Bengtson.' I did nothing to foster it, and Lombardi never once hinted at it. But it would not die. Some columnists and fans managed to convince themselves that Lombardi and I spent most of our spare time up in the throne room discussing the future, but nothing could be further from the truth. The fact is that Lombardi and I never mixed much socially, rarely talked about high level positions of power at any length, and spent very little time speculating on our coaching careers together.

"There simply was no time for politics from June to January. Every year around February 15, just before I left for my annual vacation in Arizona, Vince would stick his head in my office and ask me some mundane question like, 'How many sheets of poster board will you need to set up your depth charts for next year?' I would say, 'About six.' Then we would both smile. Something unspoken carried the message that we intended to work together for another year."

But the Packer players felt something different in Lombardi's actions. For one thing, he wasn't as hard on them as he had been in the previous Super Bowl. He even allowed the players' wives to accompany them. But at the end of the week, the players sensed something that no doubt confirmed their feelings when he addressed them in a team meeting.

Lamonica runs to his right to avoid the Packer rush.

Oakland guard Gene Upshaw offers encouragement to Wells.

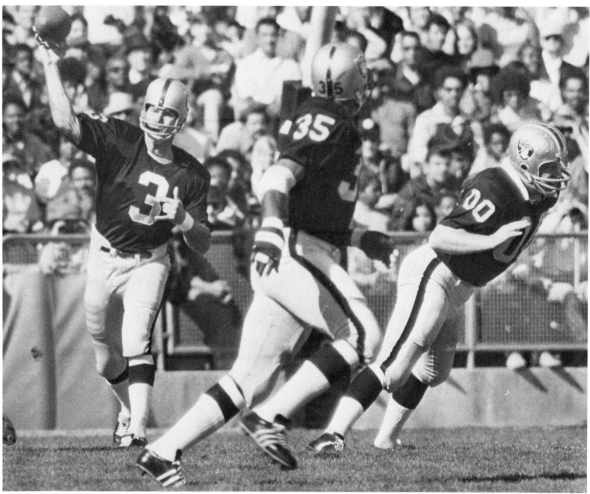

Lamonica fires a quick pass as center Jim Otto (00) and running back Hewritt Dixon (35) offer protection.

"I want to say, first of all, that we know we can win on Sunday," remarked Lombardi. "We are old hands at this game, but we also know that we will have to work harder than ever without letting up for one minute. I want to tell you how very proud I am of all of you. I have told you before that you are the finest team in all of professional football. It's been a long season, and Sunday may be the last time we are all together. Let's make it a good game, a game we can all be proud of."

Like Lombardi, Al Davis, the managing director of the Oakland Raiders, was a strong-willed individual. If there was something that gave him more satisfaction than winning, it hadn't been created yet. Davis was a fighter, a two-fisted one, but with velvet gloves, his manner had such finesse. More than anyone else, he was responsible

for such a game as the Super Bowl in the first place.

The only reason he wasn't regarded with the same awe as Lombardi was merely because he hadn't been around as long. He had rebuilt a weak Raider team in 1963 when he also served as coach. But it was in 1966 when the entire pro football world felt Davis's impact. He served a brief two-month stint as commissioner of the AFL in the spring of 1966. His game plan was to attack, and attack he did. He instituted a policy of raiding the NFL for talent. He struck right at the older league's jugular vein, the quarterback. When defection became a reality, the NFL hollered for peace.

That accomplished, Davis had returned to Oakland but given up coaching. He was still bristling over the fact that the AFL teams had to pay an indemnity to the NFL to become members. Now meeting them on the battlefield, it had all the machinations of a holy war. Davis loved the setting.

"I'm all for the merger," exclaimed Davis, "but I still think we could have licked the NFL; and I think our owners realize it. Look, I've known Vince Lombardi since I was a kid in New York and he was an assistant coach. He's pretty smart. Who's called us a junior league except Lombardi? He was the one who introduced that line of thought, and it wasn't necessary.

"A lot of people think the NFL as a league is over-rated because of weak teams like New Orleans, Atlanta, and Minnesota. But we don't happen to feel that way."

It was his way of subtly getting back at Lombardi. Only Davis could have done it so smoothly. Like Lombardi, he, too, had a way with words. The recognizable difference was that Davis used finesse. But he could be demonstrative when he had to be. He exercised extra precautions in selecting a boys' school in the woods outside of Boca Raton to shield his players' workouts for the Super Bowl game. Not only that, but he employed special security to discourage anyone in the Packers' organization from

trying to observe the Raiders' practice sessions.

Davis was strong-minded enough to enforce his policies, as he had when he took over the sickly Raiders in 1963. The city had been in danger of losing its franchise because of poor attendance, not only from the fact that they were playing their regular season games on a high school field, but from ineptitude as well. In 1961 the Raiders won just two games and in 1962 only one, losing as many as 19 games in a row. In his very first season Davis completely turned the Raiders around. He told his players tersely, "This is a dictatorship, and I'm the dictator." He finished with a 10-4 season and was named AFL Coach of the Year.

It was Wayne Valley, one of the Oakland owners, who had hired Davis over some objections by his other partners. He brazenly defended his selection of Davis.

"I hired him because everybody hated his guts," admitted Valley. "Al Davis wants to win, and he'll do anything to win. After losing all the games we had lost, I wanted to win some any way I could. We needed aggressiveness, and we sure as hell needed a winner."

There were also rumors regarding Davis's status. He, too, had been mentioned as a likely candidate for the Jets job. Like Lombardi, Davis also had New York roots. When he operated for two months out of his Park Avenue office as commissioner of the AFL, Davis made things happen. He was street wise, got things done, and had everybody talking about him and the AFL. He, too, seemed like a natural for the Jets.

"I'd be lying if I told you Sonny Werblin and I hadn't talked about it," confided Davis.

The dominating personalities of Lombardi and Davis practically overshadowed anything else. In fact, in Davis's case, his coach, John Rauch, was almost overlooked. Even though he was the coach, many felt that it was Davis who was still calling the shots. Davis could never be subjected to a lesser role. This game had far too much meaning for him. He was the symbol of the AFL. It was his war.

15

Oakland defensive back Howie Williams runs back an intercepted pass that was intended for Packers' Boyd Dowler (86).

Rauch was the extreme opposite of Davis. While Davis was dynamic to the point of being hyper, Rauch was soft and easy. He made it a point time and again to emphasize that his team didn't have any super stars. Rather, their success was the result of a team effort, both offensively and defensively. While they didn't have a household name like Bart Starr, the Raiders still had a talented young quarterback in Daryle Lamonica.

In one of Davis's better deals, he had obtained Lamonica from the Buffalo Bills. He actually took him off the bench, since Lamonica had lost his regular status with the Bills. Davis had an eye for talent, and the trade paid immediate dividends. Lamonica not only led the Raiders to the AFL championship, but he topped the league in passing.

At the beginning of the week, Lamonica came down with a case of flu. He missed a day of practice, but it didn't seem to worry Rauch too much.

"If he had an ingrown toenail, I'd be worried," said Rauch. "I think he's getting over this flu. But he had a bad case of it, and rest is the only real cure. We'll have a normal week's preparation up to game time, nothing more. Not too many people are excited about little old Oakland.

"Furthermore, there's nothing really new in football. For example, we put in what I thought to be a new play. But George Blanda told me he did the same thing his rookie year with the Chicago Bears. Blanda could do the job Sunday if necessary. But I see no reason why Lamonica won't be ready."

Rauch acknowledged that Lamonica's contribution was one of the main factors that had turned the Raiders into champions with a 13-1 record. He also pointed to the effort of running back Pete Banaszak, who came off the bench the last five games of the season when Clem Daniels was hurt. Banaszak had averaged 5.5 yards a run in 68 carries to keep the Raiders' momentum going.

"Of course, the Packers have so many outlets," mentioned Rauch. "If they can't run, Bart Starr throws to Carroll Dale or Boyd Dowler or Marv Fleming. Their personnel is fantastic, without a weak spot. Weighing their record and attitude over the years, the Packers must be rated the best team in football at this point.

"But don't get me wrong. I don't want to give anybody the opinion we're pessimistic. We're optimistic. We've faced people with winning traditions before, San Diego and Kansas City, for instance. I don't feel the Packers will intimidate us. To be honest, we're a respectable football team physically. We'll just have to play the game and find out. That's why we're here.

"We're confident. We have a good team. How good, we don't know. But we have a great togetherness and have made amazing week-to-week progress. Now we have an opportunity to play the best. It's the biggest event of my athletic career, and I'm sure my players feel the same way. We'll play cautiously on offense and looser on defense until we get the feel of the game.

"The Packers are fantastic. There's no doubt there's a certain mystique about them, the result of their winning record, their pride, their being the best in the game. I hope this Packer mystique doesn't bother us."

By the end of the week, Lamonica was sound. He shook off the flu bug and participated in all of the team's workouts. That removed all doubts that he might not be ready to play on Sunday, although he man-

Packer running back Ben Wilson manages to gain a couple of yards as Ben Davidson closes in.

Packers' Bart Starr successfully gets off pass before being brought down by Tom Keating.

aged to lose four pounds to 208. His ills cured, Lamonica's spirits were naturally high.

"I'm sound," Lamonica said, smiling. "I had a high fever, but the flu has disappeared. My only problem is that I don't want to be too ready. I don't want to be keyed too high. I'm going to try and keep my mind off football on Saturday. I won't be able to, I know. I'll be reading a magazine, and a play situation will pop into my mind. I'll have to force myself to think of other things.

"I know I'll feel the pressure at game time. But if I make a mistake, I hope it's a good honest mistake and not one that results from tensing up. We're a young club, and we haven't tensed up in any other game. We face a great challenge and opportunity. Green Bay is all you can ask for in a football team. Excellent personnel, well-disciplined, experienced, proud. They seldom make mistakes. We just have to play our best to win. We think we can.

"We've got to try to control the ball. They have a superb defense and one without a single glaring weakness, at least from what I've seen in the films. I talked recently with Lenny Dawson of the Kansas City Chiefs, and he suggested you've got to pass often to

beat Green Bay. I'm inclined to disagree. That doesn't mean we won't pass; but once the run is established, the pass becomes that much easier."

The Packers, who had only a 9-4-1 record compared to Oakland's gaudy 13-1, had had trouble with their running game at one point in the season. With the retirement of Taylor and Hornung, the Packers lost the soul of their ground game. They suffered additional woes during the 1967 season. Their replacements, Elijah Pitts and Jim Grabowski, were injured and lost for the remainder of the campaign. The new golden boy, Donny Anderson, was still learning. So, Lombardi had wisely picked up Ben Wilson and Chuck Mercein, two fullbacks nobody else wanted, and won.

Yet, Ben Davidson, the Raiders' big defensive end, could say the same thing from another view. He was with the Packers in 1961 before he was released and ultimately picked up by the Raiders two years later. He was conspicuous by his large handlebar mustache and for his eagerness in wanting to get the opposing team's quarterback.

"They say I'm a wild man, an animal, a bloodthirsty savage," snorted Davidson. "They say I broke Joe Namath's cheekbone for no reason and that I enjoy hurting peo-

17

ple. Now, every time they even suspect me of being too rough, they nail me with a 15-yard penalty. But I was pretty well beat up after that Jet game, so maybe I should start complaining. But, as befits my lower position, I just sit in the whirlpool and don't say a word.

"All this nonsense about intimidating quarterbacks is just that—nonsense. You can't intimidate a quarterback and make him afraid of you. Hell, those guys play every week; and they don't scare. They have to concentrate on the receiver, anyway. I think they feel the pressure, but they don't shake in their shoes out of fear.

"Myself, I'm looking for job security. So there are times when I just won't put up with an offensive guy holding me. He's using an illegal tactic to put my job in jeopardy. When a guy won't stop holding, you have to resort to illegal tactics yourself. What kind of illegal tactics? Kick him. Next time he'll think twice."

Starr wasn't thinking about Davidson. He'd been around too long to be intimidated by any defensive lineman. What he was thinking about was the meeting at which Lombardi had talked to the entire team. Lombardi came to the meeting dressed in a suit instead of his practice togs. That alone caught the players' attention.

"He stood up in front of us, and he told us how much he had enjoyed coaching us that year and how proud he was of us," said Starr. "He just got so choked up he had to start the projector. We all had lumps in our throats. He was so proud; he really was. But we were just as proud of playing for him.

"We felt that if we played our game and didn't make any crucial mistakes, we could win. If you only lose one ball game in the course of a season, like Oakland, you've got to have a fine football team. We can see that in Oakland's films, the way their linebackers support their linemen, the way they get help from the secondary on passes, and the way the secondary covers. You can recognize talent, and they've got a lot of talent.

"I haven't seen Lamonica in the three game films we've got. Our defense studies him, but I haven't seen him throw the first pass. All I've seen is their defense. Of course, I've seen him a few times on televi-

sion, either after we finished a game or maybe when they've played on a Saturday. The way he delivers the ball, he obviously has a great arm. And being new to a ball club, I think he's done a tremendous job of leading them this year.

"They have two very quick tackles in Tom Keating and Dan Birdwell. They get off the ball as quick as anyone we've seen. They do a real fine job along with the ends, particularly when they employ their linebackers with them on stunts and blitzes. They create a lot of havoc because, we feel, their linebackers are very quick. They move around extremely well. If they're blocked, they recover quickly. No one has hurt their defense in the three films we saw."

It was a comfortable 68 degrees when both teams lined up for the 3 P.M. kickoff. The Raiders got the ball first. After the kickoff, they didn't gain a yard in three plays and were forced to punt.

Now it was Green Bay's turn for the first time. Starr directed them from the 34 to the Oakland 32-yard line before he stalled. However, Don Chandler kicked a 39-yard field goal to give the Packers an early 3-0 lead.

Although the Raiders made some movement after the kickoff, they had to punt a second time. But Mike Eischeid put the Packers in a hole. His 45-yard punt rolled out of bounds on Green Bay's three-yard line.

But Starr was the least perturbed. After two running plays gained a first down, he hit wide receiver Carroll Dale with a 17-yard pass to get the Packers out of trouble. When the period ended two minutes later, Starr had reached the Raiders' 31-yard line.

After advancing to the 13, Starr was rushed and sacked for an 11-yard loss by Tom Keating, who was playing on a sprained ankle, and Birdwell. However, on the next play he got the 11 yards back with a pass to Fleming. It merely served to position Chandler's 20-yard field goal for a 6-0 Packer lead.

The Raiders still couldn't do anything. After the kickoff, they had to punt for the third time. This time the Packers had much better field position, operating from their own 38. On one play, Starr brought the

18

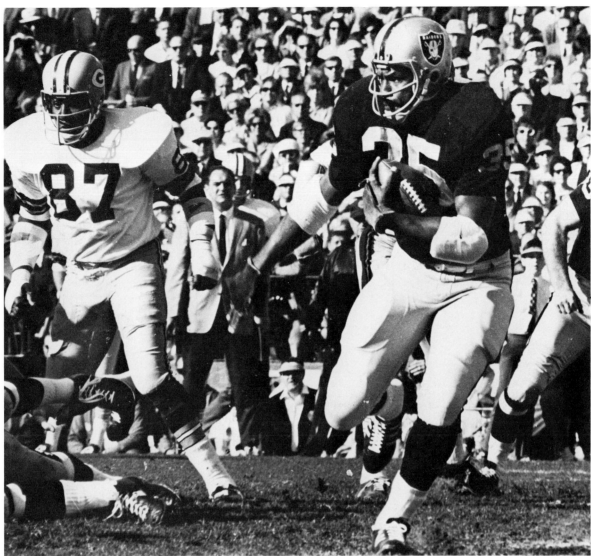

Oakland's Hewritt Dixon breaks loose as Willie Davis (87) begins pursuit.

crowd of 75,546 to its feet. He sent wide receiver Boyd Dowler on a deep pattern and caught the Raider secondary by surprise. Dowler faked a move to the sidelines and sped straight downfield. Without breaking stride he reached up for Starr's perfectly timed pass and a 62-yard touchdown that gave the Packers a 13-0 edge.

After the touchdown, the Raiders came to life. Starting on their own 22-yard line, Lamonica fired the Raiders for a 78-yard drive. The touchdown came on the ninth play, a 23-yard pass to wide receiver Bill

Miller. It was a neatly executed play as Lamonica zeroed in on Miller, who got between linebacker Dave Robinson and cornerback Herb Adderley on the five-yard line.

Fired up, Oakland's defense stopped the Packers in three plays; and the Raiders got the ball back with four minutes left in the half. But the 40-year-old Blanda missed on a 47-yard field goal attempt.

It appeared the half would end with the Packers on top by only 13-7. But Green Bay got a break. Oakland's Roger Bird fumbled a punt after signaling for a fair catch on the

Lamonica gets ready to throw as Packers' Henry Jordan moves in.

Oakland 45. The Packers recovered; and just before the half ended, Chandler booted his third field goal, this one from 43 yards.

In the third period, Starr again outsmarted the Raider secondary. Beginning on his own 18-yard line, Starr was faced with a third and one on his 40. He figured the Raiders would play the run and cooly hit his veteran 35-year-old wide receiver Max McGee with a 35-yard pass on the Oakland 25. Seven plays later, Anderson scored from the two-yard line to push the Green Bay advantage to 23-7.

Then, two seconds before the third period ended, the Packers put more points on the board. Chandler calmly booted a 31-yard field goal, his fourth of the game, to increase Green Bay's advantage to 26-7. The Packers dominated the quarter so completely that Oakland ran only seven plays.

Any faint hopes the Raiders had of catching the Packers were quickly blighted in the early minutes of the fourth period. Trying to move his team quickly, Lamonica sent wide receiver Fred Biletnikoff on a sideline pattern. But Adderley read the play, stepped in front of Biletnikoff, and sped 60 yards down the sidelines for a touchdown that sent the Packers soaring to a 33-7 lead.

Only a 23-yard touchdown pass to Miller, the last touchdown of the game, made the final score more respectable. The 33-14 triumph was Green Bay's second straight Super Bowl achievement. Lombardi was carried off the field for the last time on the shoulders of guard Jerry Kramer and tackle Forrest Gregg. Lombardi looked down on them both.

"This is the best way to leave a football field," he said, smiling.

Later in the dressing room, Lombardi would not say anything about his retirement. That would come a week later. He wanted to savor this triumph with his players. It was their moment of glory as much as his, because he also knew that some of them had played their last game. Yet, the perfectionist Lombardi wasn't completely satisfied with his team's performance.

"I told them at the half they had to put a little more pressure on Lamonica," Lombardi disclosed. "I told them that we only had a nine-point lead. But that's typical of the way we play. We get thirteen points ahead, and we go on vacation."

It was almost as if Lombardi hated the word. Only he knew that he would be going on one from coaching . . .

21

Super Bowl III

New York (AFL)	0	7	6	3	—	16
Baltimore (NFL)	0	0	0	7	—	7

It was a night for merriment. The players, owners, and coaches were there with their wives, along with selected·members of the media. But it was more than just a party. It was a significant moment. The day before, the New York Jets had reached the summit, the greatest achievement in their bedraggled nine-year history. They defeated the defending champion Oakland Raiders, 27-23, to win their first AFL title. Now, only 24 hours later, they were reveling at a private party in the Diamond Club in New York's Shea Stadium, the scene of their triumph.

New Year's Eve was only a day away, but it could very well have been that night. The wine flowed, music blared, and even strolling musicians added a soft touch at the dinner hour. The hastily prepared celebration couldn't have been better presented. It was indeed worthy of the event.

As the musicians approached Joe Namath, he was relaxing with his date, Suzy Storm, an attractive blond from Florida. It was Namath more than any other player who was the reason for celebrating. The gifted quarterback had thrown three touchdown passes 24 hours before on the field below to bring the Jets from behind in the championship game. The dramatic victory had made New York a Jets town. Namath looked up at the musicians who were serenading him. Only a few moments before, he had been informed that the Las Vegas oddsmakers had established the Jets as a prohibitive 18-point underdog against the Baltimore Colts in Super Bowl III, less than two weeks away.

"Eighteen points," exclaimed Namath while turning away from his date. "How do they figure that? Man, I wish I could bet. All those points. It doesn't seem possible."

Namath shook his head in disbelief. He

The night after the New York Jets won the American Football League championship, they were feted at a dinner party by the club's owners. Musicians honor quarterback Joe Namath, center, and his date for the evening, Suzy Storm. Author Lou Sahadi is at left.

22

had always fought the odds even as a kid growing up in Beaver Falls, Pa. And more often than not, he had won. But 18 points was too much for him to comprehend. It implied that his team and his league were vastly inferior to the long-established NFL, a league that most cronies looked upon with awe. Such reverence irritated Namath, a swashbuckling quarterback with a deep sense of pride.

He justifiably possessed it. He was looked upon as the deliverer, the one player who would lead the much-maligned AFL to parity with the sanctified NFL. That was the image he had been given the day after he signed his contract with the Jets four years before. It was a contract unprecedented in pro football annals. Sonny Werblin, then one of the Jet owners in 1964, signed Na-

math to a contract in excess of $400,000. Werblin, the one-time guiding genius of the Music Corporation of America, had extraordinary insight into the value that Namath represented. He never once wavered in the amount it required to out-bid the St. Louis Cardinals for Namath's services.

"Louis B. Mayer built the mighty Metro-Goldwyn-Mayer movie studio with the star system," explained Werblin. "It's a lesson that stuck with me. I believe in the star system. That's what sells tickets. Namath is Joe DiMaggio. He's Gregory Peck, Clark Gable, and Frank Sinatra. When he walks into a room, you know he's there. When any other high-priced rookie walks in, he's just a nice young man. This is one like Babe Ruth or Lou Gehrig or Mickey Mantle. He has that little something extra."

Namath, who threw three touchdown passes in the AFL championship game against the Oakland Raiders, packs his gear for the trip to Miami and Super Bowl III.

That's one reason why Namath had been called upon to speak last during the victory celebration. Some other players had addressed the gathering, followed by the head coach, Weeb Ewbank. Then Namath was asked to say a few words. As Namath approached the microphone, he was still limping from the previous day's game. He kept his head down until he was ready to speak.

"The coach thanked all the players' wives," began Namath. "I would like to thank all the broads in New York." The audience howled in delight. This was Namath's style.

"Seriously, though," he continued, "this championship was a great one for the players. However, I don't think anyone deserved it more than Coach Ewbank. Now, Weeb and I have had our little differences over the years, but we were both pulling for the same thing. Certainly no one worked harder than Weeb. He's a dedicated coach. I understand that he's at Shea every morning at eight o'clock. Of course, I've never seen him at that hour because it's still a bit too early for me."

Ewbank grinned. The rest of the audience roared. The charismatic quarterback was relaxed, fully at ease. But it was only a portent of things to come. On Thursday, when the Jets left for Miami and their date with destiny, the war of nerves began. It started as soon as the Jets arrived in Ft. Lauderdale that evening, as they were greeted by reporters and television sportscasters at the airport.

"Hey, Joe, what do you think of Earl Morrall?" asked one television reporter.

"I can think of five quarterbacks in the AFL better than Morrall," snapped Namath without hesitating. "Myself, John Hadl of San Diego, Bob Griese of Miami, Daryle Lamonica of Oakland, and Len Dawson of Kansas City."

Morrall, the Colts quarterback, had captured the imagination of pro football fans with his dramatic performance during the 1968 season. He had been nothing more than a mediocre quarterback throughout his 13-year career, which had been spent with five different teams. Yet, in his first season with the Colts, he took over for the ailing Johnny Unitas and guided Baltimore to its championship. He was so outstanding, he was voted "Player of the Year" in the NFL.

The very next day the Jets were scheduled to begin serious workouts for the game the following Sunday. But the Jet players had other things on their minds. Linebacker Larry Grantham, the team's player representative, informed Ewbank that the players wanted to hold a team meeting without any coaches present. They met behind closed doors.

The players had a number of grievances, mostly petty gripes, some exaggerated by locker-room rumors. But before any serious business on the field began, Grantham wanted a meeting to clear the air. The club had come too far to allow any kind of unrest to jeopardize the Super Bowl winner's share of $15,000 per man.

At the end of the meeting, Grantham asked Ewbank to join them. Ewbank listened to the grievances one by one, and quickly succeeded in satisfying the players. First, he assured them, they would be getting rings to symbolize their AFL championship. The players had earlier voted for rings, but a sourceless rumor had management substituting watches. The players then insisted the club spend $3,000 for each ring. However, Ewbank informed them that no club in the past had ever paid more than $1,000, and this satisfied them.

The players wanted the club to pick up the expenses for the wives. Ewbank again referred to past experience. He emphasized that the wives had been welcome to take the charter that the club had arranged, either flying down to Ft. Lauderdale or going back with the club the day after the Super Bowl. He pointed out that the three previous Super Bowl clubs—Green Bay, Kansas City, and Oakland—had not made any special

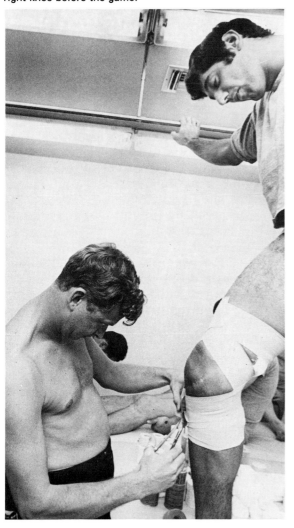

Trainer Jeff Snedecker carefully tapes Namath's famed right knee before the game.

allowances for players' wives.

The other major concern of the players was the cost required to get the field ready for the AFL championship game in New York. The figure of $42,000 for field maintenance and another $12,000 for turning on the lights, which they had heard about, was, according to rumor, going to be deducted from the winner's share of the game receipts. Ewbank explained that he did not know what the costs were because the club had not yet received a bill; and besides, it would not come out of the players' pockets.

With the air cleared, the Jets were ready to concentrate on preparing for the Colts. The players seemed relaxed, and Ewbank told them there wouldn't be any curfew enforcement until Tuesday night. He was convinced that they had earned the right to relax and have a good time until the serious practice sessions took place.

Baltimore did not arrive in Ft. Lauderdale until Saturday evening. Immediately, the local writers attempted to provoke a reaction from Morrall regarding Namath's statement a few days before. But the veteran Morrall, a quiet individual, would not allow himself to become embroiled in any inflammatory controversy.

"Joe Namath is entitled to his opinion," was all Morrall said.

Heavy rains the next day prevented any of the teams from working outdoors. So, Sunday was spent in meetings and emphasizing what was expected the rest of the week. Since Monday was photo day, there were no workouts scheduled. Photo day was really uneventful. It was an event ordered by the league in which the players were to pose for photographers in their game uniforms. It was so uneventful that Namath and the Jets' two star runners, Matt Snell and Emerson Boozer, failed to show up. Snell and Boozer claimed that they didn't receive a wakeup call. Namath much preferred to sleep anyway.

What enlivened the day was that word had gotten around that on Sunday night Namath and Lou Michaels, Baltimore's field goal kicker and defensive end, had been embroiled in a heated exchange of words that nearly resulted in a fight. Lou, the younger brother of Walt Michaels, the Jets' defensive coach, was well known for his temper.

25

Jets' Gerry Philbin applies pressure to Baltimore quarterback Earl Morrall. Author Lou Sahadi (dark glasses, squatting with hand over mouth) was the only writer allowed on field during game.

The incident had occurred in Fazio's, one of the popular Italian restaurants in Ft. Lauderdale. Namath was at the bar with his friend and roommate, Jim Hudson. Michaels, with his teammate, Dan Sullivan, approached them.

"Namath," he snapped, "Lou Michaels."

The quarterback acknowledged him.

"You're doing a lot of talking," Michaels persisted.

"There's a lot to talk about," replied Namath. "We're going to kick hell out of your team."

"Haven't you heard of the word 'modesty,' Joseph?" Michaels asked.

Hudson felt it was best that he and Namath sit down for dinner. Shortly after they were seated, Michaels and Sullivan came over to the table.

"You still here?" asked Namath.

"Damn right, I'm still here," growled Michaels. "I want to hear all you got to say."

"We're going to beat you, and I'm going to pick you apart."

"Joseph, I do believe you are the man who could do it. But you're going to find it hard throwing out of a well."

"Don't worry about that. My blockers will give me time."

"I never heard Johnny Unitas or Bobby Layne talk like that."

"I believe that."

"Even if we get into trouble, we'll send in the master, Unitas."

"I hope you do because it will mean the game is too far gone."

"Too far what!"

"Excuse me, I want to say hello to a few friends of mine."

As Namath got up, Michaels did a slow burn. Hudson sensed how upset he was.

"Don't pay any attention to what Joe says," remarked Hudson. "You've got to understand him."

A few minutes later Namath returned. Michaels looked at him.

"Suppose we kick hell out of your team?" jeered Michaels.

"I'll tell you what I'll do," answered Namath. "I'll sit in the middle of the field and cry."

Everybody laughed. The tension was broken. Later, when the check came, Namath paid for it with a $100 bill.

"You got a ride back to the hotel?" asked Namath.

"No," replied Michaels, "but we'll jump in a cab."

"Don't be silly," said Namath. "I'll drop you off."

The evening ended on a cordial note.

"You know something," Michaels said to Sullivan later, "he's a helluva guy. When everything was said and done, I was ready to take back the things I said when we first met. I learned you might as well hear Namath out. He strikes you as being cocky, but I came away thinking that he's a real gentleman. There's a lot of good in this guy.

"The only reason I showed any resentment toward Namath to begin with was because he said the Jets were going to whip us and kick the hell out of us as well. He must have had a wad of dough, close to two thousand dollars, and he peeled off a hundred dollar bill to pay the entire check. I don't know how he tips. I didn't see that."

Later Namath laughed off the incident. "It was all good, clean fun, and we parted the best of friends," he said.

Namath was certainly the central figure. It was as if no other players mattered. He was creating more excitement than the first two Super Bowls combined. He was unquestionably doing an excellent job of psyching out the Colts. Even Baltimore's excellent young coach, Don Shula, was affected. He was still peeved about the remark Namath made that "four or five quarterbacks in the AFL can throw as well, if not better, than Morrall."

"How Namath can rap Earl is a thing I don't understand," said Shula. "How the hell can you rap a guy that's the National Football League's Player of the Year? Particularly when Earl's had the percentage of completions he's had, the touchdown passes he's had, and the big yardage he's accumulated for us.

"Earl's not a guy who dumps things out in the flat to flare men to get a completion percentage built up. This guy is only interested in winning and doing the job. Na-

math can say whatever he wants to say, but I don't know how he can rap a guy who's accomplished the things Earl has for us all year.

"Anybody who doesn't realize what he's done for us is very wrong. He adapted quickly to an unfamiliar numbering system, and he recognizes how to improvise if necessary after the ball is snapped. That's the name of the game. He's done this despite coming to us late. His first appearance, in fact, was in relief of Unitas in a preseason game against Miami on August 30. He's a guy you have to chase off the practice field. He's well liked by everybody, and I have nothing but admiration for him.

"I don't see how anybody can compare Morrall and Namath. They haven't been throwing against the same kind of defenses. Namath is a heckuva thrower. He's moved their offense ever since he's been there. He has a quick release and sets up with good depth and vision downfield. He backpedals more than the quarterbacks in our league, but he doesn't get caught with the football. If his deep receivers are covered, he manages to dump the ball off. It's a problem getting to the guy because he gets back deep and

27

Baltimore linebacker Mike Curtis belts Namath after he got pass off.

gets back in a hurry. He has what we call fast feet. No over-all speed, but quick feet.

"We haven't changed our defense much for this game, but we've worked on Namath's deep set. He is able to throw quickly to the outside; and we have to be ready for that, too. But he is primarily a pocket passer. It's true that Joe has added the interest, and we've taken note of everything he's done. But about his restaurant clash with our Lou Michaels, you must remember that Joe is only the 837th guy that Michaels has threatened to deck in a career that shows only about 30 actual knockdowns."

Ironically, Shula had replaced Ewbank at Baltimore. The Colts' coach played for Ewbank, who had developed champions in 1958 and 1959. But after those glory years, the Colts began a decline that resulted in Shula's becoming the new head coach in 1963. Some of the Colt players, namely Unitas, were still with Baltimore from Ewbank's years as coach. In fact, Ewbank had the good fortune to coach two of the greatest passers of all time in Unitas and now Namath.

"They are both so great that once in a while they throw balls they know they shouldn't," revealed Ewbank. "Both have so much confidence that they simply try to force it through the defense. I think that John and Joe are the two greatest long passers, with accuracy, that I've ever seen.

"Now, you talk about the Colts' pass-rush. Well, I know about Ordell Braase. I coached him. I also know about Billy Ray Smith, and I had Fred Miller when he was a youngster. And, Bubba Smith . . . well, I hear he's supposed to be the greatest thing since peanut butter. But I've always prided myself in being able to protect the passer. Ask Unitas. He'll tell you.

"Joe is one of the best ever at reading defenses. The only time he might have trouble is when some six-foot-six defensive lineman comes through and he can't see over him that a linebacker is in position to intercept the pass. We think we can get keys and read the defenses. It's the sort of thing that Joe can do."

Namath would have to do just that more than in any other game. The Colts' defense was exceptional. During the 1968 season, they had blanked three opponents. And in the NFL championship game against

Namath lets one go before Colt tackle Fred Miller arrives.

Cleveland, they had shut out the Browns, 34-0. They finished the regular season with a 13-1 record, losing only to Cleveland, 30-20, in the sixth week of the campaign. In the past two years, the Colts were 24-2-2, the best since the Chicago Bears were 21-1 in 1941 and 1942. Their 18-point pick over the Jets certainly appeared justified, particularly since they were the first team to win 15 games in a year.

Like Namath, Ewbank could not understand the smart money's insistence that the Jets didn't have a chance. He just shook his head at the thought.

"If you listen to people talk, it would be foolish for us to dress Sunday," Ewbank said. "But we're going to. My boys are ready. As for parity of the AFL and the NFL, I think we are closing the gap. But if we are fortunate enough to win from Baltimore, I won't pop off and say we have gone past the NFL."

Later that night, Namath did. He was in Miami to receive the city's Touchdown Club's FAME Award as the pro football player of the year. The dinner was held at the Miami Springs Villa and was sold out with most of the audience lured by Namath's presence. Astronaut Gordon Cooper and Indianapolis 500-mile race winner Jim Rathman were also present, but the evening belonged to Namath. AFL president Milt Woodard presented Namath with the award and stepped back to let Joe express his gratitude.

"The Jets will win Sunday, I guarantee it," exclaimed Namath.

The statement brought a loud jeer from a heckler, obviously a Baltimore fan.

"Who's that? Lou Michaels?" asked Namath, smiling at the crowd. The audience broke out in laughter. Then Namath continued.

"I didn't intend to cast any slur on Earl Morrall when I said there were five quarterbacks in the AFL who could throw as well or better than he can. I wasn't rapping Morrall. He doesn't rate such treatment. He stepped in and took the Colts to the NFL

Curtis again lets Namath have it, but once more it's too late.

championship. That speaks for itself. But I'm entitled to my opinions and have the right to express them, just as any of you do.

"They say the Colts are going to take my statement and put it up on their bulletin board. Psychologically, it's going to lift them up for the game. If the Colts need anything like that to lift them up for the game, then they're in trouble from the beginning. In closing, I have to say it, but I'm afraid it's true: The name of the game is kill the quarterback, and you have a chance to win."

Namath's free-wheeling candor made the next day's headlines, creating more excitement. It was only 48 hours until kickoff, and ticket scalpers were asking for and getting $50 to $75 for a $12 seat. Namath had created more interest in this Super Bowl than the holy Green Bay Packers did in the previous ones, and the guys who hustled tickets for a living thought Namath was just beautiful.

Ominous low clouds moved swiftly in a northerly direction on Sunday morning. There was still a small chance of rain. It had rained heavily the night before, but now the sun was trying to struggle through. Rain would definitely favor the Colts. They had the heavy runners and a quarterback with two sound legs.

Just before noon, Namath answered a knock on the door of his suite. A bellhop entered the room holding a basket of flowers. He placed it on the table and smiled as he left the room. Namath had received flowers before from friends and admirers. This was something different. They were a dozen red roses sent by Lou Michaels.

As the Jets arrived at the Orange Bowl, one could feel the tension. The players walked into the dressing room; no one spoke. For the most part, they looked straight ahead and went about preparing for battle.

The one person who did not appear tense was Namath. He walked up behind me and gave me a playful bear hug.

"Hey, Lou, look at you, you sharp cat. You look like a native with those white pants and white shoes."

We spent a few minutes discussing his press interview for the league after the game, which I would be handling for him.

"We're going to be all right," said Joe as

29

Quarterback Johnny Unitas (19) desperately tries to get Colts going in last period.

30

if I had asked a question. "We're going to get the ball and try to get us a touchdown right fast. Got to get those points up on the board real quick. Yes, sir, everything is going to be okay."

The Jets had a chance to score first. After the opening kickoff, they managed a first down before they stalled. Curley Johnson punted, and Baltimore took over on its 27-yard line.

On the first down, Morrall hit his tight end John Mackey for a first down on the 46. On the next play, Morrall sent Tom Matte around the right side for a ten-yard advance to the Jets' 44. Two plays, two first downs. The bettors who laid the 18 points were happy. Baltimore kept driving. Finally, Michaels attempted a field goal from the Jets' 27 but missed.

Near the end of the period, the Colts had another chance to score. After catching a five-yard pass from Namath, wide receiver George Sauer fumbled the ball; the Colts recovered on the Jets' 12-yard line. However, on the second play of the second quar-

ter, Randy Beverly intercepted Morrall's pass in the end zone.

Namath took command on the 20-yard line. Like a general, he cleverly maneuvered the Jets. He took them the entire 80 yards in just 12 plays, beautifully mixing the pass and the run. Snell crashed over from the four-yard line, and the Jets went into a 7-0 lead on Jim Turner's conversion. That was the extent of the scoring in the first half as Michaels missed a 46-yard field goal try and Turner a 41-yard attempt.

The Jets got a break on the first play after the second half kickoff. Matte fumbled, and Ralph Baker recovered the ball on the Baltimore 33. After getting two first downs, Namath was sacked for a nine-yard loss. But on fourth down, Turner booted a 32-yard field goal to give the Jets a 10-0 edge.

The next time the Jets got the ball, Namath had them moving once again. He reached the Colts' 23-yard line before he injured his thumb on a second-down pass. He came to the sidelines where trainer Jeff Snedecker checked it. Then he began walking up and down, shaking his hand. Finally, he picked up a ball and shouted for someone to catch for him. Nobody responded as they were engrossed in the action, watching as Turner kicked a 30-yard field goal to stretch the Jets' lead to 13-0.

"Lou, get down there," ordered Namath.

We moved behind the bench in full view of the stands. Namath was 20 yards away, and he began to throw. He did not throw lobs, but fired with much the same force he used under game conditions. I clutched each toss as if it meant life or death, realizing the importance of his being able to warm up properly and knowing that a dropped throw would result in valuable

time lost. Namath threw four passes. Four times I returned the ball to him. Harvey Nairn, a receiver on the Jets' taxi squad, was then sent over to relieve me. On the very first toss Namath threw, Nairn dropped the ball. The crowd booed. Namath fired once more, which Nairn caught; and then Joe was ready to go again, his thumb back to normal.

Looking down from the press box, the writers had some doubts. Columnist Dick Young of the New York *News* was witnessing the warm-ups through binoculars.

"How does Namath look?" asked a fellow writer.

"He can't be looking too good because

Namath fondly embraces his father, John, after the stunning victory.

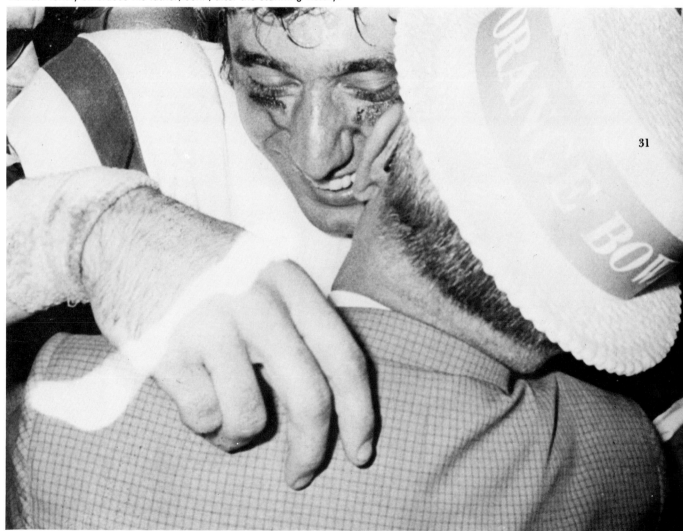

A happy Namath flanked by his dad (right) and Jets' coach Weeb Ewbank.

Sahadi hasn't dropped one yet," answered Young.

Namath stood looking at the action, waiting to return. The Colts had the ball, and Unitas was now the quarterback. Just as Namath had indicated, if Unitas got into the game, the Colts would be in trouble. They were. The third period was almost over, and they still hadn't scored.

In the opening moments of the fourth

quarter, the Jets scored again. Namath positioned a field goal with a 39-yard pass to Sauer just before the third period expired. Five plays later, Turner kicked a nine-yard field goal to give the Jets a 16-0 advantage.

Unitas tried desperately to bring the Colts back, but it was too late. The Jets were too determined and too good. All he could manage was an eight-yard touchdown drive three minutes from the end. The Jets had turned the pro football world upside down with an electrifying 16-7 upset. Namath's prophecy had come true.

The Jets' dressing room was bedlam. It was overcrowded with hundreds of people. In a tender moment, Namath and his father, John, who was wearing a styrofoam hat with the words "Orange Bowl" on the band, embraced.

"I told them you could do it!" exclaimed the father.

"You can talk," Joe said, laughing. "You didn't have to play. Where did you get that hat?"

Before the father could answer, Ewbank warmly offered his congratulations to Joe's father as he made his way through the crowd.

"Mr. Namath, you've got a remarkable son," he began. "You've got a son who makes some big statements and then goes out there and makes every one of them come true. I take my hat off to a man like that and to a man like you, sir."

John Namath's eyes were filled with tears of joy. "Thank you," he said, touching his own hat. "Joe is a good boy."

Namath's locker was so crowded with reporters that he didn't have room to undress. Time and time again the reporters were told to stand back. The heat in the overcrowded cubicle was oppressive.

"A whole lot of people were wrong," began Namath. "Eighteen-point underdog, gee whiz."

Namath didn't talk much. He didn't have to. In just one game he had brought parity between the AFL and the NFL. Never again was any AFL team an 18-point underdog . . .

Super Bowl IV

January 11, 1970
New Orleans Tulane Stadium
80,562

Minnesota (NFL)	0	0	7	0	—	7
Kansas City (AFL)	3	13	7	0	—	23

The rain had pelted the city. It was cold and damp. The cold wave sweeping across the country had somehow invaded New Orleans. A record low of 24 degrees was forecast. In New Orleans that's cold, but Jimmy Moran wasn't the least bit concerned. He had just presided over a batch of fettucini in his restaurant on Iberville Street. It was a ritual with him, a service he personally provides for his friends. And he had many of them. On this particular Monday night, he wanted to be certain that the fettucini was right for his friend Wilson Abraham. Not just right, but perfect. It was only after

Abraham agreed that Moran finally sat down.

"Don't you worry none about the weather," smiled Moran. "By Sunday, it will be sunny and warm. Ain't that right, Wils? This isn't New Orleans weather. It's some of that cold weather from the North. Some people are already saying it's Viking weather. It doesn't mean a thing. I like Kansas City with 13 points. Tell you what, Wils, the Chiefs will beat the Vikings straight up, without the points.

"I gotta go with the Chiefs. My boy Johnny Robinson will show 'em. He's a

34

In command, Kansas City quarterback Len Dawson takes snap and turns to hand off.

Defensive end Jerry Mays of the Chiefs gets a good hold on Minnesota quarterback Joe Kapp, who just did get rid of the ball.

Louisiana boy, played down the road at L.S.U. Johnny is as tough as they come. I spoke to him last week, and he'll be in for dinner with his buddy, Len Dawson. Yes, sir, Wils, I feel it already. The Chiefs will win this one easy."

There weren't many football buffs who would have agreed with Moran that Monday night, or any other night for that matter. The nation's bookmakers had established Minnesota as a solid 13-point favorite for a number of reasons. People still looked at the American Football League as a "Mickey Mouse" league, contending that last year's 16-7 upset by the New York Jets over the Baltimore Colts was a fluke. They also pointed to the fact that the Chiefs weren't even a divisional winner, but the first wild-card entry to reach the Super Bowl. Besides, they felt that the Vikings were just plain better. Their defensive line was so outstanding they were branded as the "Purple People Eaters." And in Joe Kapp, they had a tough, reckless quarterback who wasn't afraid of anybody. It was the defense and Kapp who had led the Vikings to a 12-2 season.

Their coach, Bud Grant, had shown them how to win. He had taken over in 1967 and in three years made them champions. In fact, Minnesota was the first expansion team in NFL history to win a title. Strictly a meat-and-potatoes guy, Grant built the Vikings through hard work. Nothing fancy or innovative. He concentrated on defense and let the rest of the pieces fall into place.

"Defense wins football games, offense sells tickets," claimed Grant. "You suit your style of play to your players. Doing it the other way takes too long. Here we get a strong rush from our line. On the other hand, we don't blitz that well. None of our linebackers are the Packer type, 6-5 and 240. So we play a zone defense with our linebackers helping out in the coverage. The big rush by the front four allows us to use the zone; because without the rush, the receivers have time to run down the field and stretch out the zones until they are too big to cover well.

"Since our defense is strong, our offense doesn't have to be fancy. We just line up in the basic formations and come right at you. We don't have to take chances because the defense will force turnovers and field posi-

Dawson drops back to pass.

tion. From the start of this year's camp, we have said that our improvements would come from within. We are better because we have pyramided our experience and knowledge. We can do more things because we have played together longer.

"It became evident in our 1967 training camp that we needed help at quarterback. As a result, we made a deal for Joe Kapp. At the time the transaction was made, it didn't appear as significant as it does today. Our 1967 draft helped us a great deal. We weren't going to outscore opponents, so we had to bring our opposing point totals down. It took a while to achieve. This year we allowed the least points of any team in a 14-game schedule. This was all a part of long-range discipline.

"We cut our penalties down. We cut our fumbles down to a point where the past year I think we fumbled less than any team in our division. Our interceptions were the lowest in the league this past season, and we led the league in making interceptions. I can't say at this point what month, what game, or what day we became a better football team."

Most would have said it was with the emergence of Kapp as the team leader. He, more than any other player, personified the spirit of the Vikings—a tough, hard-playing team about as subtle as a punch in the mouth. It was Kapp's free spirit and fiery play that sparked the Vikings. He was a throwback to the barroom brawler who would just as soon hit you as look at you. Every game was a personal war.

Like in the NFL championship game against the Cleveland Browns. Finding no receiver open, Kapp had taken off around end. He was about to be stopped by line-backer Jim Houston. Instead of running the other way, Kapp ran right at Houston. Like a runaway freight train, Kapp barreled into his bigger, heavier opponent. He left Houston for dead. Kapp gained his yards, and Houston had to be helped off the field.

Running back Mike Garrett slips past Minnesota's Jim Marshall (70) to score Chiefs' first touchdown in second quarter.

It didn't go unnoticed by the Chiefs' huge defensive tackle, Buck Buchanan.

"Any quarterback who can knock Jim Houston cold is all man," remarked Buchanan. "The way to stop Kapp is with a tackle, just like any other quarterback. Unlike other quarterbacks, Kapp will stick it to you when he's on the run.

"I got to have the big rush. I got to really tackle, no arm tackles, I mean really hit. I got to pressure him. I got to get to him, and I got to get to him as hard as I can."

The Chiefs' other defensive stars were also thinking about Kapp, particularly the linebackers who would challenge Kapp in the open field if he got past the line of scrimmage.

"Well, if he comes my way, it's my job to stop him," said outside linebacker Bobby Bell. "I'm sure not going to dodge him. The thing about Houston, he got caught with a knee on the chin. It was an accident. If he didn't get hit there, he just might have set Kapp back. The thing about Joe, he's been doing that all year, jumping over people, running over people. I remember a statement he made that he don't have anything to hold back—he's been around 11 years, and this is it."

"It's a question of forces," added middle linebacker Willie Lanier. "If one man is stationary and the other man is moving around, the stationary man takes the brunt. But if I'm in that situation, I'm not just going to stand there. Let's face it. You normally figure that the quarterback is the least adept at running. And we're just doing what we always do."

"The quarterback," explained Jim Lynch, the other outside linebacker, "is the hinge you hang your door on. I don't get a thrill putting anyone out of a game because we're both out there earning a living. But I'm not going to lose any sleep over it if the quarterback gets hurt."

Kapp wasn't affected by all the talk of a physical game. The tougher the game, the better he liked it. He was a street fighter.

"Nobody can guarantee a football game," remarked Kapp. "We have two good teams here, and it will be a good match. The press sometimes puts much of the responsibility for a team's success on the quarterback when actually the games are won and lost up front. Playing in the Super Bowl is a

37

Kansas City's Jan Stenerud (3) boots a 48-yard, Super Bowl-record field goal in the first quarter.

great opportunity. We've come a long way, and we're going to rock and sock.''

The ones who would do that for the Vikings were their celebrated front four. They were big and quick. End Jim Marshall was 6-4, 248, and end Carl Eller was 6-6, 250. Tackle Gary Larsen was 6-5, 255, and tackle Alan Page was 6-4, 245.

"We're all equally adept at rushing the passer,'' says Eller. "We're a team. We know they'll use a lot of formations. We know they'll give us some problems. We don't feel we have to prove anything. We're going to do what we've done all season and that is to put out our maximum effort.''

"We'll have to stop their running game,'' added Page. "When they're running well, they don't pass that much. We'll just have to play the pass as it comes. We have no ulterior motive. The key to our success is just to go out and play the best we can.''

"We just call certain defenses to fit the situation,'' offered Larsen. "It's just that each man carries out his responsibility ne-

cessary to get the job done. We've got all the incentive in the world. Just the idea that we're the first expansion team to win an NFL title is incentive enough.''

"Everyone uses the play-action pass to some extent,'' volunteered Marshall. "It's effective as can be in a given situation, but the opposition is going to adjust to it sooner or later. I don't think we need any incentive. We'll just have to play the best we can and do what we do best.''

If there was an incentive needed, it rested with the Chiefs. They had appeared in the very first Super Bowl ever played and were easily defeated by the Green Bay Packers, 35-10. But Super Bowl IV offered even more. This was the last Super Bowl between the American Football League and the National Football League. The next year the merger of the two leagues would go into full effect, and every team would be competing under the National Football League banner. One big happy family.

Hank Stram, the dapper coach of the

Chiefs, was an original member of the AFL. An innovative coach, he had successfully employed the moving pocket, play-action pass, and the "I" formation on offense, and such defensive alignments as the stack and double blitz. Some of the purists around the NFL frowned at some of Stram's inventiveness.

"We're not trying to sell our approach," pointed out Stram. "I simply have to do what I think is best for our team. The trend in the '60s in pro football was towards simplicity. The 4-3-4 defense has been popular. Most teams use only one or two offensive formations.

"Take the Vikings, for instance. Their personality is one of simplicity. On defense, they read, react, pursue, and gang tackle. Joe Kapp throws well on the move, but

(Left) Dawson holds as Stenerud kicks another field goal. (Below) Dawson pitches ball to little Warren McVea.

39

their offense is pretty much that which is used by most pro teams. Kapp is the most underrated quarterback in the business. People say he's not fancy, but he wins; and I saw films of him twice completing big passes to his right while he was running left. He puts the ball on the shelf.

"Variety in all phases of the game will be the trend in the '70s. There will be more and more of it. I'm sure we'll be competing against it soon. Most teams advertise their formations by the way they come out of the huddle and line up. I believe in the creation of formations. Different formations can create an area of doubt.

"Take our 'I' formation and the shift out of it. We think it's to our advantage if we can shrink the reaction time of the defense. If we give them a different picture all the time, we think we are causing a certain amount of indecision about what we're going to do. If we do that, we are increasing the possibility of better execution, of a more productive play. After we shift, we are set up essentially like any other pro team. Then we must depend on execution.

"Our system has some 18 basic plays. We don't use the word 'scrambler' in our terminology. Scrambling gives the connotation of a recess quarterback. You think of a kid out there on the school yard lot running around until someone comes open in a pickup game. The moves of our quarterback are by design.

"But you have to have discipline. You can't win without good discipline. Some people have the reputation of being taskmasters, but you can have it without advertising it. Discipline, motivation, and attitude: those are the things that make us win."

The Chiefs had certainly personified Stram's philosophy during the 1969 season. They had overcome adversity to earn a spot in the Super Bowl. In October, their star quarterback Len Dawson had suffered a painful knee injury. At first, it was feared that he would have to undergo surgery. An operation would have finished him for the season. Dawson rejected surgery. Five weeks after his injury, Dawson returned to the lineup. He was, in essence, a one-legged quarterback. Yet, his generalship during a game was invaluable to the Chiefs. He had inspired them to a wild-card berth and a

Appearing clam, Dawson fades back to pass.

dramatic victory in the AFL championship game against the Oakland Raiders. Despite throwing only six passes the entire game, Dawson led the Chiefs from behind to a 17-7 triumph in Oakland. One of his passes, from his own end zone, was a clutch third-down pass that got the Chiefs out of danger and on their way to a touchdown and eventual victory.

Dawson was the complete opposite of Kapp. He was a smooth, polished performer who efficiently ran Kansas City's complex multiple offense. Because he was quiet and always in control on the field, he never received the full recognition he deserved. In simple terms, Dawson was a master craftsman.

But on Tuesday night his tranquil world was shattered. A Detroit television station broke a major news story concerning a gambling figure named Donald Dawson. It further reported that one of Dawson's acquaintances was Len Dawson of the Kansas City Chiefs. The news reverberated through

Kansas City defensive back
Johnny Robinson (42) intercepts
a pass that was intended for
Viking wide receiver John
Henderson (80).

New Orleans, past the French Quarter, and to the Fontainebleau Hotel where the Chiefs were quartered.

Earlier that day the Chiefs had received word from the league that the story would break. Dawson was relaxing in his room, completely unaware of what was transpiring. As he left to attend a film session, he was met by Jim Schaaf, the team's public relations director. Schaaf appeared a bit

nervous. He motioned for Dawson to step away from the other players so as he could speak to him privately. Schaaf was almost trembling. Dawson's immediate thought was that something had happened to his family back in Kansas City.

Quietly, Schaaf informed Dawson that his name had surfaced in connection with a gambling probe in Detroit. He told Dawson that it would be revealed to the country as part of the "Huntley-Brinkley Report" that night. Dawson was shocked. He asked Schaaf to repeat what he had told him. He thought perhaps that he had heard wrong. Schaaf assured him that it was true. He warned Dawson to stay out of the lobby and urged him to change his room because the motel would be swarming with writers once the word was out.

"What about this gambling investigation?" asked Dawson. "Tell me something about it."

"I don't know any more than I've told you," answered Schaaf. "I received a tip over the phone five minutes ago. All I know is that your name was mentioned, and the story would be part of a network television newscast tonight."

A few minutes later Dawson and Schaaf approached Stram. He was in the dining room, and Schaaf quietly called him outside. He explained the situation. Stram also was stunned. Then he told Dawson to keep away from the press for the time being, at least until they could check with the league office to find out what was going on and how they should act. He instructed Dawson to go to the film room and stay there. Stram felt that nobody would look for Dawson there.

When the other quarterbacks came into the room, they had no idea of what was taking place. Every so often Schaaf would come in and whisper something in Stram's ear. Dawson knew that something was happening, but he didn't know what. Finally, when the film session was over, Stram told Dawson to remain. Schaaf had informed him that the motel was swarming with writers. So, Stram and Dawson kept rerunning the films on the Vikings. Finally, Stram took Dawson up to his suite and told him to remain out of sight in one of the bedrooms until he could get a handle on things. Dawson tried to relax but couldn't. Finally, he heard Stram talking on the phone. The league had proposed that Dawson come over to the league headquarters at the Roosevelt Hotel and meet with Jack Danahy, the NFL's head of security. The Roosevelt was also press headquarters, and Stram didn't appreciate the fact that Dawson would be an open target for the writers.

"There's no way Len is going to come over, now or later," fumed Stram. "He's going to eat with the rest of the team, and

Near end of game, coach Hank Stram congratulates Dawson for a job well done.

I'm not going to disrupt the entire organization and get the squad upset over something we know nothing about. Besides, I'm not going to subject Len to any more pressure. If you want to see him, you'll have to come over here."

Stram had made his point. They set a meeting for after dinner. Until then, Dawson still had to be protected from the press. As a precautionary measure, one of Dawson's close friends, Joe Litman from Pittsburgh, was detailed to act as his bodyguard. He was familiar to all the Chief players and was better known to them as "Pittsburgh Joe."

Litman did his job well. He got Dawson safely through the dinner hour and the scheduled meeting with Danahy. While the meeting was taking place in a far-off room,

Litman waited outside. He had safely nego-tiated the back stairs of the motel and was already planning the route back to Daw-son's room.

"I have to ask you some sensitive and personal questions, and I want you to answer me truthfully," began Danahy be-hind closed doors. "We are here to help you, do you understand?"

"Yes, I do," replied Dawson. "I have al-ways told the truth. I have nothing to hide."

"Do you know a Donald Dawson?"

"Yes, I do."

"How well do you know him?"

"He's just a casual acquaintance, nothing more. He's a restaurant owner in Detroit who I met about ten or eleven years ago when I was playing for Pittsburgh."

"How many times have you been seen with him?"

"About four or five times."

"When was the last time you spoke to him?"

"I talked to him on the telephone last November after my father had died. I was in Alliance, Ohio, for the funeral, and he con-tacted my sister to find out where I was and offer his condolences. The only other time I recall talking to him was after I injured my knee at the beginning of the season, and he expressed concern over my knee. At no time

did he ask me any questions pertaining to players, morale, injuries and such, or seek other information that may be useful in gambling."

"I believe everything you've told me. I'm confident that you didn't have any connec-tion with any of the gamblers other than knowing Donald Dawson. We'll back you all the way on this."

Later that night, Stram decided that it would be best for Len to issue a statement to the press. They had been waiting around all night for one. At 11 o'clock Dawson walked into the press room, handed out a prepared press release, and quickly left the room with Litman. In the elevator, Litman told Dawson it would be best if he stayed with him that night. He reasoned that the phone would be ringing all night. Dawson agreed. They went back to Dawson's room, which he was sharing with Johnny Robin-son. By now it was close to midnight, and Robinson was asleep. They woke him and told him what was taking place.

It was only the beginning of a week of personal horror for Dawson. He was won-dering if he was going to be subpoenaed. Of more concern, he was wondering if he would be allowed to play on Sunday; how would it affect his teammates; how would it affect his family in Kansas City, his friends?

Dawson would find out how his team-

43

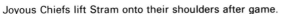

Joyous Chiefs lift Stram onto their shoulders after game.

mates felt the very next morning. After a practically sleepless night, Dawson and Litman met early with Stram before breakfast. Stram felt it would be a good idea if Len read his statement to the players after breakfast. They understood and offered Dawson their support. It was an important moment for the quarterback. He had bridged the gap.

But Dawson also had a personal bridge to cross. He had to convince his 11-year-old son, Lennie, that everything was okay. His son was puzzled by the remarks made to him at school and by all the newspaper and television and radio reports that had mentioned his father's name. Dawson repeated his innocence to his son and told him the only important thing to do now was to beat the Vikings.

By Saturday, everything seemed to quiet down. Yet, it was like waiting for a bomb to explode. It all boiled down to the game. That was where it counted for Dawson. He knew he had to win. It was as if his whole career was riding on that one game. Robinson's rib cage was still sore; Dawson still hadn't gotten much sleep; and Litman was still nervously puffing one cigarette after the other. Robinson suggested that the best thing to do was to go down to Jimmy

Moran's Artichoke Club and get some steam and a rubdown. They all agreed.

That night, Dawson tried to sleep but couldn't. His emotions were so tight that he got up from bed several times to regurgitate. It wasn't a pleasant feeling, not before the biggest game of his life. When he finally got up for breakfast with the rest of the team, he hadn't slept three hours all night. All that remained ahead of him was the game and what it meant.

As Jimmy Moran had prophesied, the weather broke by game time. The temperature had climbed to 61 degrees although the sky was overcast. But unknown to the 80,998 fans in attendance at Tulane Stadium, Stram received a phone call in the dressing room minutes before the Chiefs took the field. It was from President Nixon. He had called to say that he didn't believe any of the rumors. He made his feelings known especially to Dawson and the rest of the team, and told them to go out and play like champions.

The Vikings took the opening kickoff, but after making two first downs, they had to punt. Taking over on his own 17-yard line, Dawson drove the Chiefs to the Minnesota 41. On fourth down, Jan Stenerud thrilled the spectators with a 48-yard field goal that sent the Chiefs into a 3-0 lead.

When the period ended, Dawson had the Chiefs driving again. Beginning on his own 20, he reached the Vikings' 25-yard line early in the second quarter when Stenerud was sent out to kick a 32-yard field goal. He did, and the Chiefs were now in front, 6-0.

Midway in the period, Stenerud hit for the third time. He booted a 25-yard field goal that stretched Kansas City's margin to 9-0. The Vikings had trouble moving against the rugged Chief defense, and Kansas City was slowly building a lead.

On the kickoff, the Chiefs got a big break. Charlie West fumbled the ball after being hit, and Remi Prudhomme recovered the ball for Kansas City on the 19-yard line. The Chiefs were in a resourceful position to make something happen. If they could score again before the half, Minnesota would be psychologically down. Dawson wasn't thinking field goal now. He wanted a touchdown. After being dropped for a loss while attempting to pass, Dawson came back. On the third down he hit wide receiver Otis Taylor with a 10-yard pass on the Minnesota four. Three plays later, Mike Garrett, behind some excellent blocking,

44

Dawson answers questions in dressing room as sportscaster Frank Gifford looks on.

scored from the five-yard line. Kansas City's lead had soared to 16-0 as the half ended five minutes later.

The Chiefs took the second half kickoff and started upfield again. However, their momentum was checked by a 22-yard holding penalty. They were forced to punt, and Minnesota took over on its own 31-yard line. Suddenly, Minnesota's dormant offense came to life. Kapp was the spark. After a couple of first downs, he connected on three consecutive passes to carry the Vikings to the Chiefs' four-yard line. Then on the next play, Dave Osborn scored the Vikings' first touchdown to narrow Kansas City's edge to 16-7.

But the Chiefs were undismayed. Moving from the 18-yard line, the Chiefs reached the Viking 46. On first down, Dawson threw a quick five-yard pass to Taylor. The talented receiver broke two tackles and ran the rest of the way for a touchdown that sent Kansas City into a 23-7 lead. The pass play seemed to break the Vikings' spirit.

In what must have seemed an eternity for Dawson, nobody came close to scoring the rest of the game. Finally, with only 1:10 left on the clock, Stram removed Dawson from the game to the cheers of the crowd. His ordeal over, Dawson didn't wait until the game ended. Instead, he ran right into the Chiefs' dressing room. Alone with his thoughts, he prayed.

Before his teammates joined him, Dawson left his locker and went into the trainer's room, which is off limits to everyone except the players. He took off his helmet and sat on top of one of the tables. Not only was he drained physically, but emotionally and mentally. He could breathe easier now.

"No one was happier or more relieved than I was that we had finally won the Super Bowl," Dawson said. "I felt vindicated. I didn't have to answer to anybody again about any gambling implications. No one can appreciate how much torment I endured all week answering the questions about my supposed friendship with unsavory characters. I felt as if a tremendous emotional burden had been lifted from me."

Minutes later, the tumult and the shouting permeated the dressing room. Dawson realized that the moment of peace he enjoyed was now over. He knew he had to leave the sanctuary of the trainer's room to answer the hundreds of questions that would be asked of him. The writers were waiting for him in front of his locker. He

was there only a few minutes when he had to leave. President Nixon was on the phone, and he wanted to talk to Dawson.

"I had to dial a special number and ask for a certain operator in Washington, D.C.," revealed Dawson. "When I got the operator, I told her my name was Len Dawson. She said, 'Len who?'

"I spelled out my name. I told her the President had called, and she said, 'Just a minute.' She then got in touch with somebody else. I went through the same routine with her, and she said, 'Are you called Lennie or Len?' 'Ma'am, it really doesn't make a great deal of difference.' 'Well, the President wants to make sure that he uses the name you prefer,' she replied. I thought that was nice of him. The President then got on the phone, and I said, 'Hello, Mr. President, this is Len Dawson.' "

When Dawson returned to the crowded room, he was standing on a platform so that everyone could easily see him. He looked down and spotted his son, Lennie. He reached down and picked him up and placed him by his side.

"Dad, you done good," said the youngster.

Dawson lifted him up and gave him a kiss. That said it all . . .

With his son Lenny next to him, a tired but relieved Dawson talks to the press.

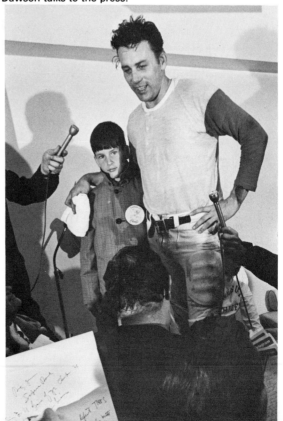

Super Bowl V

Baltimore (AFC)	0	6	0	10	—	16
Dallas (NFC)	3	10	0	0	—	13

In the beginning, they were a troubled team. They had been under strain both emotionally and physically during the 1970 season. Now, their problems were reduced to just physical ailments. That in itself was a significant relief. Physical hurts can be overcome. Emotional ones leave deep scars that can affect the performance of an entire team. That had been evident throughout most of the regular season. So much so that most knowledgeable experts had conceded that the Dallas Cowboys could never reach Super Bowl V. They certainly had had to overcome more adversities than their opponents, the Baltimore Colts.

When the season first began, Dallas coach Tom Landry had been certain of one thing, his defense. They were a seasoned bunch

Baltimore coach Don McCafferty lines up with his offensive unit during early-week practice session.

who had earned the reputation as a "Doomsday Defense." His only concern at that point was at quarterback. His regular quarterback, Craig Morton, was coming off shoulder surgery, and his reserve, Roger Staubach, was starting only his second season in the league.

But after the ninth game of the year, Landry hadn't been sure of anything. In an embarrassing display of ineptitude before millions of viewers on Monday Night Football, the Cowboys had been soundly beaten by the St. Louis Cardinals, 38-0! It left Dallas with a 5-4 record. A great many people bet that they would never play in the Super Bowl that January. The defeat was the second thrashing the Cowboys had absorbed in a short period of time. Only two weeks before, they had been routed by the Minnesota Vikings, 54-13, in a demonstration of even greater futility. Hardly championship play.

The day after the loss to the Cardinals, some 25 players had shown up at Morton's apartment. It was a moment of soul searching. The players knew that they faced certain elimination if they lost another game. They didn't want that to happen. They cleared the air of the animosities they harbored and dedicated themselves to winning the remaining five games on the schedule. Morton admittedly was down after the Cardinal defeat.

"The only thing that gave me any kind of a lift was when Ralph Neely gave me a Spiro Agnew watch as a gift," revealed Morton.

Whatever came out of that meeting had worked. The Cowboys pulled themselves together and won five straight games to finish with a 10-4 record. The defense clearly asserted itself. In the last four games, they yielded only 15 points, allowing only

46

The most dramatic kick in the history of the Super Bowl was provided by Baltimore's Jim O'Brien.

one touchdown in the final game of the season. In the playoff games, Dallas shut out Detroit, 5-0, and then handled San Francisco in the championship contest, 17-10.

"After the St. Louis game, most people wrote us off," admitted Landry. "It was up to us: we were either going to collapse or come back. If the players weren't doubting me, they were the only ones. I felt the team had to come closer together in attitude. We weren't getting much outside support at that point so we had to generate it among ourselves. It was a 40-man pickup."

Besides the players' dedication, Landry had also instituted a major change concerning the offense. He decided to put himself on the spot by calling the plays himself instead of trusting the play selection to the quarterback. It might have bruised Morton's ego, but Landry approached the change clinically.

"We felt we had to make a change in that area," disclosed Landry. "Craig burdened himself with the full responsibility for our inadequacies. After that, he loosened up and started passing much better. Craig, in the past, has always been an excellent play selector. But we had to make a change, even if it wasn't necessarily the right one."

It was an emotional change for Morton as well. Having a coach send in every play doesn't exactly enhance one's reputation as a star quarterback. From a quarterback's

Dallas coach Tom Landry watches his team warm up before Super Bowl V.

view, it makes him feel like a robot, executing a programmed play without instilling the feeling of being a leader to the rest of the team. Landry himself had recognized it five days before the Super Bowl.

"Craig feels this," conceded Landry. "He's disappointed. Every quarterback wants to call his own plays; but since we got started on this streak, we can't change.

"Craig and I are very close. I keep impressing on him that he is an excellent play selector, probably the best one we've ever had in Dallas. But we'll do everything we need to win. We used to be a finesse team, but I would rather have a power attack because it's more reliable. If you're a finesse team, you have to guess right. We're a different team than in the past two or three years. Because of our finish, we're much more confident. Earlier in the team's history, we came up against the great Packers, and we didn't win."

That was a stigma that hung over the Cowboys. They were acquiring the reputation of not being able to win the big games, the championship ones. That's why Morton approached his role philosophically.

"I had not called very good games in our two games just before Coach Landry started to call the plays," admitted Morton. "I was being too conservative with our offense. The coach and I discuss our plans when I'm

Baltimore running back Norm Bulaich is brought down after a short gain.

on the sideline. We work together. I give him some ideas that I think will work. It is not strictly a one-way thing."

What was of more concern to Morton and the Cowboys now was his physical condition. He had a number of ailments. One was laryngitis. It was left over from a severe sore throat and flu that bedded him most of the previous week. He was so sick that he didn't participate in the workouts the team held in Dallas.

But more important, Morton had a much more serious ailment, a sore elbow. He also admitted that his shoulder that was operated on was sore and that he had just recovered from a gash on his right hand. He was indeed battered. It was definitely reflected in his play in the two playoff games. Against the Lions, he had completed only four of 18 passes for 38 yards. The following week he hadn't been much better, hitting on just seven of 22 passes for 101 yards. It didn't go unnoticed by Landry.

"His arm appears to be the same," said Landry. "But he's been hurt so much he hasn't been able to develop the timing you need between a passer and his receivers. You can do that only in practice."

Morton wasn't the only Cowboy hurting. Because of his deficiencies, the Cowboys had reverted to a power running attack. And in veterans Calvin Hill and Walt Garrison and rookie Duane Thomas, they had the talent

Baltimore safety Rick Volk bulldogs Dallas wide receiver Reggie Rucker from behind.

to make it work. Thomas was the finest running back to come into the league in a number of years. He had taken over in the starting lineup when Hill was injured and led the Dallas runners with 803 yards.

However, Garrison was ailing. He was literally one of the walking wounded in a brigade of soldiers who had done battle. He limped on a swollen right ankle, had a twisted right knee, and a chipped collarbone. It would be enough to shelve any other runner but Garrison. A rough, bronco-busting rodeo rider in the off-season, Garrison is a throwback to a John Wayne type western hero.

Early in the championship game against San Francisco, Garrison had been hit by Roland Lakes and Frank Nunley. He was sandwiched so hard that his right leg was twisted like a pretzel. He was helped to the sidelines, and it appeared that he was finished for the day. But in the second period, Garrison returned, running and catching passes on a sore ankle and a throbbing shoulder. The sight of Garrison on the field inspired the Cowboys to play harder.

"When you see a guy coming back in the game, hurt like he was, still getting the yards, how can you keep from blocking your heart out for him?" exclaimed tackle Ralph Neely.

Garrison had finished the game with 71 yards on 17 carries, caught three passes for 51 more yards, and scored the winning touchdown on a three-yard run. Larry Gardner, the team's trainer, quipped that Garrison had so much tape on him that he looked like a mummy. There was even speculation that Hill would return to the lineup and Thomas would shift into Garrison's spot at fullback against the Colts.

"I'm not going to miss this one," said Garrison. "My ankle is pretty sore right now, but two, three days can make a big difference. I've never played in a Super Bowl, but I always wanted to."

Garrison's teammates believed him. They knew he had been through tougher times than football not to snap back. Two years earlier, Garrison had suffered a cracked rib while he was bulldogging a steer in a rodeo. That was the part of life that Garrison really loved. Even while he was still in high school, Garrison had traveled the small-town rodeo circuit with a buddy, going

49

Dallas wide receiver Bob Hayes waits for a long pass from quarterback Craig Morton in first period.

"Walt just takes care of himself or tries to help his friends," said Robinson. "Otherwise, he don't bother anybody. He doesn't go around actin' smart or anything. But Gawd help anybody who tries to push him around."

Garrison was a cowboy in a true sense of the word. He chewed tobacco, loved country music, and could recite poetry and tell stories about the old West in a nice easy manner. When he signed with the Cowboys in 1966, he didn't ask for a new car as a signing bonus. Instead, he opted for a two-horse trailer and got it.

One day when he was out on the road, he telephoned his wife and learned that Curt Mosher, the team's public relations director, wanted to talk to him. He phoned Mosher from a phone booth while he was waiting to have a flat tire fixed.

"I have a phone number for you to call," said Mosher. "Do you have a pencil?"

Baltimore tight end John Mackey charges out of the end zone after scoring the Colts' first touchdown on a tipped pass in the second period.

50

from one town to another in a broken-down car which also served as their sleeping quarters at night.

"Rodeo has always been a big part of my life," disclosed Garrison. "I guess I got started on rodeo back in grade school. I lived in a little town in Texas named Lewisville, and there wasn't much else to get interested in. I used to ride Brahmas, but the club isn't too keen on my doing that now. I still work the rodeos in the off-season, just riding broncos and roping."

While on the circuit, Garrison had become good friends with another rider, Bill Robinson. Bill wasn't concerned about Garrison's injuries.

Mike Clark gets Dallas on the scoreboard in the first quarter with a 14-yard field goal.

"Naw," drawled Garrison, "but I got my pocketknife."

But Thomas was a different breed. Everyone knew about him as a runner, but nobody knew anything about him as a person. While Hill was named the 1969 Rookie of the Year, Thomas, by gaining 803 yards, was virtually assured of winning the award for 1970. As a football player, he was someone Landry admired. But as a person off the field, he was hard to figure. The way he dressed was not exactly in line with Landry's style. On this particular day, he wore love beads around his neck and the peace symbol hanging from a leather armband on his left wrist. Yet, he smiled and was fairly talkative.

"Life to me is a movie," began Thomas. "I relate the characters in a movie to characters right here. I'm a part of all I've met. I want to find out what things mean, because I want to find out what I mean. By nature, I feel I'm part of everything. I'm trying to figure out the whole Super Bowl scene. What I'm really trying to figure out is what it means to everybody else.

"People have always said I had a bad attitude because I have never been close to anyone. My mother sent me to school in Los Angeles in the fourth grade to live with an aunt because she thought it would be good for me. I lived in a black ghetto in Los Angeles and never knew much else. I used to daydream a lot, sort of Utopia type of dreams. I always found peace by going to the beach. It was a good place for meditating. I would think of a better day and how I could improve myself by the experiences I had that day. I was a loner as a kid.

"Football is a sport and something you enjoy, but I try never to lose my composure and resort to any type of physical violence. Running is becoming tougher each week because of success. Defenses are out to stop you. A few blows are thrown to impress me, but I don't believe in retaliation unless I have to.

"Baltimore's defense, from watching films, is a lot more physical than most people realize. They've got two good safeties in Rich Volk and Jerry Logan, along with those linebackers Mike Curtis and Ted Hendricks. This is a swarming defensive team. I don't pattern myself after anyone. It's all me. I just do the best that I can. I am a better runner than I was in college.

"I worked on my peripheral vision to where I glance from side to side as I run.

Morton hits running back Duane Thomas (33) with a touchdown pass in the second period that gave Cowboys 13-6 halftime lead.

This has helped a great deal as the hole is not always open, and I can pick up yardage elsewhere. Sometimes I feel like a gladiator, especially the other week in San Francisco because we came through the tunnels, fenced in on both sides from the fans, for the introductions; and everyone was screaming and yelling at us."

The success of the Cowboys centered around their running attack and defense. Morton's arm miseries were only part of the reason for the defused Dallas air game. Lance Rentzel, one of the team's primary wide receivers, was suspended for the remainder of the season because of personal problems resulting from a morals charge. The club's other wide receiver, Bob Hayes, was not only a deluxe pass catcher but a dangerous punt returner as well. However, the speedy Hayes, whose total of 34 pass receptions was the lowest of his career, nevertheless led the Cowboys in touchdowns with ten. Part of his mediocre performance was the result of being benched for two full games and part of three others. Landry felt that he didn't meet with Cowboy "performance levels." Hayes admitted that he spent most of the season swapping dirty looks with Landry.

"I didn't like being benched," Hayes said emphatically. "I feel I'm good enough to play for anybody's first team in football. Why should I sit on the bench when I'm at my best?"

Part of Hayes' problems with Landry probably came from the fact that he hadn't signed his 1970 contract. He was involved in a salary dispute with the club and threatened to play out his option. Despite his return to the regular lineup and the fact that the Cowboys were in the Super Bowl, Hayes still harbored resentment.

"I'm damn serious about playing out my option," he added.

That was why the Dallas running game took on even more significance. Morton was looked upon by many as the least impressive quarterback ever to play in the Super Bowl. But while he had his problems, so did his counterpart, Johnny Unitas of the Colts. There was a feeling among many that the veteran 37-year-old Unitas couldn't throw the long ball effectively any more, but he was also beset by personal problems. There were rumors, but nobody knew then that a week after the game Unitas's wife would file for divorce.

Still, Unitas had led the Colts to an 11-2-1 record. He had completed 166 of 221 passes for 2,213 yards and 14 touchdowns. But the most glaring statistic was that he had 18 interceptions. The year before, when Baltimore had finished with an 8-5-1 record, people had started to whisper that Unitas was finished. He completed 187 of 327 passes, had only 12 touchdowns, and 20 interceptions.

"I can't throw as far, and I can't run as fast," said Unitas in response to the criticism. "Quarterbacks can't permit themselves to think of injuries or they'll leave their game in the locker room. The Cowboys' linebacking unit is a great one. They are not as big as some, but they are strong as they can be; and they have great speed and mobility.

"Probably the biggest thing they have going for them is that they have been playing together a long time. With all that experience, they know exactly what they are doing and the best way to do it. Up front, I think the Cowboy rush is better than most we've played against this year. If you want to beat the Dallas defense, you've got to figure out some way to beat them."

(Left and above) Unitas leaves game in second period after sustaining a rib injury when hit by Dallas' defensive tackle Jethro Pugh. The Baltimore quarterback retired to the bench and never returned to the game.

While Unitas attracted most of the attention, reserve quarterback Earl Morrall was hardly noticed. It was a strange paradox. Two years before in Super Bowl III, Morrall had been the center attraction. While Unitas was injured, Morrall had stepped in and led the Colts to the Super Bowl. Because of his great performance, he was named "Player of the Year." But Super Bowl III was a lingering nightmare for Morrall.

"Sure, I think about the game," confided Morrall. "I still get flashbacks. I keep seeing Johnny Sample reaching around Willie Richardson to make an interception. I keep seeing Jimmy Orr wide open on the flea flicker play. I keep seeing the ball bounce off Tom Mitchell's shoulder pads, and Randy Beverly's interception. All my flashbacks are bad.

"You always remember the mistakes, not the good things. I'll be on the phones on the sidelines Sunday. I'm sure if I get a chance to go in it'll mean we are losing, and I don't want it to go bad for John. But that doesn't mean that I wouldn't want to play. I'm ready to go in any time."

Morrall wasn't the only one sharing the

Morton is hit from behind by Baltimore defensive end Roy Hilton (85).

"We'll save the vacations until after the game. We want to eliminate all the distractions, to concentrate on just one thing, the Dallas Cowboys. When there is family around, there are other things to take up a player's time. Our whole season is wrapped up in this week; and the players agreed that it isn't too much to ask that for this amount of time, football remain the only thing on their minds.

"We want to make sure we work on artificial turf, too. Dallas has an edge on us there because they play all their home games on artificial turf and played something like nine games this season on such surfaces. We played three games and won two."

McCafferty was a sharp contrast to his predecessor, Don Shula. Although he had been in the NFL for 12 years as an assistant coach, he was probably the least known among the head coaches. He was a quiet type, who portrayed a fatherly image to his players. Most of the players knew him well as an assistant coach with the club for ten years. They felt comfortable with him.

"I'm the patient type," disclosed McCafferty. "You learn that by teaching, and I taught classes all the time I was at Kent State. Coaching is teaching, too. Some people have the idea that playing football qualifies someone to coach. But there is more involved in coaching than experience as a player, and I was a lousy pro end."

The only lousy thing that surfaced in pro football in 1970 was a players' strike. A

54

nightmare of Super Bowl III. All the Colts remembered it much too vividly. This time, they were relegated to a monastic life at the Miami Lakes Country Club where they were billeted. No wives or other members of the family were permitted, a sharp contrast to two years before.

"This is strictly business for us," emphasized Colt coach Don McCafferty.

Baltimore running back Tom Nowatzke scores Colts' second touchdown in the fourth quarter, as quarterback Earl Morrall (15) jumps with joy.

principal figure in the brief strike was the Colts' tight end John Mackey, who was also the president of the National Football League Players Association. Wisely, he postponed discussing the problems that still remained despite an apparent agreement that had been made with the league.

Mackey had had a painful summer. In the first place, he spent time recovering from a knee operation. Then, too, he had had to lead the players' negotiating team in their heated and often bitter talks with the owners. While a peace had been agreed upon, no official contract signings resulted. Just agreements. All season long Mackey had had to live with the serious problems of player-owner relationships. He tried not to get into any lengthy discussions on the subject but was more concerned with recovering from a pulled hamstring muscle he had suffered in a playoff game three weeks earlier.

"I'm only thinking Super Bowl now," Mackey said, smiling. "The negotiations are still in the hands of our lawyers. I'm concentrating on the game. When the game's over, I'll begin to think about the other situation.

"All the players have been nice enough to leave me alone lately. They know what it's been like to get ready for a playoff game, and then a championship game, and now a Super Bowl game. And when the game Sunday is over, they know I'll be available. Our contract hasn't been signed yet. In the confusion of getting a settlement, some misunderstanding developed. But don't get me talking about it. I want to think football.

"You know, I think of sitting around at halftime in that game two years ago and how bad it was, how unprepared we were. And I remember that the night before, that was the only time that my wife ever stayed with me before any game."

But Mackey remembered more. He remembered dropping a few passes in the game. But he also revealed that those unpleasant memories hadn't bothered him in the years that passed.

"Those things happen," observed Mackey. "On one pass, I lost it in the background of the spectators. It's hard to see in this stadium because of the colorful crowd. All the people in different colored clothes,

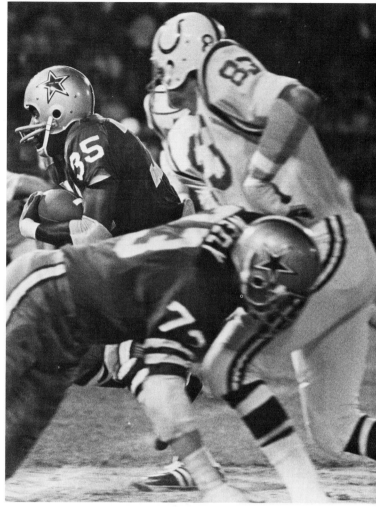
Dallas running back Calvin Hill gets past linebacker Ted Hendricks (83) for a few yards.

orange, red, green, white. But the loss bothered me. I remember feeling like I wanted to dig a hole and hide until the next season started.

"Everybody knocked our team this year. But it got progressively better as the season went on. We had new players; we were in a new league; we had new defensive alignments to face. It was an adjustment for the veterans as much as for the rookies. Early in this season we had to think. Now we don't have to think."

At least nobody had to think about the weather. At game time, the temperature was 70 degrees. The Cowboys received the opening kickoff and couldn't do anything. Neither could Baltimore when they got the ball. Dallas got the ball again and still

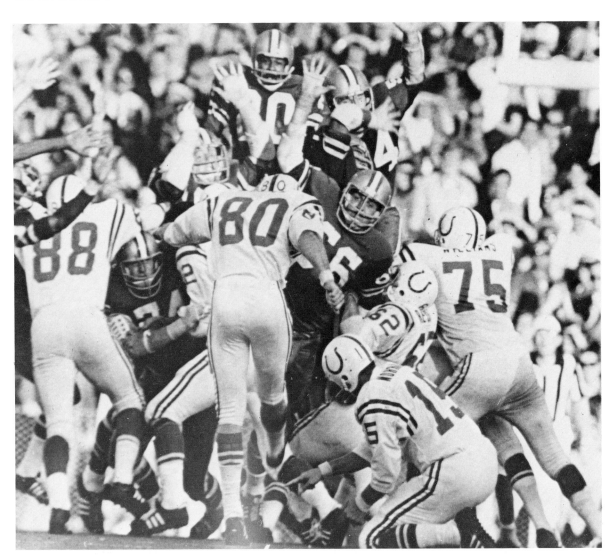

56

(Pages 56 and 57) With just five seconds remaining in the contest, Jim O'Brien calmly kicked a 32-yard field goal to give the Colts an exciting 16-13 triumph.

couldn't move it. When Baltimore got the ball a second time, the Colts had excellent field position. On first down from the Baltimore 47, Unitas wanted to pass short to his back, Norm Bulaich. However, Chuck Howley, the seasoned Dallas linebacker, intercepted the ball on his own 32 and ran it back to the Baltimore 46.

But Dallas couldn't capitalize. Then, when Ron Widby punted, they got a break. Ron Gardin fumbled the kick on his own nine-yard line, and the ball was recovered by Cliff Harris. The Cowboys had a great opportunity, but the Colt defense stiffened and prevented a touchdown. Instead, the Cowboys had to settle for a 14-yard field

goal by Mike Clark, which sent them into a 3-0 lead.

Early in the second quarter, the Cowboys scored again. This time Clark booted a 30-yard field goal that put the Cowboys in front, 6-0. But the lead was brief. On the ensuing kickoff, Baltimore struck quickly and without warning. After two passes failed, Unitas tried a third pass from his own 25-yard line. He tried to hit wide receiver Eddie Hinton, but the pass flew over Eddie's head. Hinton leaped and tipped the ball toward Dallas cornerback Mel Renfro. He, too, couldn't control the ball; it fell into the arms of Mackey, who ran the rest of the way for a touchdown. The 75-yard pass

Unitas and defensive tackle
George Wright congratulate
each other as they enter Colts'
dressing room.

58

play tied the score at 6-6 as Jim O'Brien missed the conversion that would have put Baltimore on top.

Midway into the quarter, Dallas got their second break. Attempting to pass on third down from his own 21-yard line, Unitas, finding no one open, began to run. He was hit hard by linebacker Lee Roy Jordan, and fumbled. Jethro Pugh recovered the ball for Dallas on the 28. Three plays later Morton hit Thomas with a seven-yard touchdown pass for a 13-6 Dallas edge.

Unitas tried to get the Colts going on the next series but failed. On third down, he was hit hard by defensive end George Andrie. His wobbly pass was intercepted by cornerback Mel Renfro, and Unitas trotted off the field holding his side. He was hurt. The next time Baltimore got the ball before the half ended, Morrall took over. He led

the Colts to the Cowboys' two-yard line before he was turned back on a fourth-down pass.

When the third period began, Jim Duncan fumbled the kickoff, and Richmond Flowers recovered the ball for Dallas on the Baltimore 31. Keeping on the ground, the Cowboys moved for a first down on the Colts' two-yard line. But Thomas fumbled, and Duncan redeemed himself by recovering the ball on the one-yard line. No one seriously threatened to score after that, and the quarter ended with Dallas still in front.

On the first play of the fourth period, Morrall's third-down pass was intercepted in the end zone by Howley, which killed another threat. However, after a Dallas punt, Morrall had the Colts moving again. On a first-down play on the Dallas 39, Morrall lateraled the ball to Sam Havrilak, who passed to Hinton on the five-yard line. Hinton fumbled, and the ball rolled out of the end zone for a touchback. It was the *seventh* Baltimore turnover.

Just as quickly, Dallas gave the Colts the ball back. On third down from his own 23-yard line, Morton's pass was deflected by Duncan and intercepted by Volk, who ran it back to the three. Two plays later, Tom Nowatzke went over for the tying touchdown.

It appeared that the game would end in a 13-13 tie and go into overtime. With just over a minute to play, Morton tried to pass from his own 27-yard line. His pass bounced off halfback Dan Reeves' hands and into the arms of Curtis, who brought it back to the 28. Morrall was thinking field goal. Two runs advanced the ball to the 25. On third down, Jim O'Brien was sent in to attempt a game-winning 32-yard field goal. With only five seconds showing on the clock, O'Brien came through. The Colts prevailed in an error-filled game, 16-13. So frustrated was Dallas' All-Pro tackle Bob Lilly that he threw his helmet about 40 feet into the air.

O'Brien, the game's hero, appeared calm in the Baltimore dressing room. He told about a dream he had a week before the game.

"Right after we got down here, I had a dream that a long field goal was going to win this game," revealed O'Brien. "I didn't know who was going to kick it or how far or when it would happen, but now I know. All the guys had confidence in me, and that was the big thing. When we went out there, Earl just told me to kick it straight through, that there was no wind, just to kick it. I hurt my knee on the kickoff before the field goal, and I was concerned that it would get stiff. But I didn't think about it when I made the kick."

The winning kick made McCafferty the first rookie coach to win a Super Bowl. Naturally he was happy when the players handed him a game ball along with O'Brien.

"The turning point had to be Curtis's interception," said McCafferty. "That set it up for us. We had a lot of bad breaks in the first half, but we hung in there. I kept Morrall in the game, although the doctor said Unitas could return, because I thought Earl was doing a real fine job; and I saw no reason to make a change."

Landry was quite subdued. It was obvious that the loss affected him. He knew the charge of not being able to win the big one would surface even more.

"This hurts pretty bad," he disclosed. "You don't measure disappointment. I couldn't say anything to the team. I tried, but you can't say anything. We just beat ourselves. The fumble by Duane Thomas and the two interceptions by Rick Volk and Mike Curtis killed us. Thomas's fumble undoubtedly was the big play of the game. If he had scored, they would have had a lot of catching up to do. We would have been in firm control."

In retrospect, it was an error-filled game. Nobody really had control . . .

59

Super Bowl VI

January 16, 1972
New Orleans Tulane Stadium
80,591

Dallas (NFC)	3	7	7	7	—	**24**
Miami (AFC)	0	3	0	0	—	**3**

They were somewhat of a Cinderella team. They had a fish on their helmet; wore summer colors of aqua, orange, and white; played in a hip, resort city; and were poked fun at their first four years in the league. They even had a dolphin named Flipper for a mascot that they kept in a water tank at one end of the end zone. Some diabolical writer figured the dolphin was put there to take the fans' attention away from the football field. The team's performance was so inept that Flipper got more cheers than the players. But that was only until 1969.

The following season the Miami Dolphins began a new era with the arrival of coach Don Shula. Overnight, he transformed the ragamuffin Dolphins into winners. Flipper was gone, and Shula was the new hero. In 1972, only two years after he became coach, Shula had the Dolphins in Super Bowl VI.

It didn't promise to be an exciting week in New Orleans where the Super Bowl returned for the second time. Not when considering what the Dolphins had done in the championship playoffs. In their opening game, they defeated the Kansas City Chiefs, 27-24, in an overtime game that lasted 82 minutes and 40 seconds. It was the longest game in NFL history. Then, in the AFC championship game the following week, Shula defeated his old team, the Baltimore Colts, by a convincing 21-0. Dolphin fans bordered on hysteria, so much so that they stormed the team's offices in Miami to get Super Bowl tickets.

Winning was a strange new experience for the Dolphins. Their opponents, the Dallas Cowboys, knew what winning was all about. They had experienced five consecutive winning seasons, participated in the championship playoffs all those times, and had appeared in Super Bowl V the previous year. It was understandable why they were established as a seven-point favorite to defeat the Dolphins, Miami madness or not. The experts felt that Dallas was long overdue.

With all the excitement surrounding the quarterbacks the last three years, Super Bowl VI offered no such drama. Both Bob Griese of the Dolphins and Roger Staubach of the Cowboys disdained publicity. Both were similar in nature in that they were teetotalers, happily married, placid, and religious. The fact that both led their teams to the Super Bowl should say something about clean living.

The biggest action in New Orleans was finding hotel rooms. Even Joe Robbie, the owner of the Dolphins, needed rooms badly. He put out the word all over town in an effort to accommodate the requests made to him. People were willing to pay $100 a night for a room, a lot more than scalpers were getting for a ticket to the game. Hotel rooms were so scarce that the American Society of Refrigerating and Air Conditioning Engineers, Inc., had to postpone its convention until the following week.

No sooner did the two opposing teams arrive in New Orleans than the action heated up. Duane Thomas, the Cowboys' star runner, refused to show up at the press interviews the first day. He had sent word through a club official that he wasn't talking to any writers that day, the next day, or the rest of the week. In fact, the word was out that Thomas wasn't talking to anybody, including his teammates and his coach Tom Landry. He was strictly unapproachable. It was ironic. Duane Thomas, who withdrew

The sphinx that Miami couldn't stop: Duane Thomas.

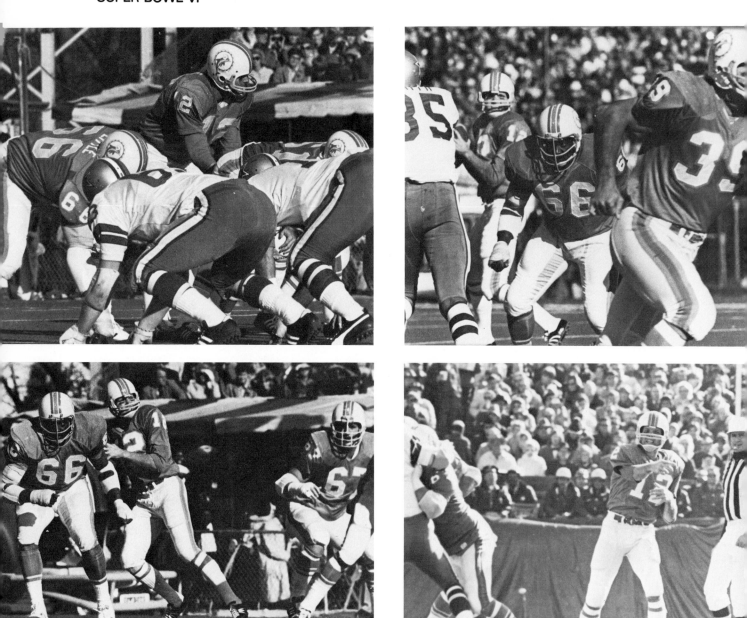

Miami quarterback Bob Griese spent a frustrating afternoon against the powerful Dallas Cowboys as the Dolphins' offense could only produce a field goal.

completely behind a cloak of silence, was making news. The Thomas mystery even left some doubts whether he would show up for the game on Sunday. After all, he had missed a day of practice the previous week in Dallas. The Cowboys never explained why. Nobody really knew how Thomas felt because no one was able to talk to him.

Dewey Wong couldn't understand it at all. He was Chinese and had talked to people, even writers, long before President Nixon made his historic trip to China. Wong owns about the finest Chinese restaurant in New York. His restaurant is frequently visited by athletes. At the time of the Thomas incident, he was having lunch in Jimmy Moran's place on Iberville Street with Robbie and Gene Ward, the widely read sports columnist of the New York *News*. Wong couldn't believe that Thomas wasn't speaking to anybody. He shook his head and removed a cigar from his mouth.

"You know, when he was in my place last month, we sat and talked for at least 45 minutes," disclosed Wong. "He liked my food; and after he ate, we talked about everything. We didn't even talk about football. He's a very intelligent person. When he got up to leave, he said, 'Good-bye, brother.'"

Robbie just shook his head. "Well, at least you're one person he spoke to," he said.

"Where are the Cowboys staying?" asked Wong.

"At the Hilton Inn," answered Ward.

"Maybe I should give Duane a call," offered Wong.

"Say, Dewey, I have a great idea," Ward said and smiled.

"What's that?" inquired Wong.

"Why don't you call Thomas, find out what he has to say, and tell us about it?"

"That wouldn't be a bad idea," added Robbie. "At least we'll find out if he's going to play on Sunday."

Later that day, Robbie had another matter to worry about. It concerned his team. A story broke out of Miami that George Wilson, whom Shula had replaced as coach after the 1969 season, was quoted as saying, "Joe Doakes could have taken this Miami team to the American Football Conference championship and the Super Bowl." It was a direct slap at Shula and the Miami organization. Wilson was still bitter about being fired. He pointed to the parallel situation involving Vince Lombardi and Scooter McLean at Green Bay. McLean was fired, and Lombardi replaced him and turned the Packers into a winning organization.

"You know, it's a funny thing," said Wilson. "McLean started building Green Bay the year before Lombardi took over. It was McLean who made a halfback of Paul Hornung, built the offensive line, and made most of the moves Lombardi got all the credit for. Not to knock Lombardi, but he got the praise and acclaim for building the Packers while McLean was forgotten.

"I brought Don to Detroit as an assistant

Big Bob Lilly was the spearhead of the Cowboys' tight defense as he constantly applied pressure from his tackle position.

63

when I was coaching the Lions and recommended him to Carroll Rosenbloom at Baltimore after I had to decline an offer of a five-year contract to take over the Colts. It just seemed to me that it would have been only common courtesy for Shula to call me and let me know he was being offered the Dolphins job. It wouldn't have taken a two-hour conversation, just a simple call. I came awfully close to learning over the radio that I had been fired. Wouldn't that have been great?"

The assembled writers tried to elicit a response from Robbie when he returned to his hotel. A feisty owner, Robbie has been known to lose his temper at times. They had hoped that a sharp retort from Robbie would enliven the feud, but Robbie kept a cool head.

"I'm sorry George made a statement like

that," answered Robbie after being told about Wilson's remarks. "It's the first I've heard of it. We've always considered George a part of the Dolphins. He played such an important part in the formation of the club at its beginning. We always give George season tickets for himself and his family. Why, if he wants to see Sunday's game, he can come as our guest. Gentlemen, I don't think any further commentary is necessary. It just doesn't sound like something that George would necessarily say."

The next morning at his press conference, Shula treated the matter lightly, in a humorous fashion. It was the perfect ploy. The writers were hoping that Shula would retaliate, but he wisely refrained. Starting or continuing feuds was not Shula's way.

Introduced as head coach Don Shula, he immediately interjected, "Or Joe Doakes, whatever you prefer to call me." A few minutes later a writer, confusing him with Landry, began to ask him a question, "Tom, er, uh, Don . . . " Shula quipped, "Just call me Joe." The writers all laughed. Then Shula got serious.

"I don't know what Wilson's reasons

Dallas running back Walt Garrison hurdles for some extra yards.

64

Griese hands ball to second back coming through, Jim Kiick (21), as Larry Csonka (39) leads the way.

were for making those remarks at this time," remarked Shula. "I'm disappointed to hear that he made those comments. I've never been one to step forward and say I'm a coaching genius. But as far as taking over a ready-made team is concerned, there are only 18 players with us now who were on the squad I took over.

"I learned a great deal under Wilson, particularly in the art of handling men. There was no better psychologist in the business. I had heard that he was upset because I didn't call him, but the reason I didn't was that I had promised Joe Robbie I would keep it confidential. Before I ever agreed to talk with Robbie, I asked him if Wilson was out regardless of whether I took the job. He told me he was. If Joe Doakes could have taken this team to the Super Bowl, all well and good. But let's get all of this out of the way now so that we can get back to talking about the football game."

Shula didn't want all this budding controversy to upset his club. He was well aware of any added pressure and didn't welcome it. He had been in too many big

Miami tight end Marv Fleming looks for running room after catching a pass from Griese.

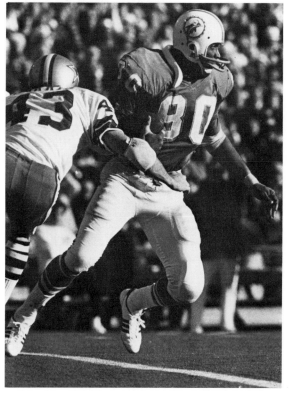

games not to realize its impact. He had been part of the confusion that surrounded Ft. Lauderdale and Miami Beach when he had been preparing his Colts to meet the New York Jets in Super Bowl III. He wanted to avoid any duplication, especially this time around. He had a young team who had never been exposed to the pre-game ballyhoo from writers, broadcasters, and photographers from all over the world. Shula tried to limit the press interviews with his players. He attempted to have a training camp atmosphere amid all the excitement, but it was difficult. At night after supper the team reviewed films. They were instructed to be in their rooms by 11 P.M.

"We have to overcome our lack of experience with aggressiveness," reasoned Shula. "The important thing now is how our young people react to their offense. We don't want our aggressiveness taken away by indecision. I think we have achieved our identity as a mature, contending team by the way we came through under pressure against the Chiefs and Colts. Now our players don't just think they can do it, they know they can win against the best."

Yet, Griese was still considered a young quarterback. It was only his fifth year in the league and only his second winning season. He led the new American Conference in passing with 145 completions in 263 attempts for a percentage of 55.1. He had also thrown the most touchdown passes, 19, in the conference. It was all still new to him. However, he had a game-breaking receiver in Paul Warfield that presented a threat to any opposing team.

"I'm trying to prepare for the game just like any other," revealed Griese. "But there are so many people around and there is so much emphasis on the game that you could let it bother you if you're not careful. I have used every waking moment since Monday night to study. The only pressure I feel is when I talk to the writers. That's why I don't read the newspapers.

"I'm more of an introvert than an extrovert. I am not loud or outspoken; but if there is a bunch of football players ready to play football, somebody has to be in command. Taking command, that's something that somehow I have always been able to do. In a game I think of myself looking on

65

Dallas quarterback Roger Staubach is looking up from somewhere near the bottom of this pile.

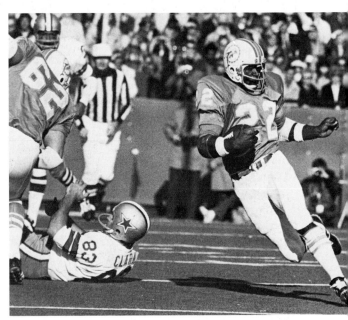

Mercury Morris almost broke one for Dolphins after taking a second-half kickoff.

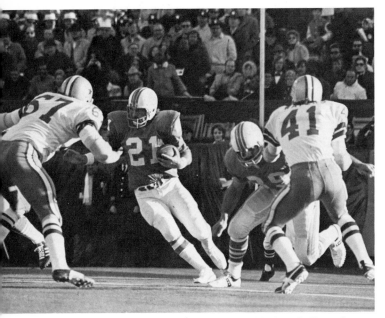

Csonka (39) prepares to throw a block on Dallas safety Charlie Waters (41) in attempt to give Kiick (21) some running room.

the situation from above like a chess player moving pieces. I can see moves coming, and I'm ready to make them. When you're a rookie, you feel like one of the pieces. You can't see everybody because you're down among them, and things aren't clear. But when you have a total grasp and knowledge of what's going on, then you feel you can maneuver people around, manipulate your offense to take advantage of what the defense is showing.

"Warfield changed me as a passer. When he came to Miami, he brought defenses with him. I had been taught not to throw into double coverage. But Warfield always gets double coverage, and he showed me he could beat it. I didn't know much about Paul at the time he joined us, but I heard a great deal about him. I thought maybe there was something physically wrong with him, or that he was over the hill and that's why he was traded.

"He has had two great years for us, and he should have three or four more. He has opened up the passing game for us. Before, we never had a receiver who could go deep. In one way, I suppose you could say it has meant more work for the quarterback because Paul has brought a lot of coverages we hadn't seen before, double coverages and combinations. Like I said, I had been taught that when a man is double-covered, go to another receiver. One thing I had to learn was to stick with Paul because he can beat double coverage."

But what **Shula** also liked about Griese was his knowledge of the running game. In that respect, Griese was the complete quar-

Miami middle linebacker Nick Buoniconti had a busy day trying to lasso Cowboy runners.

terback. He would stay with whatever was working during a game. If he had the pass, he would take it. If the run was open, he would utilize it. And in Larry Csonka and Jim Kiick, the Dolphins had a strong running attack. They had gone through the entire 1971 season and the playoffs with only one fumble between them. They opened the defense for Griese's play-action passes to Warfield.

"We follow the blocking the way it's set up," explained Csonka. "And it's set up for four yards plus. You stay within your blocking and take what you can get and maybe fight for a little more. Once you break away from it and try to bust a long one, you'll get the long gainer every now and then; but your average will take a plunge, and you'll hurt the team. You'll hurt the whole concept of what it's trying to do."

What Csonka did well was run during the 1971 season. He led the Dolphins with 1,051 yards. He was a jarring runner and a bruising blocker. Whether running or blocking, he liked contact. He especially liked blocking for Kiick, who gained 738 yards. Csonka and Kiick were close friends off the field. They were inseparable, as close as two players could be. They were affectionately known around the league as "Butch Cassidy and the Sundance Kid."

"We're two of a kind," said Kiick, smiling. "We enjoy running over people. We like to hit. Larry really runs over people. I feel sorry for those defensive backs who have to stop him. He absolutely destroys them. I can't really run over that many people because of my size. Larry just bowls them over.

"I can honestly say I get as much satisfaction when Larry has a good game running with the ball as I do myself. If he's running well, it simply means that I am blocking well and doing my job. Larry may look slow, but he's not. He's so big that people get the impression that he can't be very fast. But just watch him when he runs to the outside."

Csonka and Kiick's friendship was low-keyed. They didn't have to make anything big out of it. It was natural to them. Each knew that one would help the other. They possessed that kind of deep relationship. They could sit together quietly without saying a word, yet, each would know what the other was thinking.

"Jim and I are of the same mold," admitted Csonka. "We're just a couple of beer drinkers who like to have a good time together. Statistics come second to us. I like to play, and so does Jim. There's only one way to gauge a runner, and that's by how many yards he makes. What I like to feel after every season is that I've gotten every inch I possibly could have.

"I'm not too swift sometimes when it comes to blocking some defensive linemen. I try to get them where they have to cross

Garrison is in full stride as he turns upfield around end.

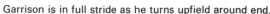

Dallas's linebacker Chuck Howley comes up fast to stop Kiick, who had caught a pass from Griese.

68

my path to get to the runner. You can sort of trap them if the play is near the sideline. It's like the difference between chasing a hog in a big pen and one in a little pen."

Csonka remembered one such experience. It occurred in the 1971 Pro Bowl. Csonka

Miami wide receiver Paul Warfield is sandwiched by Cowboy defenders.

thought he had set up Dallas's perennial All-Pro tackle, Bob Lilly, for the crusher.

"I was going to blast him, wipe him right out," recalled Csonka. "The next thing I knew, he wasn't there. I swear, Lilly must have been six feet up. I mean he actually leaped right over me, and I'm six-feet-two. I never touched him."

Csonka looked at Kiick.

"We know Dallas is tough to run against, but we still have to establish our running game," pointed out Kiick.

"Yeah, they're tough; and the fact that they resemble Kansas City doesn't make me feel real well," added Csonka. "They've got those tackles, Jethro Pugh and who's that fellow on the other side?"

"Bob Lilly," answered Kiick, "and he's the one reason they're so tough to run against. Lilly is so quick. Some people say the best thing is to run right at him, that he's so quick sometimes he jumps out of his own position. Even though they play great defense as a team, the name Lilly comes up when we talk about Dallas. His name just stands out.

"Lilly's speed and pursuit symbolize the entire Dallas defense. When you watch Dallas films, you hone in on their pursuit. That's what makes great defense. Most teams, when you turn the corner on a sweep, you know you're going to make 10 to 12 yards. But when you play Dallas, you get that off-side pursuit, and nothing is assured."

By Thursday, Landry wasn't sure of the availability of his own running star, Calvin Hill. The big running back's knee had given out in the NFC championship game, and his status for the Super Bowl was questionable.

"If we had to go into the game today, our starting backs would be Walt Garrison and Duane Thomas," disclosed Landry. "Hill worked out yesterday, and most of the soreness is out of his knee; but he's still not moving at full speed yet. Assuming the turnovers are equal on Sunday, the team that runs best against the other team has the best chance of winning.

"I know nothing at all about the Miami defense except that I do know Shula, and I have to assume we'll see a lot of the same thing we saw when he was coaching Baltimore. If we are going to run the ball, we're

Dallas running back Duane Thomas (33) is escorted through the line by Walt Garrison (32) and John Niland (76).

going to have to get somebody to block their middle linebacker, Nick Buoniconti. He has freedom back there, and he's not guessing. We don't give freedom to anybody. They have many young, developing players on defense, but Buoniconti is a real veteran, the key to their defense. His experience gives him the ability to read plays and get to the ball."

Still, Landry didn't appear too concerned about Hill's knee. When he had first hurt it earlier in the season, he had been sidelined for seven weeks. Yet, Thomas had filled in for him and the Cowboys began to win consistently, finishing the season with a nine-game winning streak. With Hill, Thomas, and Garrison, Landry had three fine runners he could rotate effectively. Hill had hopes that he would start against the Dolphins.

"The knee is a discouraging, frustrating thing," conceded Hill. "But day by day it seems to be getting better. I don't have as much lateral motion as I did before the injuries this year and last year. I'm more of a slasher now. I'm stronger than I've ever been, and I've run over more people this year. The knee locked, like a trick knee. If I can do okay in practice the rest of the week, I will play Sunday. But one of the good things about our situation of having depth is that I don't feel the pressure to go half-speed.

"Look at our record since Thomas came back. Duane reminds me of a lot of guys I know coming out of college today. His whole life isn't football and getting smashed and picking up broads. I was a

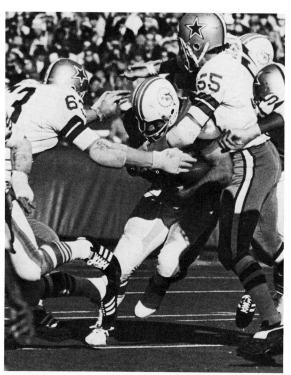

Big running back Larry Csonka is stopped by Cowboy linebacker Lee Roy Jordan (55) and defensive end Larry Cole (63).

Garrison is in trouble as Dolphin linebacker Mike Kolen (57) closes in behind line of scrimmage.

(Left and above) Duane Thomas, the star Cowboy running back who wasn't talking to anybody before the game, showed the Dolphins his many moves as he ran for 95 yards.

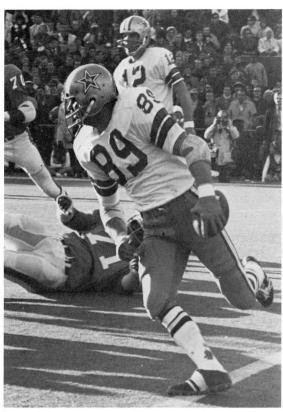

Dallas tight end Mike Ditka churns upfield after catching a pass, picks up a blocker in John Niland (76), then goes in for a touchdown in fourth period.

black history major at Yale, and he and I talk a lot in that area. I found out he was reading a lot of that stuff. He was put on the spot this year, and people are more aware of what he's doing. But he's the same man this year as he was last year. He has some real depth as a man.''

Staubach felt the same way. While much was made of Thomas's withdrawal from the press and his refusal to talk to people, his behavior didn't affect his concentration or upset the rest of the team.

"Duane is a quiet individual right now," disclosed Staubach. "He's an intelligent man, you know. I don't know what's bothering him right now, and I don't intend to ask him. We don't have any communication problems in the huddle. As I said, he's very bright. He knows our plays, our formations, and all of his routines perfectly. Once in a while he'll goof up a pass pattern, and I chew him out for it just like anybody else. He knows right away when he's made a mistake.

"I don't mean I ridicule him or raise my voice, but I tell him he didn't execute properly; and he takes it just fine. By the same token, if I give him a bad hand-off, I apologize to him. You haven't seen Duane in practice this week, but I want to tell you he runs every play out 15 or 20 yards downfield. Anyway, I know I won't sleep well Saturday night before the game; and that's to be expected. Before the championship game against San Francisco, I went to bed at 10:30, and three hours later I was still going over those plays in my mind. It doesn't do me much good to sit here and talk about what I would like to do. The only place I can do that is on the field Sunday."

Super Sunday dawned bright, clear, and cloudless. The radiant blue of the sky framed the rooftops of the nineteenth-century houses in the French Quarter. Yet, the sun was deceiving. It looked warm, but it wasn't a Miami sun. A cold wind rattled the large, old windows of the Quarter. Out-

Dallas defensive back Charlie Waters is brought down after running back a kickoff.

side it wasn't more than 28 degrees, too cold for New Orleans. Yet, it was much more pleasant than the rain that had pelted down on Super Sunday two years before.

When the Dolphins received the opening kickoff, the temperature had climbed to 39 degrees. The second time they got the ball, they had a mild drive going. Csonka swept around his right end and gained 12 yards before he was brought down on the Dallas 46. But on the next play, he fumbled for the first time all season, and linebacker Chuck Howley recovered for the Cowboys. Twelve plays later, Mike Clark kicked a nine-yard field goal to give Dallas a 3-0 lead with just over a minute left in the period.

Near the end of the half, Dallas struck again. With Thomas and Hill running for sizeable yardage, Dallas had a first down on the Miami seven-yard line. Staubach then fired a perfect pass to wide receiver Lance Alworth in the left corner of the end zone to give the Cowboys a 10-0 advantage.

There was only 1:10 left when Miami got the ball again. Griese hit Warfield with a couple of passes and Kiick for another as he drove the Dolphins to the Dallas 24. With just eight seconds showing on the clock,

Dallas quarterback Roger Staubach gets set to throw before a charging Manny Fernandez.

Garo Yepremian booted a 31-yard field goal as the Dolphins went into the dressing room trailing 10-3.

Dallas had controlled the play during the first half. They made 13 first downs to Miami's five, gained 174 yards to Miami's 74, and held Kiick to 19 yards and Csonka to just 15. That was the total of the Dolphins' running attack.

Yepremian's last-second field goal gave the Dolphins hope, as did the fact that Griese moved them 44 yards in about a minute. With such success, a 10-3 lead was not insurmountable. After all, the Dolphins did have the power to strike back; and with a half-hour respite, they were ready to come back strong.

However, things immediately got worse for the Dolphins when the third quarter began. The Cowboys took the second half kickoff and went 71 yards in just eight plays. Thomas scored a touchdown on a

third-yard run to send Dallas into a 17-3 lead.

But then Mercury Morris made the fans leave their seats as he almost broke loose for a touchdown. He gathered in Clark's kickoff on the goal line and dashed to the 37 before he was upended. There was still 9:25 left in the quarter, and Griese tried to get the Miami attack going. He couldn't. The Miami offense managed to get the ball three times in the quarter, but the Dolphins failed to get a single first down. Miami had only eight plays from scrimmage during the entire period. They just couldn't get it going at all.

In the opening minutes of the final quarter, Dallas killed any chances the Dolphins might have had for coming back. Howley picked off Griese's pass at midfield and started downfield with no one in front of him. However, the 35-year-old veteran stumbled and fell on the nine-yard line. It

Duane Thomas lunges for some additional yards through the center of the line.

didn't matter. Three plays later Staubach threw a seven-yard pass to tight end Mike Ditka in the end zone for a 24-3 bulge. Miami was finished.

The win was especially satisfying for Landry. He had lost last year's Super Bowl, and his teams had been criticized as not being able to win the big games even before that. The dressing room was quiet for a few minutes as he received a phone call from President Nixon. When he finished, he faced the writers.

"This was our best overall performance of the season," exclaimed Landry. "Considering the caliber of competition we have faced in the playoffs, allowing each of them one touchdown or less, the defense has been fantastic. This certainly is my biggest thrill.

"We changed a few things on offense, but basically we went with our best plays. We ran a much stronger counterattack. We usually run to the strong side. We tried to run both sides; but I guess when we were successful, we stayed right most of the way. A lot of our success running came as a result of handling Buoniconti. You either block

Dallas's swift wide receiver Bob Hayes catches up with a Staubach pass.

74

Staubach cleanly hands the ball off to Thomas.

Buoniconti, or you don't run. I was surprised with the yards we got. In the second half they came out with three men and a linebacker in spots where we had opened holes in the first half, so we went the other way.

"Of course, the defense was the strongest part of our game. But I really didn't think that we could shut off their runners as well as we did, holding them to 80 yards."

The Dolphins took the loss hard, especially Csonka.

"There's no doubt about it—my fumble was the big turning point of the game," he lamented. "I was reading the defense before I got the ball and was a little higher than usual for the handoff. I think I hit it with my knee. If I hadn't done that, it would have been an easy 20 to 30 yard gain as both tackles were stunting and we got a good block on the linebacker. That play could have given us momentum, but it gave it all to Dallas instead.

"Anyone that plays in the Super Bowl has to feel the pressure. We didn't think it

Dallas running back Calvin Hill is hit and fumbles on goal line near end of game.

Veteran Dallas linebacker Chuck Howley starts downfield with intercepted pass in final quarter.

would affect us, but it's there. You can't hide from it, but that's part of it all. If you want to be a champion, you have to handle it."

Shula was even more disappointed. He was the losing coach in two Super Bowls now.

"They completely dominated us," said Shula. "My big disappointment was that we never really challenged in the big game. I say they have a great football team, but I say it grudgingly. They tore us apart on defense and controlled our offense. We were worried about stopping Dallas's running, and we weren't able to do it. We had good pressure on Staubach, but their running game broke it open."

Even though he led all runners with 95 yards, Duane Thomas still wasn't talking . . .

Super Bowl VII

January 14, 1973
Los Angeles Memorial Coliseum
90,182

Miami (AFC)	7	7	0	0	—	14
Washington (NFC)	0	0	0	7	—	7

They were something else. There had never been a team like them before in the long and cherished history of professional football, not even the eulogized Green Bay Packer teams of Vince Lombardi or the powerful Chicago Bear teams of George Halas. None of those teams had ever done what the Miami Dolphins did in 1972. It was unbelievable. They had gone through an entire season unbeaten. They had won every game in the regular season, 14 in all. Then they added two more victories in the championship playoffs. When they arrived in Los Angeles to face the Washington Redskins in Super Bowl VII, the Dolphins were 16-0. Unparalleled. Unprecedented.

Yet, despite their perfect season, the Dolphins were rated as underdogs! An undefeated team listed as an underdog? It didn't seem possible. Yet, the smart money boys, the oddsmakers, established the Redskins as three-point favorites. And, there was a lot of money wagered on Washington. Besides being the money favorites, the Redskins were the sentimental favorites as well. They were an assorted collection of discards and retreads, older than any other team in the league and affectionately called the "Over-the-Hill Gang." It was admirably put together by coach George Allen, who, outside of President Nixon, was perhaps the most powerful individual in Washington.

Allen was a dedicated, strong-willed person who always appeared in total control. Yet, during the hectic activity that has become associated with Super Bowl week, Allen became edgy, a bit testy. He looked with dismay at all the press interviews scheduled and the constant freeway driving that kept him away from his preparations for the biggest game in Washington history. It just wasn't his style. Anything that takes

him away from his year-long approach to football isn't. In fact, the two most important things in life, besides his family, are football and ice cream. His players loved him for that and for his dedication to winning.

"We have fun," said Diron Talbert, a defensive tackle that Allen had brought with him to Washington in 1971 after both had been with Los Angeles. "It's a known fact we call him 'Ice Cream.' Well, I'm captain of the huddle. And every once in a while we'll yell, 'I scream, you scream, we all scream for Ice Cream.'"

One of Allen's assistant coaches, Marv Levy, was more serious. While the players were having fun, he didn't want to lose perspective. After all, football was a very serious business.

"I've seen him eat other foods," pointed out Levy. "The image isn't totally right, but he is tremendously dedicated. He does want to be the best in the world. Just like someone who wants to be the best ballet dancer in the world.

"The main thing is his year-round approach to football. He gives everything he has to getting the team ready. He's always concentrating on the players' needs. He doesn't say on a Monday, 'Hey, this week we're going to work on motivation.' It's a total thing, an all-year-round thing, and the players know this. The cheers are a fun thing. They remind the players of the fun that goes with winning."

Ron McDole, the Redskins' 34-year-old defensive end, knew the feeling. In his third season with the club after being acquired from the Buffalo Bills in a 1971 trade, McDole enjoyed playing and winning once again under Allen.

"I've never seen a guy so dedicated to one

Miami safety Jake Scott, who intercepted two Redskin passes, starts upfield on a 55-yard run.

Before the game, Washington coach George Allen (left) and Miami coach Don Shula exchange views.

thing," added McDole. "His life is football; he lives football; he'll die football. Being around him, he forces us to try to have the same dedication. He puts in so much time and effort, it embarrasses you if you're not doing as much.

"I've played for five or six coaches, and I've never been better prepared. In the playoff games we held Green Bay and Dallas without a touchdown, but that's expected of us. The offense expects us to do it; we expect the offense to score, and everybody expects the kicking team to do their share.

"Yeah, we're older; and Allen relies on us not making mistakes, mental mistakes. It's different with young guys. When I was with Buffalo and we had lots of young kids, one week we'd look like Superman. We'd have a real good game. The next week, nothing. No consistency. They'd see something a little bit different than they'd seen before, and they'd screw it up.

"We know a lot of short cuts. For example, the mistake that most young defensive linemen make is chasing a back from be-

Washington wide receiver Charley Taylor stretches to pull down a pass.

Squatting low, Washington
running back Larry Brown looks
for an opening.

hind. What good does it do to chase a guy in a big circle? I'm not gonna catch a guy like that from behind. So I head down the line of scrimmage. If he cuts back, he cuts back into you."

The strength of the defense was the main reason why the Redskins were favored. No team in football that year played the run better than Washington. They had stopped the Packers in the opening playoff game with a five-man front. The following week they repulsed the Cowboys' high-powered offense in the NFC championship game. And to Allen, defense was what counted.

His players were well aware of it. Larry Brown, the Redskins' star runner, for one. In Washington, he had played for both Allen and Vince Lombardi before him. No one could have played for two finer coaches.

"George Allen has not spoken to me more than a few times since he joined the Redskins," disclosed Brown. "I ever hardly get to talk to him because he is primarily a defensive coach. I mainly talk to our offensive coordinator, Ted Marchibroda.

"Allen is constantly talking with the defensive players, and they have a lot of togetherness. Lombardi, on the other hand, was the offensive coordinator as well as the head coach, and I talked to him a lot. This is the first time that I have ever played for a

defensive coach in my career. Lombardi took a lot of personal interest in individual players, whereas Allen's interest is in the team as a whole.

"Pro football players like money, and Allen has been able to get it for us. Besides, we all have tremendous respect for him. He has put together a super football team. George Allen's philosophy is, 'You play together, this team,' and we have all bought that philosophy."

What Allen wasn't buying was the daily press routine. By the end of the week, he was visibly annoyed. While the player interviews ended on Thursday, he had to attend a special coach's press interview at Newport Beach. He didn't like making the long trip or the time required away from his players. The more he talked to the contingent of writers and sportscasters, the more upset he became. He said the interviews caused a delay in his team's Thursday workout, and it resulted in the worst practice they had all week. And, because he was now in Newport Beach, it made him miss a team meeting, the first one he had ever missed in the 23 years he had been coaching. It was only because it was mandatory by the league that Allen tolerated the interviews. But nevertheless, he let his feelings be known.

Although Miami coach Don Shula wasn't

enamored of the press conferences, he showed some of his displeasure in a jocular way. It was refreshing, too, because Shula was under a great deal more pressure than Allen or anyone else for that matter. He had coached in two previous Super Bowls, in 1969 with Baltimore and the previous year with Miami, and had lost both times. Like Allen, Shula was also a perfectionist.

"I've been answering the same questions since Monday," Shula said, and smiled. "New reporters come in every day. I don't mind, but it takes me away from my players. The concentration isn't there.

"Why don't you guys drop over to our hotel at ten in the morning? I know there isn't any interview scheduled, but I've gotten so used to seeing you at that time, I'll get lonesome.

"We're thinking of moving our last practices to Tijuana. I'll say that now so that George can begin scouting the area for our practice field. Seriously, though, when you're going against a George Allen-coached team, you're in tough. They play defense, as evidenced in the playoffs. They are strong offensively, able to strike quick, and they've got a fine kicking game. This is a team that is good in all departments, and that's our main concern. We know, going into the game, that we just have to scrap and battle and come up with the plays that will somehow win for us.

"We feel the run is our main strength; and even though Washington is strong against it, we think we can get our running game going. We feel we have the offensive weapons to take advantage of a five-man line if Washington plays it. There are some things we like to do against it."

What Shula had to do was to decide who would open at quarterback. It had been a delicate decision made before the team left Miami. His regular quarterback, Bob Griese, had broken his ankle in the fifth game of the season. Earl Morrall, a 38-year-old, $100 waiver pick-up from the Baltimore Colts the year before, took over and led the Dolphins to nine straight wins. He had continued as the quarterback into the playoffs before he was lifted in the second half of the AFC championship game against the Pittsburgh Steelers. Griese brought the Dolphins from behind for a 21-17 victory. In a private meeting before de-

Miami defensive end Bill Stanfill has only one thing on his mind—sacking Washington quarterback Billy Kilmer.

parting for Los Angeles, Shula called Griese into his office. The press never knew about it.

"How do you feel?" asked Shula.

"I feel fine, coach."

"Any physical hurts from the Pittsburgh game?"

"No, I'm real good."

"How's the ankle?"

"The best it's felt since I hurt it."

"Good enough to start in the Super Bowl?"

"I'm ready to play if that's your decision."

"Well, Bob, I am thinking very seriously about starting you."

Griese's eyes lit up. When the meeting was over a few minutes later, Shula and Griese walked out together. Shula wanted to find Morrall and tell him of his decision. It was a rough thing to do. After all, how do you tell a player who led you to 11 straight victories that he wasn't going to start in the Super Bowl? Although he was disappointed, Morrall understood Shula's thinking.

"I explained to Earl that the big reason I made the decision was that I felt our team would be stronger with a healthy Griese starting," disclosed Shula. "The last few games we were having trouble getting across the goal line, and that caused me to make the decision to start Griese.

"I wanted Morrall ready to come in just in case something happened to Griese or because he wasn't getting the job done on the field. I much preferred having Morrall in reserve rather than Griese because due to Bob's inactivity, I wouldn't really know what to expect if he got into the game.

"Naturally, I realized I left myself open for criticism when it became known that Griese would start. I would be second-guessed because similar decisions had back-

fired on other coaches who had recently switched quarterbacks. Only the week before, Dallas, with Roger Staubach at quarterback, had looked very bad against the Washington Redskins. Coach Tom Landry had decided to start Staubach in that game after considerable inactivity, and to bench Craig Morton, who had done a good job for him. Staubach showed signs of rustiness and never did get the Cowboys off the ground.

"The same thing happened with the San Francisco 49ers a couple of weeks earlier. Coach Dick Nolan had to decide between starting veteran John Brodie or Steve Spurrier. Brodie was coming off an injury, and Spurrier had done an excellent job in his absence. Nolan went with Brodie; and as it turned out, the 49ers lost to Dallas.

"Judging by the results, I might have been inclined to stay with Morrall instead of starting a rusty and inactive Griese. But I believe that you have to make every decision on the merits as they affect your team, and that's exactly why I made Griese the start-

Defensive tackle Manny Fernandez of the Dolphins has Redskins' Larry Brown in his sights.

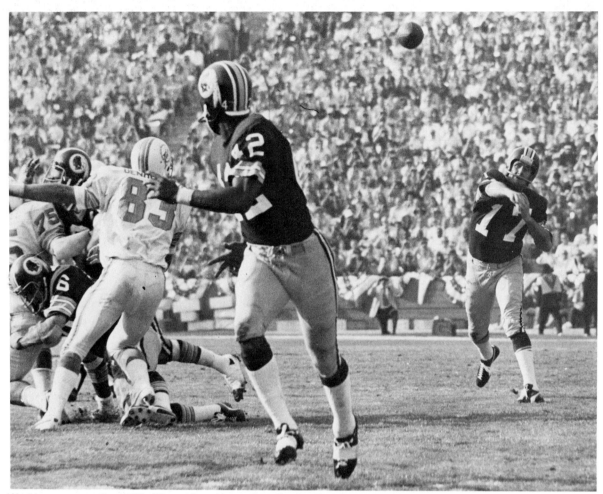

Washington quarterback Billy Kilmer hits wide receiver Charley Taylor with a quick pass.

ing quarterback. I was confident Griese could get the job done. There's no sentiment involved. At the start of the season we felt the team was strong with Griese as the number one quarterback and Morrall as a good backup, and the situation hasn't changed."

Except for Morrall. Suddenly from a starter, he was now relegated to a reserve role. It was tough to live with.

"Of course, I do not agree with the decision," Morrall said, "but I'll abide by it. I thought I had a fine year. I feel I should get the shot Sunday. Coach Shula just called me in his office and told me of his decision. He's that kind of guy. If he has something he wants to tell you, he gets right to the point and gives you all his reasons. You might not agree with him, but you have to respect the way he is.

"He told me the entire coaching staff had

a meeting and felt that as a team we'd be stronger with Bob healthy and ready to play again, going as the starter. Sunday, I'll just be ready. I'll watch the Redskins' defense and try to figure out what they're doing and how they're reacting to our offense. It generally takes a period or two to get the feel of a defense. Some people feel it is difficult to come off the bench and play. I'd rather start, but I don't think it's that tough coming in. At least I don't think there is any secret about it."

Like Morrall, Griese did have experience in playing in a Super Bowl. Morrall had started in Super Bowl III and came in off the bench two years later in Super Bowl V to spark the Baltimore Colts to victory. The year before Griese had a horrible experience in Super Bowl VI as the Dallas Cowboys easily won, 24-3. In defeat, Griese learned.

"We fell for the theory that the first team

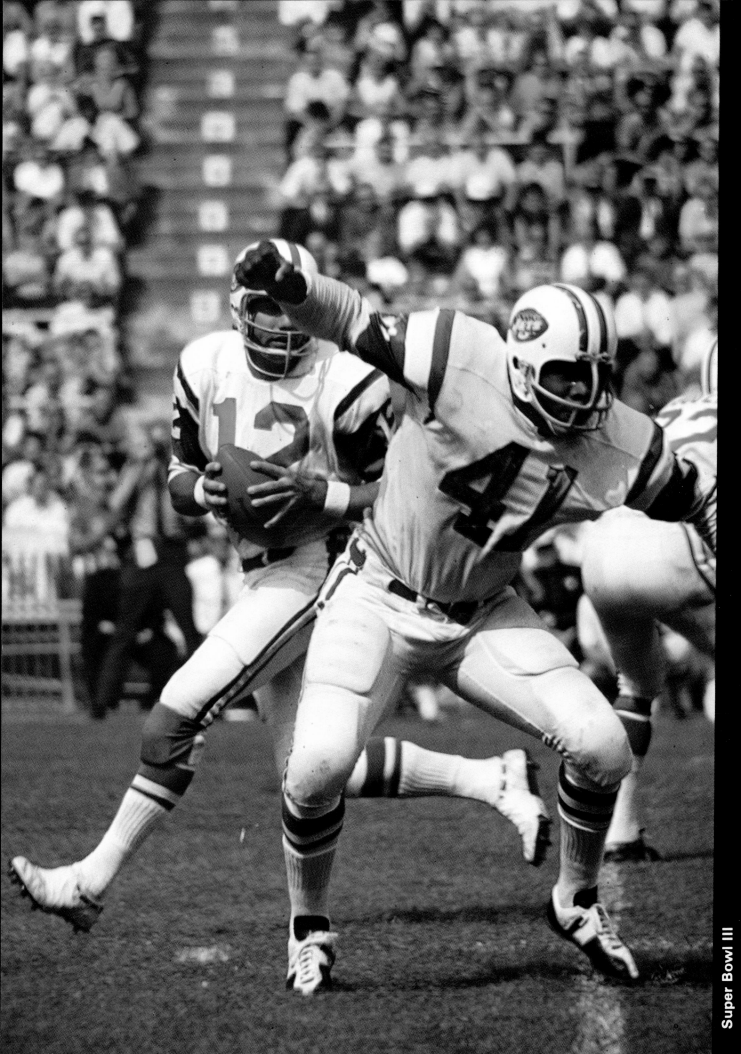

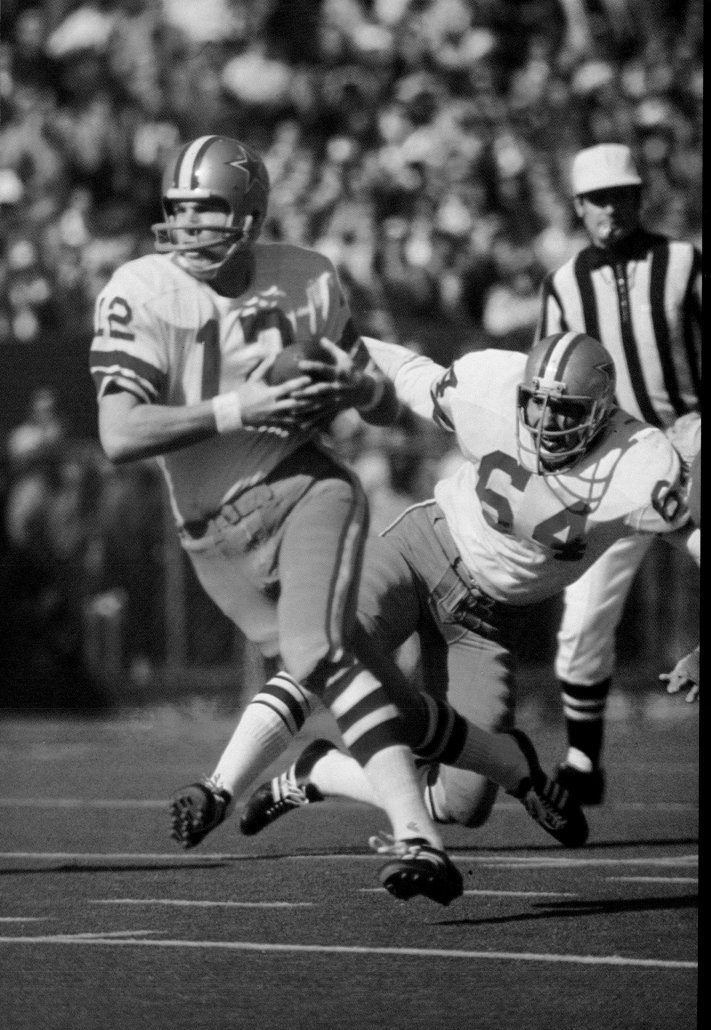

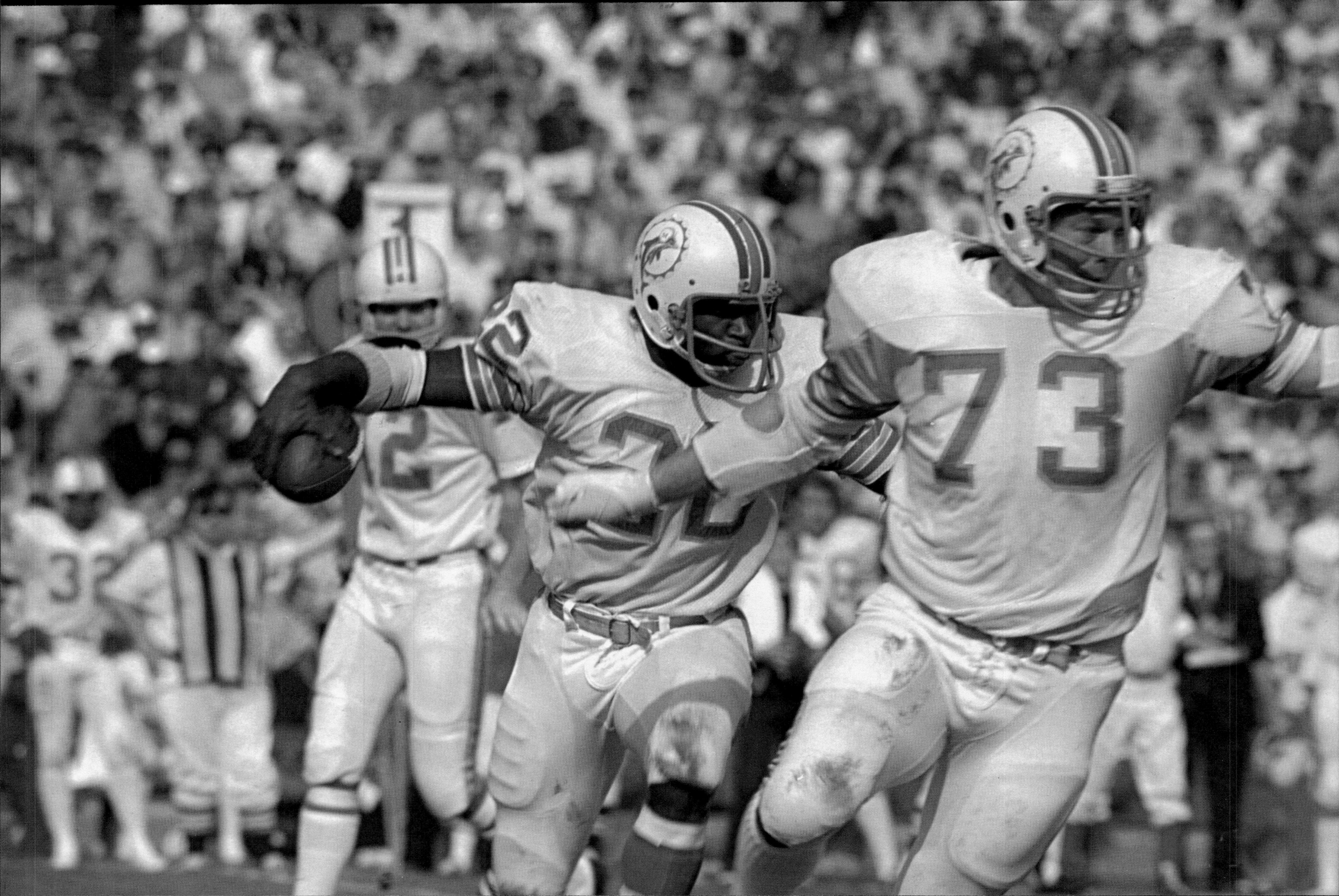

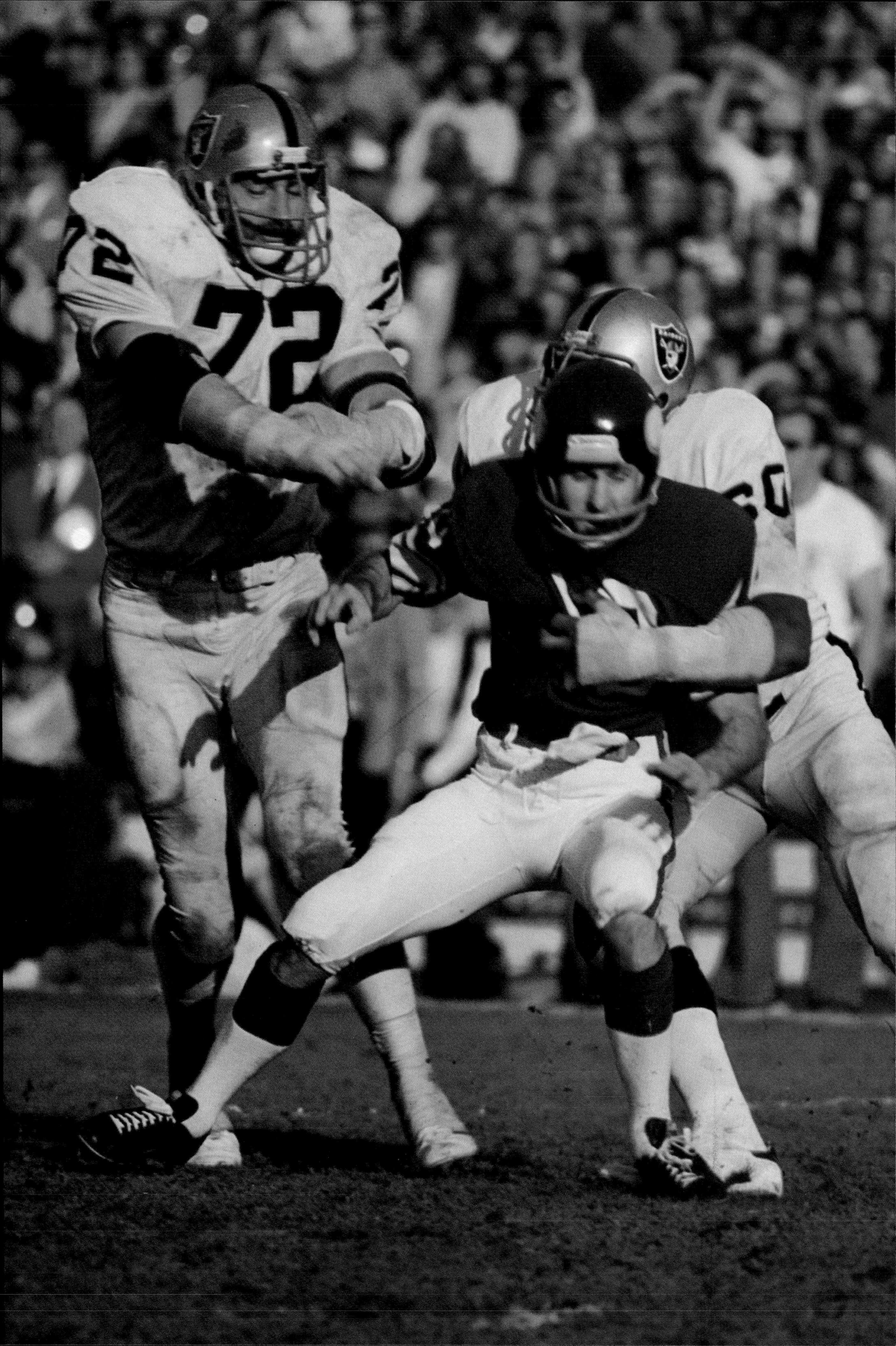

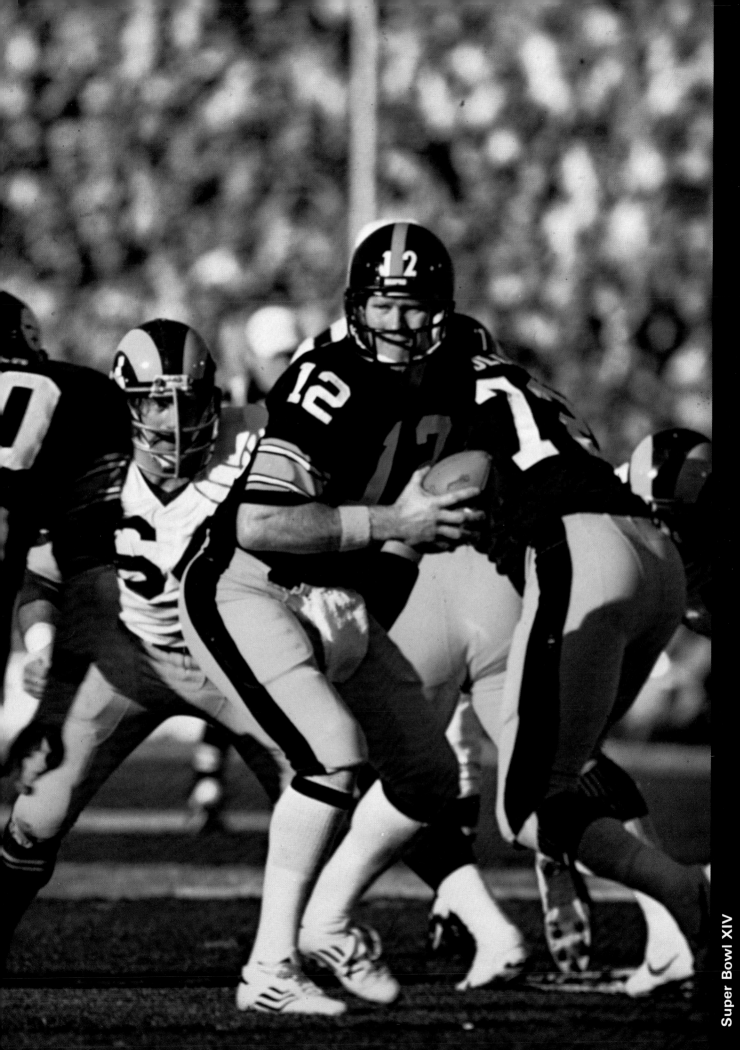

to get on the scoreboard will control the tempo of the game and go on to victory," explained Griese, "and it cost us the ball game. You get fixed on a goal like that, and two things can happen—you can score first and let down, or the other team can score first and put you at a tremendous psychological disadvantage.

"Last year we departed from form to try to get a quick score against Dallas. I threw on the first two downs, and both times the receivers were covered. When we didn't score, it hurt us psychologically. Then, when Dallas scored first, we were really shook. I think there's a definite advantage to having been here before. There are so many distractions. But at least if you've experienced them before, it's easier to adjust to them.

"Just like playing. This time we're going out to play a sixty-minute ball game and win it. Our goal isn't to score first, but to score the most."

His adversary at quarterback, Billy Kilmer, felt the same way. Like Griese, Kilmer had a good feel for the running game. Like the Dolphins, the Redskins depended on the run. While the Dolphins had a three-pronged attack in Larry Csonka, Jim Kiick, and Mercury Morris, the Redskins rested their hopes in Larry Brown.

Most experts gave the edge at quarterback to Kilmer for two reasons. One was the fact that Griese was playing after a long layoff. The other was that at the age of 34 and playing in his twelfth season, Kilmer had more experience. Although he didn't have a strong arm, Kilmer had a way of making things happen mainly by effectively throwing off the run. He was most effective when his running game was working.

"I think there's been too much emphasis

83

Miami linebacker Nick Buoniconti motions for Jake Scott to stop after intercepting Billy Kilmer's pass in the end zone.

on the importance of scoring first," said Kilmer. "It's a valid objective, but you can't let it get out of proportion. The way to look at it is that it's important but not essential. That's the big thing. You can't go off on a tangent if something goes wrong. You stay with your game plan and keep the pressure on.

"We won't do anything different. We can't. I always start off trying to establish the run and use it as a pressure point. It holds the linebackers at home and puts enough burden on the linemen to keep them from rushing me when I go to the pass. I can change up a lot, go to play-action and other stuff.

"I like to get the running game going because when you don't and you get into a third-and-ten situation, everyone expects you to throw; and the linebackers drop back. It doesn't give you much leeway. I'm sure they're scared of Brown. We design our attack to run to daylight. He can do a lot on his own, cut back, turn the corner, or just hit the line and burst through.

"Some have that talent—like O. J. Simpson, Ron Johnson—and some don't. Csonka and Kiick don't. They're different types. The Miami attack, like ours, primarily is set up to do what they do best. People talk about attacking a zone by running against it, but that's not easy to do on Miami's. They play their force men certain ways and are probably better against the run than any zone I've seen.

"I've been studying game films all week and will right up through Saturday. It's not a glamorous way of preparing, and you keep wondering what you possibly can find after seeing them 1,000 times. But maybe you can see something you didn't before, and that one thing could be worth it all."

Shula defines it as the winning edge. The game meant more to him personally than anyone else. He and Allen were the central characters of the unplayed scenario. But Shula more than Allen. He had come away unfulfilled in two other Super Bowl games. And for the third one, he had been faced with a command decision about which quarterback to start. Strangely, his team was entering the game as an underdog despite having won all 16 games it played. A perceptive individual, Shula realized that his squad did not look strong in winning the

Shula has a big hug for one of his players coming out of the game in the last quarter.

two playoff games. That more than anything else had influenced his decision to revert to Griese and break a winning combination for Super Bowl VII.

Yet, Shula suffered an added, personal strain. It disturbed him deeply. So much so that he couldn't sleep well the night before the game. A few days earlier, Carroll Rosenbloom, the owner of the Los Angeles Rams, had made a personal slur on his character. Shula had coached for Rosenbloom for seven years in Baltimore.

Rosenbloom was quoted in a newspaper article as saying, "These are two coaches who broke all the rules in football." He said that all Allen did was cheat on some rules involving waivers. The inference was that Shula had done something more than that. It affected Shula emotionally. His entire family was with him in Los Angeles. His oldest son, 13-year-old David, read the article before Shula had a chance to talk to him about it.

"Dad, I always thought that you were

honest and as fair as you possibly could be."

"That's right, son."

"Yet, in the newspaper Rosenbloom says that everyone knows that Shula and Allen have broken all the rules in football. What does it all mean?"

"I've always tried to do everything according to the rules, David. If I've broken any rules, I don't know about them."

"I'm sure of that, Dad."

"I'll find out the answers, you can be sure of that."

Shula privately made his feelings known to Commissioner Pete Rozelle. He had remained quiet and didn't reply publicly to the newspaper article. Rozelle remarked that he hadn't read the article. So, Shula read it to him over the telephone. He didn't want to wait to arrange a private meeting with Rozelle. He complained to Rozelle that his entire family was upset. He firmly told the commissioner that he was at a loss trying to explain to his family about the inference that he had broken rules. Rozelle said that he would look into the matter and get back to him. By Saturday night, Shula still had not heard from Rozelle.

Shula kept tossing and turning. He couldn't sleep. He wondered whether Rosenbloom's remarks would have an adverse effect on his team's play the next day. After much thought, he felt that the remarks would have a positive effect on the players. The Dolphins' entire unbeaten season came down to one game. Surely they weren't about to lose their first game now and lose their place in NFL history.

He was comforted by the fact that his team had accomplished so much. They had broken the NFL team rushing record by gaining 2,960 yards. In Csonka and Morris, the Dolphins had two runners who had gained 1,000 yards for the first time in history. And he, Shula, had collected his one hundredth coaching victory in the ninth game of the season. It was the first time any coach had achieved 100 wins in his first ten years of coaching. But for Shula and the Dolphins, nothing would be bigger than a victory the next day.

Sunday turned up Dolphin weather. It was a warm, sunny day with the temperature at 84 degrees. Maybe it was an omen. Shula certainly hoped so. He couldn't bear the thought of losing all three Super Bowls he was involved in. A record crowd of 90,182 fans turned out in shirt sleeves in the Los Angeles Coliseum to see if that would happen. By game time the odds hadn't changed. The Redskins entered the game as three-point favorites.

The Dolphins received the kickoff. Griese, remembering to remain patient and not worry about a quick score, started the game with two running plays that gained a total of four yards. After a safe pass to Csonka lost a yard, Miami punted the ball to Washington.

Kilmer went right to Brown. After two runs, he hit Brown with a swing pass and the game's initial first down. Then Brown carried again for five yards. He was involved in Washington's first four plays; but the Redskins stalled, and they had to punt.

That set the tempo of the game. The Dolphins got the ball and after moving for one first down had to punt the ball back to the Redskins. The Redskins couldn't do

Victorious Dolphin players lift Shula on their shoulders in final tribute to an unbelievable 17-0 season.

anything, and they had to punt the ball to the Dolphins. It appeared that the defenses of both teams had asserted themselves.

When Miami got the ball back for the third time in the period, there was only 2:55 left on the clock. They had the ball on their own 37-yard line. Kiick ran for three yards and then eight yards. When Griese hit his deluxe wide receiver with a 14-yard pass, the Dolphins were suddenly on Washington's 34-yard line. Csonka got two yards and Kiick four. Griese now was analyzing a third and four on the Redskin 32. He had to throw. As he dropped back, he looked to his right and threw a perfect pass to his other wide receiver, Howard Twilley. The little veteran receiver made his move on the five-yard line, shook his defender, caught the pass, and scored standing up. As the Dolphin fans waved their white handkerchiefs, Miami was in front, 7-0, one second before the quarter ended.

No team mounted a serious threat in the second period. Just when it appeared that the half would end without any further scoring, the Dolphins came up with a big play on defense. With only two minutes remaining, Miami's middle linebacker, Nick Buoniconti, intercepted a Kilmer pass on the Miami 41 and raced all the way down to the Washington 27 before he was upended.

Griese remained calm. Two running plays gained six yards. On third down, Griese fired a sideline pass to his tight end, Jim Mandich. Jim caught the ball on the two-yard line and rolled out of bounds to stop the clock with only 28 seconds remaining. Kiick got a yard, and the Dolphins called time out. Then Kiick carried again and went over for a one-yard touchdown as Miami increased its advantage to 14-0 as the half came to a close.

Griese was the difference. He was perfect in the first half. He completed all six passes he threw. What's more, he was in control. Shula's decision to start him certainly appeared to be a stroke of genius. But there was still another half to go, and the Redskins had always been tough in the final 30 minutes of a game.

Kilmer brought the Redskins storming back in the third period. He started on the Washington 30-yard line and drove the Redskins to the Miami 17. However, on third down he was sacked for an eight-yard

loss by Manny Fernandez. At that point Mike Bragg tried a 32-yard field goal that went wide to the right.

Griese later got the Dolphins moving on a drive that began on his own 17-yard line. Two running plays got the Dolphins to the 35. Then Csonka broke loose like a runaway truck up the middle and ran for 49 yards before he was brought to the ground on the Washington 16. Three plays later the Dolphins were on the five. However, Griese's pass was intercepted in the end zone as the quarter neared its end.

Kilmer had the Redskins moving on a long drive that began on the Washington 11. He marched the Redskins to the Miami ten-yard line before his third-down pass was

In the spring, hope blooms eternal. A loyal Redskin fan looks toward Super Bowl VIII.

intercepted by safety Jake Scott in the end zone. Once more the Redskins were repelled.

It didn't appear as if Washington would score. With 2:07 left in the game, Garo Yepremian attempted a 42-yard field goal for Miami. However, Bill Brundige blocked the kick. Yepremian picked up the ball and attempted to pass. He fumbled, and Mike Bass caught the ball in midair and went 49 yards for a touchdown. It was the final blow. Less than two minutes later the game ended. Miami prevailed, 14-7. They had won their 17th straight game for an unbeaten season, and Shula was the happiest person alive.

"This is the greatest team I've been associated with," said a beaming Shula in the Dolphin dressing room just five minutes after his first Super Bowl victory. "It's hard to compare it with other great teams of the past, but this team has gone into an area no one has gone into before. It went through the season undefeated and won it at the end, and they have to be given credit for their achievement. There was always the empty feeling of not having accomplished the ultimate. This is the ultimate.

"All phases of our football team won. We had the poise to hang onto the ball and not make an error at the end. And remember that they didn't score against our defense. We knew they were tough to run against. We came out with the run, mixed in some passes to take advantage of their stacked defense against the run. On defense, we made them lay the ball up. We figured if they had to do that, we could come down with something. Griese's fine performance didn't surprise me. If he was 18 for 18, I wouldn't be surprised."

Actually, Griese was eight for 11 for 88 yards and a touchdown. He mixed his plays so well that Csonka gained 115 yards on only 15 carries. Shula's choice in starting Griese was justified indeed.

"I felt I was mentally prepared today," said Griese. "I knew what I wanted to do and what they like to do defensively. I had a very good week of practice. I threw the ball very well and went into this game with lots of confidence. This is a very satisfying moment. When I was injured in the fifth week of the season, I was in a very depressed state."

Perhaps tight end Marv Fleming put it all into perspective. He had played on the great Green Bay teams that easily emerged victorious in Super Bowls I and II.

"This is without question the greatest team I have ever played on," exclaimed Fleming. "It is better than all the Packer championship teams I was part of. I have three Super Bowl rings now, but I will cherish this one the most. Coach Shula deserves a lot of credit for the way he handled this team. We never accomplished a perfect season in Green Bay, and that's why this is a better team."

There was nothing more to say . . .

87

Super Bowl VIII

January 13, 1974
Houston Rice Stadium
71,882

Minnesota (NFC)	0	0	0	7	—	7
Miami (AFC)	14	3	7	0	—	24

It was a strange week. Not too much attention was focused on the game, at least during the early part of Super Bowl week. Instead, when the Miami Dolphins and the Minnesota Vikings gathered in Houston for Super Bowl VIII, most of the talk centered around what was taking place off the field. It reached the point where it became humorous. If nothing else, that alone made it different from any previous Super Bowl game—which is the way it's supposed to be, anyway.

In the first place, Minnesota's coach Bud Grant was upset at the training facilities allocated to him by the league office. He felt the practice field was strictly high school level at best. He was even more vehement about the locker room and even conducted a tour through the facility, pointing out the sub-par conditions. He saved the best for last. He told various members of the press corps that he found sparrows nesting in the shower. Really! He protested to the league. Naturally they couldn't do anything about making other arrangements. He voiced his displeasure for a couple of days until a directive from the league office told him to "cool it," which he finally did but not until after the league managed to rid the locker room of the intruding sparrows. The remainder of the week, Grant became a bit more subdued.

His adversary, coach Don Shula of the Miami Dolphins, was also barraged with complaints. Only his was a club matter. But rather than become upset over his problem, he handled the situation in a light manner. It was wise. If anything, Shula faced a much more volatile situation than Grant. His crisis occurred before the team left Miami. It surfaced in Houston, and that's when Shula took control.

"Prior to leaving for Houston, I informed our squad, as in the past two years, the Miami Dolphins would fly the players' wives to the Super Bowl so that they could be on hand to see their husbands play," explained Shula. "Any subject brought up at our team meetings is open for discussion. I informed the players what the club policy was. If there is no discussion, that's it.

"When I told the players that our owner, Joe Robbie, would pay for the wives, several of the single players brought up the question of whether the club would pay for the mothers of the single players. To their way of thinking, the club's decision to pay for only the wives was discriminatory. What they suggested was a one-man, one-woman rule.

"I told them that I would take the matter up with Robbie, which I did as soon as we arrived in Houston Sunday night. I presented the single players' point of view, but Robbie said he would only pay for wives. At our Monday morning team meeting, I told the players of Robbie's decision and thought that was the end of the subject. But as usual at the Super Bowl, subjects such as this tend to get blown out of proportion. A few of the single players discussed the situation with the press later in the day during our photo session."

Everyone the early part of the week seemed to have forgotten about football. The Miami mothers and the Minnesota sparrows were making headlines all around the country. Shula realized that the subject of mothers would be the main topic of questioning at his press conference on Tuesday morning. Since he felt that the whole matter was blown out of proportion, he decided to handle the subject humorously. Shula's press conference created quite

The story of Super Bowl VIII was Larry Csonka. The powerful Miami running back ran for a record 145 yards against the Minnesota Vikings.

a stir. After elaborating on his team's preparations for the game, he threw open the conference for questions.

"How are all the mothers this morning?" was the very first question asked. The entire room broke out in laughter.

"The mothers . . . the mothers. I like mothers," answered Shula. "The policy of the Dolphins for the last three years has been to bring the wives. This came up last year. But it wasn't as big a problem as it turned out to be this year because last year and the year before, we had a charter jet; and you were able to put as many people as you wanted on them. This year Joe Robbie decided not to take a charter and instead use a commercial jet. This year when the announcement was made 'wives only,' some of the single players brought up the question of mothers; and some other single people brought up the question of girlfriends. I think the line has to be drawn somewhere, and that's the policy Joe Robbie has set."

"How many players are involved?" asked another writer.

"Let's see," began Shula. "Larry Little is single. Jim Mandich is single. The ones that voiced complaints were Marv Fleming, Jake Scott, and Mandich, although I'm not sure whether that was a mother or a girlfriend in that situation."

Again the writers broke out in laughter.

"Who else do we have?" continued Shula. "Marlin Briscoe, Bill Stanfill. Stanfill didn't complain last year because he was married. This year he's divorced."

That evoked more laughter.

"Did that have anything to do with his divorce?" a question was raised.

"I can't answer that," remarked Shula. "Stanfill will be here later; you can ask him."

Again the writers laughed out loud.

"Can married guys bring their girlfriends?" Shula was asked.

Now it was Shula's turn to laugh.

"No, it's not an either-or situation," he replied.

Once more the writers laughed.

"Do you have the tapes of the meeting with Robbie or were they erased?" came another question.

"I hope to heck there were no tapes of that meeting," answered Shula.

The writers broke out in loud laughter at that one.

"Does a thing like this cause any concern for you . . . It wouldn't cause any dissension, would it?" Shula was asked.

"I'd rather not have this situation," said Shula. "It's something that was discussed at the meeting, and the policy was set. I'd like to think that Griese, who is married, is going to throw the ball to either Fleming or Mandich, who are both single."

That made the writers laugh.

"Will the wives be in the same hotel as the players?"

"No," answered Shula.

"Will the wives' hotel be off limits to the players?"

"No," replied Shula. "We're not going to attempt to follow them around and see where they go. A lot of players voiced the opinion that they would prefer to have the wives in another hotel, and a lot of wives voiced the opinion that they would prefer to be in another hotel."

"What about the old Tuesday rule?"

"The Tuesday rule . . . the Tuesday rule," pondered Shula. "I've never been able to check on that."

"What's the Tuesday rule?"

"The Tuesday rule is that the players can't be with their wives after Tuesday," explained Shula. "From then on you dedicate yourself to the task of getting ready for the game."

The writers laughed again.

"I've mellowed quite a bit," added Shula. "That's gotten down to a Saturday night rule for me."

Once more the room rang with laughter.

But Shula had other disturbing elements during the week. Stories began to break that his defensive coordinator, Bill Arnsparger, would become the new head coach of the New York Giants. It disturbed Arnsparger. While trying to concentrate on his preparations for the game, he had to answer questions every day to explain his position. Then other rumors began to circulate that line coach Monte Clark was also leaving the Dolphins to become head coach of the Cleveland Browns. That created further distractions.

However, the only concern among the players was Paul Warfield. The gifted wide receiver strained a hamstring muscle during a workout. Warfield's leg was immediately packed in ice. It wouldn't be known until game time whether he would be able to

Csonka (39) applies a block to Viking linebacker Roy Winston to give Mercury Morris (22) some running room.

play. Two other Dolphin regulars were pronounced ready. One was star guard Bob Kuechenberg, who had broken his arm in the next to last regular game of the season and played in the playoffs with a cast. The other was defensive tackle Manny Fernandez, who was just about fully recovered from a torn leg muscle.

Despite all the flack centering around the Dolphins, they were established as the favorites. The oddsmakers listed them as six to seven points better than the Vikings. And with good reason, too. The Dolphins were being talked about as being as good or perhaps better than the powerful Green Bay Packer teams of Vince Lombardi. That was high praise, indeed.

Since their miraculous 17-0 season in 1972, the Dolphins continued to appear unbeatable. In 1973, they finished with a 12-2 regular season record before winning their two playoff games. No team has yet equaled its combined two-year record of 31-2. The most pronounced characteristic about the team was its running attack. They had power in Larry Csonka and speed in Mercury Morris and a quick, smart offensive

line that blocked with precision. In fact, the offensive line was praised almost as much as Csonka and Morris. Tackles Wayne Moore and Norm Evans, guards Bob Kuechenberg and Larry Little, and center Jim Langer were the most efficient unit in the league. Clark was proud of them.

"Moore has a lot of tenacity," said Clark. "He's a guy who can play with adversity, play with pain, and he's had a lot of it. He had surgery and came back right at the end, and he played when 99 percent of the people wouldn't have. He's a very underrated lineman, but he's been hurt so darn much it's been difficult for him to get the recognition.

"Kuechenberg is better than anyone else at turning up in a hole and putting his man on the ground. He can turn upfield, looking back inside; and when he does, it's almost vicious. He hasn't got great speed, but he's got great foot movement.

"Centers have a man on their nose more often now because of the odd defenses. We try to utilize Langer as a guard because he has played some guard. Langer is never out of fundamental position because he's able to seal people off and handle the man on his nose by himself with great position and strength.

"Little's been outstanding for us. He's the kind of guy you're glad is on your side because he does everything well. He has an attitude when he leads a sweep that there's 'no way I can lose,' and that's just about what happens.

"Evans is an expert at knowing the details of his assignment. He makes it a point to know his duties better and study harder and know more detail than the next guy. He fights, and he scratches, and he digs; any way that will help him win."

Because of the Dolphins' devastating running game, Miami quarterback Bob Griese didn't have to throw the ball much. In the AFC championship victory over the Oakland Raiders, Griese had thrown only six passes. That was how much Miami's offensive line and running attack dominated the game. Csonka had finished the season with 1,003 yards and Morris with 954 as Miami's ground game averaged a remarkable five yards a play. Since the Vikings averaged yielding 4.4 yards against the run, finishing eleventh in the NFL in that category, it was expected that the Dolphins would attack on the ground.

The amazing part about the entire week was that hardly anybody talked with great intensity about the game. Maybe it was because the weather was murky and unstimulating. Perhaps it was because the Dallas Cowboys weren't participating, and Texans didn't care much about the game one way or the other. Inasmuch as ticket scalping was legal in Texas, the excitement of purchasing a ticket was missing. Then, too, the Dolphins themselves weren't awed by the spectacle, having appeared in the Super Bowl for the third consecutive year.

"This wasn't what it was the first two times," admitted Csonka. "I wouldn't say that the Dolphins are bored. It just isn't the great exciting adventure it was the first two times around. That first Super Bowl game was sheer excitement. We even loved the practice sessions. Can you imagine that?

"I came here to talk about the football game, and I hear so little talk about our game with the Minnesota Vikings that I really don't know what to say anymore. They want to hear me talk about faith and morals. That's fine, but I'm a football player. That's not the biggest thing in my life. It's a means of a livelihood. It's fun, and I love the game. But is just isn't the most important part of my life.

"I'm honestly not worried about whether this football team is one of the great ones of all time or not. That sounds funny, I know. The object is to get to the Super Bowl. How history judges the Miami Dolphins of the 1970s is nothing I'm worried about. Being remembered is not the same reward as doing something. I'm here, right now, and we're doing something. That's the reward.

"A lot of people think we have already won this football game. There are no scientific means of predicting the outcome of a football game. It's all sheer guesswork. A man told me that we are seven-point favorites. Suppose I wake up on Sunday morning and feel sick? Suppose I fumble four times? What does that do to all the predictions? I only know what happens after there is a kickoff.

"I sincerely hope that if we play well and lose that it will not be held against us. America loves professional football because the country loves action. This game will eventually spread to other parts of the world, to the Orient, to South America, and to Western Europe. I hope that somebody in this country will recognize the fact that not everyone can be the champion. The stress on winning isn't good for America. There has to be a place for sportsmanship that is appreciated when it does not result in total victory."

While Csonka was deep in philosophical thought, Fran Tarkenton, the Vikings' heady quarterback, was experiencing the thrill of playing in his first Super Bowl much like Csonka and his teammates did in 1972. Only Tarkenton had to wait longer. It took him 13 years. Yet, at the age of 33, Tarkenton was the key to the Vikings' success. He had his best season ever, completing 61.7 percent of his passes, and was only intercepted seven times.

Tarkenton was somewhat of a marvel. Just barely six feet, he nevertheless had a complete view of the field. He managed it

92

Miami cornerback Tim Foley intercepts a pass that was intended for Minnesota wide receiver John Gilliam.

that we'll be a scatter-gun team. The Vikings have more backfield speed than we've had before. I'll throw the ball on first down and feel I can throw deep against a zone defense

"I think there's a tendency many times when a team gets in an important game that it's so worried about making mistakes that it doesn't play as well as it can. We hear people say, 'Let's don't make any turnovers.' We hear that so much. They don't take any chances because they feel they're good enough to win if they don't make any turnovers.

"There are different philosophies. People may have played it cautious and won playoff games. Our attitude is not that. It is not unique, I'm sure, but we believe that for better or for worse we're not going to play to keep from losing in these playoff games. We'll play to win, use our full complement of plays.

"If throwing the ball from our end zone is dictated as the thing to do, then we'll do it. If taking fourth-down chances is right for the situation, we'll do that, too. Sometimes the tempo of the game dictates different things. In the Dallas game when we went for two fourth-down plays, it was obvious at that point that our offense was moving the ball pretty well. If we hadn't, we might have made a different decision. You don't go for a fourth-down play just for the heck of it.

"For years I've been hearing a scrambler couldn't win. Then Roger Staubach and Bob Griese quarterbacked Super Bowl winners. I haven't heard anyone say it lately. It was the greatest lie ever perpetrated on professional football's public. The Dolphins' 53 defense is somewhat different, but all that means to me is that you have to approach it a little differently.

"Some teams defy it. They think they can run their own stuff against it, but that doesn't seem to work. I think you've got to prepare for the 53 defense, you've got to make it so the Dolphins don't know what to expect."

The Dolphins had a great deal of respect for Tarkenton. If they decided to rush four men, they hoped to keep Tarkenton in the pocket. He was less effective in that situa-

93

by an unconventional move—not staying in the pocket to pass. Rather, he rolled out or scrambled around until his receivers were shaken loose. He was the type of quarterback who made things happen during a game. He wouldn't hesitate to throw on a first down, whether he was deep in his own territory or close to his opponent's goal line. Tarkenton had starred in the Vikings' two playoff victories over Washington and Dallas and had a hot hand.

"This is going to be a more wide-open game than you've seen in the Super Bowl in several years," exclaimed Tarkenton. "Our team isn't afraid to gamble. I don't mean tion. However, when employing the 53, the Dolphins had to be alert to protect the short zones 15 yards down the field. Middle linebacker Nick Buoniconti put Tarkenton into proper perspective.

"He's a marvel," exclaimed Buoniconti. "He has a sixth sense that tells him when he's in trouble. He just seems to know when and where the pressure is, and he moves away from it so fast that he never gets hit a shot from the blind side. He does everything by instinct so there's no way we can anticipate where he'll be. So the whole thing has to start with our defensive ends, Bill Stanfill and Vern Den Herder. They've got to contain Tarkenton. If they let him roll out and throw, it's going to be a long afternoon. Oh, he'll do it a few times, of course, but we can't let him do it all day.

"Who knows what the Vikings will do. Tarkenton has transformed the team. The Vikings used to have a lot of tendencies on offense. You pretty much knew when and where they'd pass or run. Now they have no tendencies at all. Tarkenton is a great play caller in that respect."

Grant wasn't surprised by what Tarkenton did on the field at any time. He had come to expect the unexpected.

"He's very consistent with what we've set up," disclosed Grant. "He has great command, a great capacity for using plays we have set up. Half of the time when he comes out of the huddle, I can predict the play that he has called."

The only thing that wasn't predictable was the weather. When the 68,142 fans gathered in Rice University Stadium, the weather was cloudy and humid; and the threat of rain was present in the somewhat foggy atmosphere. There wasn't any wind, and it felt warmer than the 50 degrees simply because of the 80 percent humidity.

The Dolphins had the first opportunity to score. They received the opening kickoff, and Griese had his offense in formation on the 38-yard line. He began the game by giving the ball to Morris, who gained four yards around the right side. Csonka was next, and he picked up two yards inside. Griese then hit a clutch third-down pass to Mandich for 13 yards and a first down **on**

the Minnesota 44-yard line. After Morris was stopped, Csonka broke through for 16 yards to the Viking 27.

Griese picked up six yards on a quick pass to Briscoe. Then Csonka drove up the middle for five yards and another first down on the 16. Csonka carried again and got all the way down to the eight-yard line. Griese went back to Morris, who reached the five-yard line for another first down. The Dolphins were running as smoothly as a computer. On the next play, Csonka went all the way for a touchdown and a 7-0 lead. Miami had moved 62 yards in just ten plays as the Viking defense offered no resistance.

After Minnesota failed to mount a drive, the Dolphins took over again on their 44-yard line. Once more the Dolphins moved unchallenged. It took Griese another ten plays to score. He took the Dolphins 56 yards, mostly on the ground, completing the only two passes he threw. Csonka's buddy, Jim Kiick, punched over from one yard out to send Miami into a 14-0 lead. The two times the Dolphins had possession of the ball, they scored easily. Csonka in eight carries had already gained 64 yards!

After the first five minutes of the second period, the Vikings still hadn't excited anybody on offense. Midway through the quarter, the Dolphins were moving again. They reached the Viking 21-yard line when Csonka was stopped for no gain on a third-and-one play. Nevertheless, Garo Yepremian proceeded to kick a 28-yard field goal to send Miami's margin to 17-0.

Finally, Tarkenton and the Vikings came to life. With 5:56 left in the first half, Tarkenton got the Vikings moving. Beginning on his own 20, Tarkenton led the Vikings to the Miami 15-yard line. On first down, he rolled out and ran for eight yards to the seven. Oscar Reed then lost a yard to the eight. He carried again and picked up two yards to the six. It was now fourth and one. Only one minute remained to play in the half. The Vikings had to get on the scoreboard. Instead of a field goal, the Vikings were going for a first down. If they could make it and then score, they could perhaps stop Miami's momentum and come charging back themselves in the second half.

Despite Miami's second straight Super Bowl victory, it was a tearful ending of mixed joy for Dolphin defensive coordinator Bill Arnsparger, who left team to become head coach of the New York Giants.

Tarkenton handed the ball to Reed for the third straight time. He was met head on by Buoniconti, who jarred the ball out of Reed's grasp. Jake Scott recovered the ball, and the Minnesota threat was stopped.

It was a disappointing and discouraging first half for Minnesota. They managed only 103 yards and four first downs and got into Miami territory only one time near the end. Meanwhile, Miami had made 13 first downs, gained 162 yards with Csonka accounting for nearly half the total with 78 yards. The methodical manner in which they controlled the game didn't allow any time for excitement.

The second half started the same way. The first time the Vikings got the ball they were in trouble. A scintillating runback of 65 yards by John Gilliam on the kickoff was nullified by a clipping penalty. Operating from the 11-yard line, Tarkenton had poor field position; and four downs later the Vikings had to punt.

Miami got the ball in excellent field position. Griese went to work on the Viking 43-yard line. It took him only eight plays to take the Dolphins in; Csonka plunged over from the two-yard line to send the Dolphins into a commanding 24-0 lead.

The remainder of the action in the quarter was inconsequential. It ended without any further scoring. But what NFL officials were now busy watching was Csonka's yardage. He was on his way to surpassing the record of 121 yards set by Matt Snell of the New York Jets in Super Bowl III. Csonka had accumulated 115 yards in 23 carries, and there was still another quarter to play.

After three minutes of the final quarter had elapsed, Minnesota fans finally got the opportunity to cheer. Tarkenton himself put the finishing touches to a ten-play, 57-yard drive by running over for a touchdown from the four-yard line. Still, with the score at 24-7, Miami wasn't seriously threatened

All that was really left to witness was Csonka's assault on a new record. On the next series of downs, he only carried one time for three yards. He now had 118 yards. When Miami got the ball for the last time, Csonka broke the record. On his first carry, he broke through for seven yards to give

him a total of 125; but he wasn't through. He carried the ball seven more times to finish with 33 carries and 145 yards, both new records. The final score of 24-7 was anticlimatic. By halftime, it was apparent that the Dolphins would win. When they finally did, they became the second team in history to win two consecutive Super Bowls. The die was cast. The Dolphins were being compared to the great Super Bowl teams of Vince Lombardi. There was no getting away from it. Those were the first questions everyone was asking in the happy Miami dressing room.

"It's really not my job to assess whether the Dolphins are the best team ever, although it's natural that I feel that way," Shula said. "And my opinion is just that— my opinion. I'll leave that up to the media to say. When we won Super Bowl VII, I wondered how we would ever come up with anything better than a 17-0 record. I can't begin to tell you how proud I am of our team this year.

"We were better this year not only because we won Super Bowl games back to back but because we had Bob Griese with us all year. The only adjective you could put on this team today is 'great.' We got better from week to week in the playoffs. You just can't deny football players of the type that I have on the Dolphins. They are completely unselfish and entirely dedicated.

"We gave two game balls, one to Csonka and the other to Bill Arnsparger, who is supposed to be getting the Giant job as head coach. All I can say is that the Giants are getting one helluva coach. That ought to take care of that rumor."

Other members of the media crowded around Csonka. They were asking him mainly about his record-setting day, but Csonka wasn't concerned about records.

"It's a great team without an individual leader," he remarked. "We don't really need one in this outfit. Our linemen are no longer knuckle-dragging low I.Q. people. They have intelligence, and they mean something to the team's success."

Although Shula wouldn't come out and say his team ranked right up there with the legendary Packers, Carl Eller did. That alone is tribute enough, especially when it comes from someone else, like an opponent.

"Miami is the best team I have ever played against, and that includes the Green Bay Packers of 1967 and 1968," exclaimed Eller. "This club has a great combination of talents. Today, they just utilized a wide-open attack and scattered their running, sweeps, traps, whatever. Their offensive line got off the ball exceptionally well. What else is there to say? They are an outstanding team."

Carl Eller said it all . . .

Super Bowl IX

January 12, 1975
New Orleans Tulane Stadium
80,997

Pittsburgh (AFC)	0	2	7	7	—	16
Minnesota (NFC)	0	0	0	6	—	6

Nobody could understand it. The quarterback wasn't playing, and the star runner was complaining that he wasn't carrying the ball enough. But after a slow start, the Pittsburgh Steelers began to put it all together. They overcame instability at quarterback and an early season injury to their number one running back to finish with a 10-3-1 record. And for the first time in the 42-year history of the franchise, the Steelers competed in the playoffs. That was what the contribution of Terry Bradshaw at quarterback and Franco Harris at running back meant to Pittsburgh.

It also meant a great deal to Art Rooney, the venerable 73-year-old patriarchal owner of the Steelers. Rooney had owned a NFL franchise longer than anyone except George Halas, the founding father of professional football. He had paid the unlikely sum of $2,500 in 1933 to launch the Steelers into the NFL. For all those years he had never won anything. Even then he never complained nor quit hoping for the day that his beloved Steelers would win a championship. So, about ten days before Pittsburgh was scheduled to meet the Minnesota Vikings in Super Bowl IX, Rooney invited some of his players to his 115-year-old Victorian home for a quiet dinner. It was a special moment for him.

Harris was there, as was Joe Greene and Dwight White, two of the star defensive players. The atmosphere was warm and informal, and Rooney regaled his guests with his tales about horse racing. Outside of the Steelers, Rooney's other great love was race horses. He bet them, owned them, and was also the proprietor of several race tracks. It was such a relaxed atmosphere, Rooney puffing on his ever-present cigar, with very little talk of football.

Rooney liked to talk about the past. He was telling his players what it felt like when he had won his first daily double.

"The horses came into the stretch, and I was jumping up and down," said Rooney, smiling. Then in a serious tone of voice, he somewhat likened the Steelers to that winning horse.

"I believe if we can hold this club together, I think they will be a strong ball club for five or six years," he said. "We might not win every time, but at least we'll have the team that can do it any year."

The players agreed. Then Greene looked at Rooney and said, "I think we'll hold the key for awhile."

Rooney's boys wanted to make it happen. They were a colorful bunch: Bradshaw, who was branded as dumb and didn't play until half the season was over; Harris, who was half-Italian and half-black; Greene, who hated the nickname "Mean Joe" hung on him by writers; Rocky Bleier, a runner who was a Vietnam hero with a Bronze Star and Purple Heart; L. C. Greenwood, a defensive end who was conspicuous with his yellow high-top cleats; and Chuck Noll, the coach who was somewhat of an expert on wines.

Despite their early season troubles, the Steelers were rated a three-point favorite over the Vikings, who were making their third Super Bowl appearance. What im-

If Larry Csonka of the Miami Dolphins was the big story in Super Bowl VIII, running back Franco Harris of the Pittsburgh Steelers was the hero of Super Bowl IX. The big running back set a new Super Bowl rushing record of 158 yards. He moves for some of those yards behind guard Gerry Mullins.

98

pressed the oddsmakers was the strong finish of the Steelers that was keyed by a strong defense and a runner like Harris who could control the tempo of a game.

But most of that week in New Orleans, Harris didn't feel good. The weather was cold and damp, and Harris caught a heavy cold. He didn't feel much like practicing, but he did and never complained. The game meant too much to him.

"The first couple of days after winning the conference championship I was thinking, 'I'm going to the Super Bowl,'" remarked Harris. "I wasn't thinking of winning the Super Bowl, but just being here wasn't where it was at.

"But the team talked it over. Now our minds were made up that we were the Pittsburgh Steelers, and we didn't want to be second best. This game was a lot different. It had more significance than the other games that got you here. This was *the* game to decide the championship of the world.

"We realized that it would take all that we had to beat Minnesota. Anything less would not do it, but we were a hungry team. This was something brand new for us; and we were strong now, not tired. We had to overcome many adversities to get here, and I thought we were a great team.

"Confidence is important, but I never really want to get that attitude of having too much. I never want to get that sure of myself. I don't ever want to take the position that we're definitely going to win the game. I feel we're capable of winning, but I don't want to be absolutely sure of anything."

The Steelers' game plan was to run at the Vikings. Noll felt that was one way, and perhaps the easiest way, to beat the Vikings. Led by tackle Alan Page, Minnesota had a fierce pass rush. Noll was hoping to evade the rush by sending Harris through the defense on draws and quick traps. One such play was called P-10. It was a play in which Harris started up the middle and then ran wherever his instincts took him. It was the one play the Steelers went to when they were in trouble. Harris usually came through.

"I really try to work at it," disclosed Harris. "I know that in a lot of ways things come naturally for me. But I feel better when I know I really work for something rather than thinking it's just going to come.

Most of the time when you work for something it usually pays off, and it doesn't matter how rough it may be during that time. I need to carry the ball often to be effective.

"When the season opened, I felt ready. Then all of a sudden, boom! I missed three games. I didn't want to miss any at all. I hate to lose that much time. The injury was frustrating, but I tried not to let it get to me. I told myself to just forget it, not to favor the ankle. I figured that if it was good enough, fine. If it wasn't, I wasn't going to hurt the team. More than anything, I was worried about cutting, but I told myself to just put it out of my mind.

"Running is like anything else. You try to find a good groove. When you find that groove, well, you don't want anything to mess it up. When I get going good, I want the ball as often as possible. I don't mind the heavy workload. I don't even think of it in those terms at all."

In the first three games of the 1974 season, Harris had gained only 125 yards. When he returned to the lineup for the sixth game, nobody was thinking about a 1,000-yard

Minnesota quarterback Fran Tarkenton gets off pass through the outstretched arms of Pittsburgh defensive end L. C. Greenwood.

100

season; but Harris was. He gained 881 yards in the final nine games to finish with 1,066.

Bradshaw was not so fortunate. When the season began, he was on the bench. Instead, Noll went with a third-string quarterback, Joe Gilliam, who had a hot exhibition season. The strong-armed Gilliam had completed 65 percent of his passes and thrown 12 touchdown passes in six games. Gilliam had continued to throw the ball a lot and set a team record by firing 50 in one game. Bradshaw became quite discouraged and had a private talk with Noll.

"I can't understand why Chuck is doing this," said Bradshaw. "Joe has looked good throwing, and we've been winning. But you can't make it just passing. You have to use your running game."

When Bradshaw returned to the lineup, he took over as the team's leader. It was something that Noll had wanted. The players realized the transformation in Bradshaw and responded. He led them to both victories in the playoffs. In the AFC championship game against the Oakland Raiders, Bradshaw brought the Steelers from behind with three fourth-period touchdowns in the 24-13 victory. He had arrived.

"That dumb quarterback rap has been on my back for five seasons," complained Bradshaw. "Some Pittsburgh writer hung it on me. I'm sick of talking about it. Every writer wants to discuss it. If I'm so stupid, how did Pittsburgh ever make it to the Super Bowl with me at quarterback?"

On the other hand, the Vikings reached the Super Bowl on the resourcefulness of their quarterback, Fran Tarkenton. It was Tarkenton's guile that caused many experts to pick the Vikings. Tarkenton had appeared in the previous Super Bowl, and there were others on the squad who had played in the 1970 affair. While the Steelers led the NFL in sacks with 52, the Vikings' offensive line permitted Tarkenton to get nailed only 17 times.

"With the front four the Steelers have, they might be able to play without their linebackers," mused Tarkenton. "Usually, I can scramble away from a strong rush, but the Steelers are so quick that it would be suicide to make it a track meet out there on every pass play. That's why we will be using a lot more play action to slow down their rush.

"In the Pittsburgh scheme of defense,

they double on the outside receivers more than anyone else in the league. They do it because their outside linebackers can cover the running backs one-on-one better than any team in history. This is a game between two pure, physical rock-'em and sock-'em teams."

Actually, it was a play against Tarkenton, when he was with the New York Giants, that earned Greene his nickname which he doesn't like. Greene talked about it as he relaxed before a workout.

"It seemed our defensive team was on the field the whole third quarter when we were playing against him in New York," recalled Greene. "I kept chasing him and chasing him, and I didn't get him. I honed in on him like I had tunnel vision. He was all I could see.

"When I finally hit him, I didn't realize that he had thrown the ball about five minutes before. I was just so frustrated by that time. Yeah, I got flagged for it and got escorted off the field. The New York writers asked: 'Who is that crazy man?' I already had the nickname, but that made it stronger." I like 'Joe' better, but 'Mean' has been good to me.

"Tarkenton breaks containment all the time. We can't let that happen. We're going to have to find a way to stop him. Whatever he can do to hurt you, he will. He scares me more than any other quarterback we've played against because he's so clever. He thinks so damn well on his feet."

The only thing that was worrying Minnesota coach Bud Grant was the condition of Tarkenton's shoulder. Actually, Grant was only mildly concerned and just mentioned it in passing. In fact, he tried to make light of it.

"It's a good omen," said Grant and smiled. "Francis always has a good day when his arm is sore. He's like all the great ones when they get nicked or have a temperature or something of that nature. They work twice as hard. If he has a sore arm on Sunday, I'm sure he'll have a great day."

Grant appeared surprisingly at ease despite losing two previous Super Bowls. He tried a different approach with his players. He allowed them more free time, didn't rule the French Quarter off limits, and permitted the players to fly their wives down for the game.

"We're making better use of our free

101

Viking defensive tackle Bob Lurtsema lunges at Pittsburgh quarterback Terry Bradshaw.

102

time," explained Grant. "The players are not running off every chance to see something, but they're getting out. As a result, we're more relaxed and not as edgy as we've been in the past."

Since it was the Steelers' first time in the Super Bowl, Noll couldn't determine his squad's mood; but it didn't appear to concern him. What did, was the game itself.

"I can't tell if the players are ready to play emotionally," remarked Noll. "I've given up trying. All I do is prepare them for

the game and what to expect from the opposition rather than worry about the mental aspect.

"You win this game with good, basic fundamental football. No gadgets. Just blocking and tackling. That's what it's all about. Blocking and tackling. There's a lot of hoopla attached to the Super Bowl, but it all comes down to blocking and tackling."

Because of the nature of the teams, Super Bowl IX was expected to be a low-scoring game. Although the Viking defense wasn't as awesome as it was in the past, it was still strong. However, its chemistry changed. It used to be a dominant force, intimidating the opposition into mistakes with its excellent speed and determination. But age had begun to surface in defensive ends Carl Eller and Jim Marshall. Instead of being an offensive type of defense by attacking its opponents, the Vikings have resorted to a bend-but-don't-break type of play.

In this regard, Minnesota rarely gave up the big play. Teams could throw against them but not for long yardage. They could also be run on but again not for big chunks of yardage. In attacking the Vikings, it was obvious that Bradshaw would have to use patience.

"I don't think this team is as good as the two we've had in the Super Bowls before," disclosed Alan Page, the Vikings' star tackle.

Apparently Grant felt the same way. During the course of the season, Grant had reverted to unconventional gimmicks on defense. At various times he had employed the 14-man defensive huddle, the five-man defensive line on long yardage situations, and the extra defensive back on obvious passing downs. Still, to stop Pittsburgh's ground game, namely Harris, the Vikings had to get strong games from both Page and tackle Doug Sutherland.

The rain that had pelted New Orleans all week finally subsided by Sunday morning. But the weather was cold and windy, and the day was unusually dark. It was so dark that the lights were turned on before the game began in aged Tulane Stadium. Since both teams were from the North, they were at least used to the unsavory weather, even if the 79,065 fans weren't. The weather conditions didn't appear to bother Harris. In the dressing room before the players went on the field to limber up, he was completely relaxed and went around snapping pictures of his teammates with his camera.

By the time the Steelers were ready to receive the kickoff, the fans were trying to find ways to keep warm. Some started small fires, while most bundled up with heavy overcoats, gloves, and scarves that seemed out of character for New Orleans. Although it was Viking weather, the sentimental choice of the fans was the Steelers and their owner, Art Rooney.

The Vikings got a big psychological lift on the first series of downs. Beginning on the 37-yard line, Bleier ran for three yards; but Harris lost one, and Bradshaw was dropped for a four-yard loss. The Steelers had to punt.

Tarkenton came out throwing. He hit wide receiver John Gilliam for 16 yards and a first down on the Vikings' 34-yard line. But he missed on two other passes, and the Vikings were forced to punt.

After the Steelers moved for a first down, they had to punt a second time. Page was responsible. On a third-and-nine play, he sacked Bradshaw for an eight-yard loss. This time, however, Bobby Walden's punt pinned the Vikings on the 14-yard line.

With poor field position, Tarkenton couldn't get anything going. Mike Eischeid had to punt from the eight-yard line, which would present the Steelers with good field position on the return. When he did, Bradshaw set up on the Minnesota 44. He managed one first down before getting stopped on the 20. It was still close enough for Roy Gerela to try a field goal from the 37, but his kick sailed wide to the left.

Just before the opening period ended, the Steelers had another shot at a field goal from the 33-yard line. But the snap from center went askew, and the period closed scoreless. At least the Vikings accomplished two things. First, they blanked the Steelers. They also did a fairly effective job in stopping Harris. In seven carries with the ball, Harris gained only 24 yards, 14 coming on one run.

The Vikings had an opportunity to score early in the second quarter. Bleier had run for an eight-yard gain when he was hit hard and fumbled on his own 24-yard line. After a two-yard advance, Tarkenton missed on two passes; and Fred Cox tried to get the Vikings on the scoreboard with a 39-yard field goal. However, his kick went off to the right.

Midway through the period, the Steeler defense broke through. On a second-and-seven play from the ten-yard line, Tarkenton tossed a poor pitchout to Dave Osborn. He fumbled but recovered the ball in the end zone for a safety. Pittsburgh had a 2-0 lead. Ironically, that was the only scoring in the first half. The game was indeed a defensive struggle, which most experts had predicted.

Harris was kept pretty much in check. He

103

managed to break loose on a 25-yard run on his last carry of the first half. When the half ended, Harris had 61 yards on 11 carries. Up to now he was not a factor, and the freezing fans were wondering if anyone was going to score.

When the third period opened, the Steelers got a break. Veteran Bill Brown, who was playing his last game at the age of 37, fumbled the kickoff. Pittsburgh recovered on the Minnesota 30-yard line. They were primed. Bleier tried the right side and was stopped for no gain, but Bradshaw displayed patience. Instead of passing, he handed the ball to Harris. The big running back broke loose around the left side and bolted for 24 yards before he was finally brought down on the Vikings' six-yard line. The crowd sensed a touchdown.

Bradshaw stuck with Harris. However, on the first down Harris was dropped for a three-yard loss when linebacker Wally Hilgenberg came up fast to stop him as he tried to get outside around right end. Bradshaw called Harris's number again, this time around left end. He didn't fail. Harris broke loose and went over standing up for the game's first touchdown. When Gerela kicked the extra point, the Steelers shot into a 9-0 lead.

The Vikings were now placed in the position of playing catch-up football, something they didn't like to do. The Steelers applied pressure to Tarkenton and contained him the rest of the quarter. Minnesota didn't get close enough even to attempt a field goal. When the quarter ended, the Steelers appeared in control with a 9-0 lead. The defense had limited the Vikings to only 23 yards on the ground and only 99 yards in the air. They were taking it to the Vikings.

When the final period began, all the Steelers had to do was control the action. One way would be to give the ball to Harris. In three periods, he had gained 118 yards. Although the Vikings concentrated on stopping Harris, they couldn't do it effectively. He was the Steelers' chief offensive weapon.

Yet, early in the fourth quarter, Harris fumbled on the Pittsburgh 47. The Vikings recovered and had an excellent chance to get back in the game. Tarkenton didn't wait. On first down he threw a long pass to Gilliam that was incomplete on the five-

yard line. However, interference was called on safety Mike Wagner, and the Vikings got a chance at life.

It was snuffed out on the next play. The Vikings' reliable Chuck Foreman fumbled on the seven-yard line, and Greene pounced on the ball like a big cat. It appeared that Pittsburgh was out of danger.

The Steelers moved the ball to the 15-yard line when Walden was sent in to punt on fourth down. Suddenly, Minnesota fans had an opportunity to cheer for the first time all day. Linebacker Matt Blair broke through and blocked Walden's kick. The ball rolled into the end zone, and it was recovered by Terry Brown for a touchdown. Just as quickly, the Vikings were back in the game. However, Cox missed the important extra point when his kick hit the left upright.

There was still 10:18 remaining in the game when the Steelers' offense went back on the field following the kickoff. They realized that a 9-6 lead was not secure. So, Bradshaw went to work from the 34-yard line. Harris was stopped for no gain but then churned for eight yards to the 42. On a third and two, Bradshaw crossed up the Viking defense. He tossed a 30-yard pass to his tight end Larry Brown on the Viking 28.

Now Pittsburgh was threatening. Bleier ran the ball three straight times and reached the 16. Then on a key third-and-five play from the 11, Bradshaw tossed a six-yard pass to Bleier on the five. The Vikings keyed on Harris. He gained two yards, but on his next carry he was dropped for a yard loss. On a big third-down play, Bradshaw faked a run to the right and hit Brown with a four-yard touchdown pass that clinched a 16-6 victory.

In the final period, Bradshaw gave the ball to Harris an almost unbelievable 12 times. Yet, it wasn't until his last carry of the game that Harris set a new rushing record. On his 34th carry, Harris burst through for 15 yards to give him a total of 158. He surpassed the record of 145 set by Larry Csonka of the Miami Dolphins in the 1974 Super Bowl game against these same Vikings.

After 42 years, the Steelers had won a championship. Bleier was the first one into the Steeler dressing room. All the world knew that the Steelers had defeated Minnesota, but nobody knew of a tender interlude

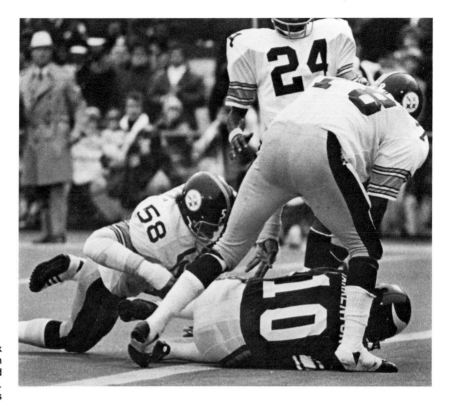

Steeler middle linebacker Jack Lambert (58) drops Tarkenton in the end zone as defensive end Dwight White (78) makes sure. The referee signals a safety as Steeler defenders raise arms in agreement.

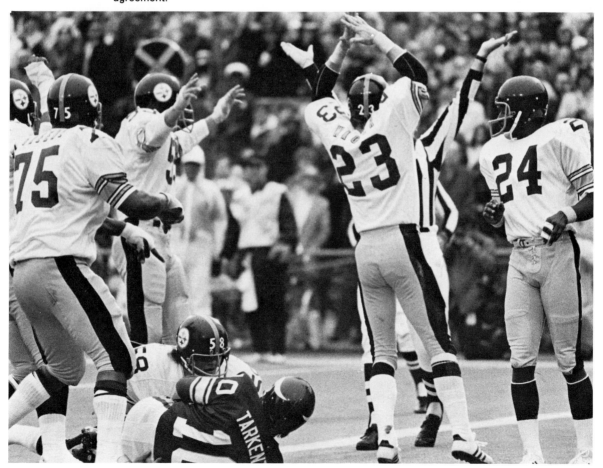

just minutes after the battle. Bleier walked up to Rooney and gave him a hug. Tears were trickling down Rooney's time-weathered cheeks.

"Thank you for giving me the chance to play," whispered Bleier.

"Thank you for being part of the championship," murmured Rooney.

The Steelers' joy in winning the game for Rooney was contagious. It was an emotional edge they carried onto the field. Winning made it all worth while.

"Art Rooney is the greatest man who ever walked," exclaimed Bradshaw. "Winning this for him was the big thing. He's the kind of man who'll get all of those boxing buddies of his together for a party, and he'll let them take that beautiful trophy out to the back alley to admire it.

"I'm glad our victory happened in Louisiana. I love this state. Winning the Super Bowl here is kind of like the hometown boy comes back and wins the Super Bowl in his own back yard. That is a thrill. I didn't win the Super Bowl. We all won it.

"I don't think I'm a bench warmer, but early in the season I certainly was that. I've certainly looked at all sides of life now, the good and the bad, the hero and the jerk; and I think I can handle this.

"It was a long year. A lot has been said and written about that situation, but a quarterback is judged only as a winner or a loser. As I walked off the field, I just savored the noise and all the emotion. It was just a great, satisfying feeling.

"I've faced a lot of adversity. I withstood the trials; and they enabled me, that and my personal faith in God, to do this. They can say all they want to. We've got the rings, and we're the champs. I'm doing personally what I think I'm capable of doing. It takes time and patience."

Almost lost in the well of emotion was Harris's record-shattering performance. He proved again that he was the constant of the Steelers' offense.

"One hundred and fifty-eight yards?" asked Harris excitedly. "You have to be kidding me. I can't believe it. I never thought it could have been that high. Winning the Super Bowl is very important to me and all of us because it means that you're number one, and that's what it's all about.

Super Bowl IX was also a warm story for Steelers owner Art Rooney. The venerable 73-year-old owner holds the game ball and the Super Bowl trophy presented to him by NFL commissioner Pete Rozelle commemorating the first championship in the team's history.

"The most significant thing that can happen to a running back is to gain 1,000 yards in a season and contribute to winning a title and getting a Super Bowl victory. Since all of that happened this season, I would have to say this is the most significant year of my life.

"I had a head cold for a couple of days and really didn't feel all that well. But there was nothing much I could have done about it because they say there's really no cures for a head cold, so I wasn't looking for one.

"Terry had us all relaxed in the huddle. Not that we were cracking jokes or anything like that, but we had control of the situation except for that one time when I fumbled. But when I was coming off the field, Joe Greene told me to relax and don't worry about it. 'We'll get it back,' he said, and they did. They did it all afternoon.''

Led by Greene, the Steeler defense had a perfect game. They didn't yield a touchdown and embarrassed the Vikings by limiting them to only 17 yards on the ground. It was unheard of. They picture him as mean, yet he is a compassionate individual.

"I don't care too much about the nickname," remarked Greene. "I think a man should be whatever he wants to be. I don't play a dirty game. A lot of teams have conned me on the field saying, 'Nice day, Joe, nice going, Joe.' They say nice guys finish last. I don't want to be last, and I don't want to be mean, either.

"Even in my wildest dreams I didn't think I'd get as big a charge out of winning the Super Bowl as I have. Winning is a lot bigger than I thought it would be. I love it, man. I really do. I feel so good I'm almost weak.

"It's more than wearing the ring and being number one. This is our first time. We've never been here before, but we never considered losing. It's not all fun and games. We knew we had a job to do. The Vikings were a worthy opponent. I feel compassion for them.''

It was just like Greene. He was also quick to shower praise on the other members of the defense. Like L. C. Greenwood, the end with the yellow shoes. He felt that Greenwood didn't get all the credit he should have. And while Greene anchored the middle of the line, Greenwood protected the outside. He not only played the pass but the run as well.

"Our defensive team did a helluva job," emphasized Greenwood. "My job was to contain Tarkenton on the sprint outs, protect the outside, and then pursue him from behind. We concentrated on stopping the run, then the pass. I thought the Vikings looked a little tight.''

Perhaps Rooney was more relaxed than anyone. He felt all along that his team would win. Five minutes before the end of the game, he made his way to the Steelers' dressing room and waited for his players.

"I just wanted to see if my hair was combed," he said, smiling.

The whole world smiled with him . . .

107

Super Bowl X

January 18, 1976
Miami Orange Bowl
80,187

Dallas (NFC)	7	3	0	7	—	17
Pittsburgh (AFC)	7	0	0	14	—	21

The wind blew off the ocean, sending a week-long chill across Miami Beach and its environs. It most definitely wasn't the typical Miami weather where sun followers eagerly pay $75 a day for a hotel room. When it wasn't cold it rained. The chemistry of the two elements made it very uncomfortable. Out-of-towners shivered in summer clothing; the beach boys couldn't hustle any Super Bowl tickets because nobody was by the pool; and the only action was at the hotel bars where there was day-long drinking. Like New Orleans the year before, Miami was cold; and pro fans were beginning to wonder if there would ever be a Super Bowl played in warm weather as advertised.

The Dallas Cowboys couldn't have cared less about the weather. They had somewhat unexpectedly become a participant in Super Bowl X, and dramatically so. They had executed two startling upsets in the playoffs. In the opening playoff game, they defeated the Minnesota Vikings, 17-14, on a last-second touchdown that fans in town for the Super Bowl were still talking about. The one play that people were discussing over and over again was quarterback Roger Staubach's final pass of the game to wide receiver Drew Pearson. Staubach later called it his "Hail Mary pass." With just 24 seconds remaining to play, he threw a 50-yard pass to Pearson, who made a miraculous catch of the ball on his hip. It gave Dallas one of the most exciting victories in NFL history. Then the following week the Cowboys easily trounced the favored Los Angeles Rams, 37-7.

On the other hand, the Pittsburgh Steelers had reverted to form. They were the defending champions, having beaten the Vikings, 16-6, the previous year in Super Bowl IX. They had finished the 1976 season with a 12-2 record and were established as

seven-point favorites over the Cowboys, who had entered the Super Bowl as a wild-card entry with a 10-4 mark. It was only the second time in the history of the Super Bowl that a wild-card team had reached the championship game.

The surge of the Cowboys and the repeat of the Steelers had made tickets for the game scarce. Commissioner Pete Rozelle had remarked earlier during the week that there was more demand for tickets than in any previous Super Bowl. Some enterprising individual or individuals figured to cash in on the demand. A number of counterfeit tickets were discovered in the possession of eager ticket buyers. It was no wonder that legitimate ducats were attracting anywhere from $100 to $150 each.

Author James Michener was impressed with it all. He was the guest of Miami Dolphins owner Joe Robbie at the sumptuous $75,000 NFL party at Hialeah Race Track. He was discussing his latest book, *Centennial*, and mixed football talk with Phil Shalala, a Chicago trade magazine publishing executive who had flown to Miami especially for the game, leaving business aside for a day.

So was Larry Mulloy, the public relations director for the International Longshoremen's Union. He arrived at the party by limousine with Bob Francisco and other members of his party from New York. Mulloy, who had attended a number of such functions throughout his career with the ILU, seemed to know just about everyone at the party. He approached one friend in particular, Jack Danahy, the head of NFL Security, who'd had a busy week trying to track down the counterfeit ticket ring.

"Hey, Jack," Mulloy greeted him, "you have any tickets?"

"Which kind?" kidded Danahy.

Pittsburgh wide receiver Lynn Swann, who was considered a doubtful performer before Super Bowl X, reaches high over Dallas cornerback Mark Washington to catch a pass.

109

"The right ones," answered Mulloy. "You know I only deal in the good ones."

The parties, the drinking, the revelry, the story telling, the incessant radio and television interviews, the reams of newspaper articles, were all part of the Super Bowl scene. It was strictly a fan's delight. The competing players didn't have an opportunity to enjoy the social whirl of activities. They still had to maintain somewhat of a spartan life in their week-long preparation for the game itself. The players could get affected by it.

Farther inland, the Steelers, who were billeted at the Miami Lakes Inn, were getting a bit ornery, particularly Ernie Holmes, the mean-looking defensive tackle. They had an unusually violent workout on Wednesday, and by Friday they were just biding their time until Sunday.

"I'll be glad to get out of here and into the game," growled Holmes. "I'm so mad I can eat these damn palm trees. I don't like this place. It's for people with arthritis. They come here to play golf or die. All that's out here are these damn mosquitos and space. It's depressing. This is no place for champions."

Actually, Holmes could have been surly for other reasons. One was the fact that he hadn't been named to the All-Pro team while his teammate, Joe Greene, who had missed six games during the season, had been. The other was the questionable status of another teammate, Lynn Swann, for Sunday's confrontation.

The lithe wide receiver was still shaken from a concussion he had received in the AFC championship game against the Oakland Raiders only two weeks before. He was hit so hard that he had been hospitalized for two days. During those 48 hours, Swann lay awake wondering if he would ever play football again. When he was finally released from the hospital, the doctors insisted that he should rest and forget about football. It was highly possible that Swann would miss the Super Bowl.

As the Steelers engaged in their workouts, Swann looked on. He still wasn't feeling good. Doctors checked him every day. They finally told him that he would be able to play but left the decision up to Swann. They had warned him that if he took another severe shot to his head, it could cause further damage. Swann was under a

Steelers running back Franco Harris rumbles for yardage as Rocky Bleier gives Dallas linebacker D. D. Lewis a bump.

great deal of pressure. He was the only one who would make the decision on whether or not to play.

Just a couple of days before the game, Swann worked out. All he did was run. He ran some pass patterns, worked on his timing, and refrained from any contact. He had to see if his legs were weak or if his head bothered him. The Steelers were as concerned as Swann. They implored him not to overdo anything but to take it nice and easy. Swann wasn't exactly bubbling over with confidence after his workouts.

"I'm not 100 percent," admitted Swann. "I'd like to play Sunday, but I value my life and health more than one football game. I'm a bit worried. My timing was off. I didn't get dizzy, but I just didn't feel right. I dropped a lot of passes. I also have to decide whether it would hurt the team or help the team if I played."

Ironically enough, Swann got the encouragement he needed the next day. Cliff Harris, the Cowboy safety, gave it to him.

"Now, I'm not going to intentionally hurt anyone," remarked Harris. "But getting hit again while he's running a pass route has to be in the back of Swann's mind. I know it would be in the back of my mind.''

When Swann read about Harris's remark in the newspaper, he decided to play. He felt that Harris was trying to intimidate him. That was all that Swann needed to see. Overnight his cautious mood changed.

"I read the stuff that Harris said," fumed Swann. "He was trying to intimidate me. He said that because I had a concussion I would be afraid out there. Well, he doesn't know Lynn Swann or the Pittsburgh Steelers. He can't scare me or this team. I said to myself, 'To hell with it. I'm going out there and play 100 percent.' Sure, I thought about being reinjured, but it's like being thrown by a horse. You've got to get up and ride again immediately or you may be scared the rest of your life. The doctors left it up to me

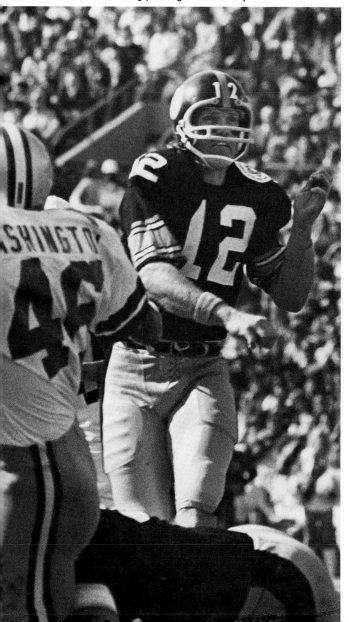

Pittsburgh quarterback Terry Bradshaw grits his teeth as he throws a long pass against Cowboys.

whether I wanted to play or not I decided to play."

Besides Swann, Greene was also not quite 100 percent physically. The big defensive tackle had injured his arm during the season, and it deprived him of some of his strength. Besides missing six games, he had also been relieved in others. In Greene, Holmes, and defensive ends Dwight White and L. C. Greenwood, the Steelers possessed one of the most formidable front fours in the league. With their aggressive linebackers and secondary, the Steelers' defense was solid. So much so that it impressed Fran Tarkenton, the Vikings' veteran quarterback, who picked Pittsburgh to win.

"The Pittsburgh defense is the most dominating I've ever seen in football," disclosed Tarkenton. "It is also the most frustrating defense I've ever played against.

"Contrary to much opinion, the best thing the defensive line does is play the run. I don't think they're the greatest pass-rushing line that's ever played, but against the run they may be.

"Their linebackers are as excellent as everyone says they are. They are able to play the pass as well as any linebackers I've ever seen. The secondary plays double coverage, covering the wide receivers with a safety and a cornerback and leaving their mobile linebackers to handle the tight ends and backs. Frankly, I don't see why more teams haven't gone in more for this type of coverage. The Steelers are the only team that does it that well.

"The Cowboys at the moment are playing by far their best football. They probably played their best game ever against the Rams, and they played very well against us. But when it gets to this point in the season, it gets down to defense.

"Pittsburgh is less of a defensive problem to Dallas than vice versa. The Steelers have geared themselves to a very conservative offense that depends on Franco Harris. Dallas should be fairly successful in defensing Pittsburgh."

The Cowboys' strategy was to stop the run, which meant curtailing Harris. They utilized a strange defense called the "flex." They were intent on preventing the run and forcing the other team to pass. They had used it so effectively against the Rams that the sum total of the Los Angeles running attack was an anemic 22 yards.

With their concern for the run, it was felt that Dallas might be vulnerable to the pass; but they were not alarmed. They regarded Harris as more of an offensive worry than quarterback Terry Bradshaw, making note of the fact that Bradshaw was intercepted five times in his two playoff games.

Most experts contended that if the game were close, the edge at quarterback would belong to Dallas's Roger Staubach. Like Bradshaw, he had the ability to run if necessary; but in the clutch, he was regarded as a far superior passer than Bradshaw. With just an average running attack, Staubach demonstrated his skill all season long in converting third-down passes to maintain possession. His main target was Pearson; but he also had other excellent receivers in wide receiver Golden Richards, tight end Jean Fugett, and running back Preston Pearson.

In Harris, the Steelers no doubt had a dominant force. He had rushed for 1,246 yards during the regular season. He could get the big first-down yardage taking the pressure off Bradshaw in obvious passing situations. Like Staubach, Bradshaw also had prime receivers. Besides Swann, the Steelers had big play performers in wide receivers John Stallworth and Frank Lewis.

"I see the game as a match between our offense and their defense," observed Staubach. "The Steeler defense will provide the biggest challenge we had all year. I probably run too much, but that's just my instinct. I've always run when a play breaks down. I'd like to be more like Fran Tarkenton. He scrambles and throws, picking up receivers downfield. I don't have the ability to do that. When I scramble, I usually run.

"We also use the shotgun formation at times. It gives you more time and confuses the defense. However, it's not a major part of our offense. We only use it on third-down passing situations. I've learned to look for a receiver and try to hit him wherever possible. I've tried to scramble in this situation and came up short of a first down too many times."

Because of Staubach's presence in the game, Bradshaw had to take second spot in the pre-game limelight; but he wasn't affected in the least. He was only concerned with winning the game.

"We'll set up a formation and run a play, and we'll soon see whether they give us the defensive front that we anticipated," explained Bradshaw quite calmly. "If they do, fine; then we'll know where we are. Then we'll run another play to see how they react. If they don't react the way they normally would, then we'll throw our first pass and take a look at what they do on their coverages.

"If they give us what we thought they would from scouting reports, fine. If they don't, then we chart it down, look at it on paper, and say, 'Look, they're not doing this'; and then we'll change everything on the sideline. And this keeps going on and on and on."

Bradshaw made it sound so easy. That's how relaxed he was. His approach to the game was simple: run Franco and try to control the game. If that doesn't work, then throw the ball. Naturally, the Cowboys were counting on their flex defense to corral Harris. They would much prefer to defend against Bradshaw's passes, figuring that he was susceptible to interceptions. On offense, they wanted to come out throwing and score quickly and make Pittsburgh play catch-up football.

On Sunday, the weather had turned sunny. Still, at 57 degrees, it was far from being warm enough for sun bathing. For a football game it was ideal. The sky was cloudless; but there was a chill in the air nevertheless, chiefly because of a 17-mile-per-hour wind from the north.

Right after the kickoff, the Cowboys did try to throw the ball. They were unsuccessful. On first down Staubach was hit by Greenwood and fumbled, but the ball was recovered by his center, John Fitzgerald. Then on third down he tried to hit Preston Pearson over the middle but overthrew him.

After the punt, the Steelers did what they were expected to do. They ran five straight plays in an effort to establish a ground game. After succeeding in moving for one first down, the Steelers were forced to punt. As he had done so many times before, Bobby Walden waited to punt the ball. However, when the snap from center came, he bobbled the ball and was tackled on his 29-yard line.

The turnover provided the Cowboys with an excellent opportunity to score, and Staubach didn't hesitate. In the huddle, he looked up at his favorite receiver, Drew Pearson, and called his number. The play was a crossing pattern in the middle. Pearson caught the ball on the Pittsburgh 15-yard line without breaking stride and ran the rest of the way untouched for a touchdown. When Toni Fritsch added the extra point, the Cowboys jumped out in front, 7-0.

Bradshaw took over on the Pittsburgh 33-yard line following the kickoff. He remained cool. He wasn't going to panic into making any mistakes. After six years in the league he had matured and developed patience. He kept the ball on the ground. One run, two, three, four. He now had a second and five on the Dallas 48. He still hadn't thrown a pass.

Then he struck. He threw a 32-yard pass to Swann down the right sideline. The Steelers were on the Cowboys' 16-yard line. Bradshaw went back to his ground game. Rocky Bleier moved for five yards, and Harris got four. Pittsburgh had a third and one on the Dallas seven. Bradshaw figured that the Cowboys would play the run in an attempt to prevent a first down and force a field goal. He also felt that they wouldn't be paying much attention to Randy Grossman, a reserve tight end behind starter Larry Brown.

Coming out of the huddle, Bradshaw looked over the Dallas defense. He figured right. They began to bunch up at the line in an effort to stop the run. Bradshaw was ready for the kill. He called out his signals slowly and clearly. At the snap of the ball, Grossman moved inside, faked a block, and broke outside to his right. As he turned in the end zone and looked back, Bradshaw hit him with a perfect pass for the tying touchdown. He had effectively moved the Steelers 67 yards in just eight plays, completing the only two passes he threw.

The touchdown at that point of the game, early as it was, was very important to the Steelers. In scoring quickly on Pittsburgh, Dallas had gained great confidence. If they could prevent the Steelers from scoring in their series of downs following the kickoff, then the Cowboys' momentum would start to build.

Yet, as it turned out, the Cowboys scored again the next time they got the ball. They began to mount a drive from their own 35-yard line. When the first period ended, they had moved all the way down to the Steelers' 14-yard line. Staubach had efficiently made

Harris leans forward, looking straight ahead for an opening in the Dallas defense.

use of his ground game. He threw only one pass, that a first-down, nine-yard strike to Fugett. But the famed Steeler defense began to fuse together. Dallas' last two running plays only gained a yard.

When the second period opened, Staubach was looking at a third and nine. An illegal motion penalty sent the Cowboys back to the 19. Staubach had to pass. He tried to hit Fugett again, but safety Glen Edwards broke up the play. Still, the Cowboys were close enough for Fritsch to boot a 36-yard field goal that sent them back on top again, 10-7.

Pittsburgh reached the Dallas 36-yard line after the kickoff but was stopped on a fourth-down play. Later, after both teams exchanged punts, the Cowboys were threat-

Roy Gerela, Pittsburgh's soccer-style kicker, closely follows his field goal attempt.

114

ening again. Beginning on his own 48, Staubach led his team to the Pittsburgh 20. He had completed three of four passes, two of them on third-down calls.

With a first down on the Pittsburgh 20-yard line, it appeared as if the Cowboys would add to their lead; but the Steeler defense got angry. On first down, Robert Newhouse was dropped for a three-yard loss by veteran linebacker Andy Russell. Staubach tried to pass and was sacked for a 12-yard loss by Greenwood. Facing a third and 25, Staubach ordered another pass. This time he was sacked for a ten-yard loss by White. The Cowboys were rudely driven back to the Pittsburgh 45.

Mitch Hoopes' punt pinned the Steelers on the six-yard line with only 3:47 left to

play in the first half. Still, Bradshaw didn't quit. On a third and six from the ten-yard line, he sent Swann deep. Locking the ball into his arms, Swann made a magnificent tumbling catch on the Dallas 37. The noisy crowd of 76,892 applauded Swann's efforts. Hurrying to get more points on the board before the half, Bradshaw drove the Steelers to the 19. Two plays failed to advance the ball any further, and Roy Gerela was sent in to attempt a game-tying 36-yard field goal. However, with the clock showing only 26 seconds, Gerela's kick sailed off to the left.

At the half, Bradshaw was instructed to stay with the original game plan, emphasizing the run and then the pass. The feeling among the Steeler coaches was that they were moving the ball well against the Cowboys. They had gained 194 yards to Dallas's 98 and with a break or two, would have scored more points.

They realized, too, that the strong Steeler defense had the Cowboys pretty much under control. They just felt that the players would have to assert themselves a little more the rest of the game to keep Dallas in check while giving the offense the opportunity to score more points. They were convinced that the game was still close enough for the defense to make things happen. That's how much confidence they had in themselves.

Three minutes into the third quarter, the Pittsburgh defense did make things happen. Cornerback J.T. Thomas picked off Staubach's pass and ran it back 35 yards before he was brought down on the Dallas 25. The

Steelers had a threat going. Three running plays produced a first down on the 14. After Bradshaw lost two yards, he tried two passes to Swann that were incomplete. Once again Gerela was sent in to tie the game, and once again he missed. His 33-yard field goal attempt was wide to the left.

When the final period began, the defenses of both teams were in control. On one defensive play, Pittsburgh turned the game around. On fourth down, Hoopes was standing on his goal line waiting to punt. Just as he got the kick off, the Steelers' Reggie Harrison broke through, blocked the ball, and sent it rolling out of the end zone for a safety. Dallas's lead had dwindled to one point, 10-9. But more important, the Steelers were certain to get good field position now because the Cowboys had to turn

Defensive tackle Steve Furness of the Steelers locks his arms around Dallas running back Bob Newhouse.

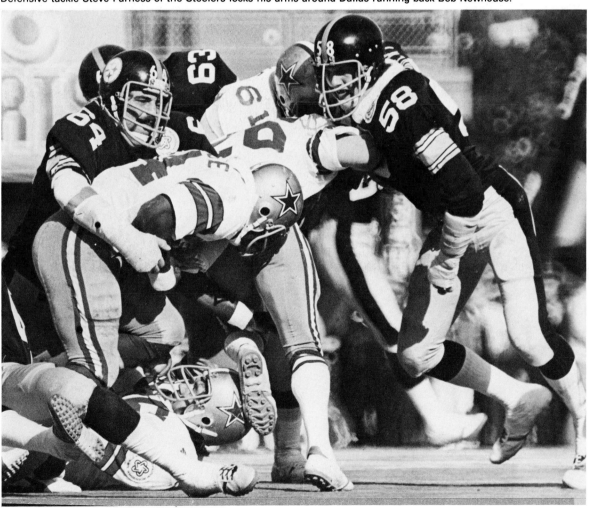

115

over the ball on a free kick from their own 20-yard line.

Hoopes managed to kick the ball to the Steeler 30-yard line. But Mike Collier ran it back 25 yards to the Dallas 45 before he was tackled. Calmly, Bradshaw kept the ball on the ground. He got one first down and reached the 20. But on third and one, Harris was stopped; and Gerela came in to try another field goal from 36 yards away. This time he made it, and Pittsburgh led for the first time, 12-10.

The Pittsburgh defense made things happen again immediately after the kickoff. On first down, Staubach tried to hit Drew Pearson with a pass on the 26-yard line. But safety Mike Wagner quickly moved in front of Pearson, intercepted the ball, and raced to the Dallas seven-yard line before he was stopped. Steeler fans were now jumping up and down in the aisles of the Orange Bowl as they sensed how the momentum of the game suddenly changed.

But they got a scare. On third down from the one-yard line, Harris fumbled; however, he managed to recover the ball. Gerela then booted an 18-yard field goal that gave the Steelers a 15-10 lead with 6:37 left in the contest.

Yet, the final outcome of the game was still in doubt. Less than a touchdown separated the two teams, and one big play could turn the outcome around. It appeared that the Cowboys would get the opportunity to do so. With only 3:02 showing on the clock, Bradshaw was faced with a key third-down-and-four play on his own 36-yard line. Dallas played for the pass, figuring Bradshaw would throw short in an effort to get the important first down. The pressure was on Bradshaw because he realized that the Cowboys would be coming after him.

Bradshaw called perhaps the most important play in his six-year professional career. He instructed his players in the huddle, "69 Maximum Flanker Post." That was Swann's play. It was designed as a deep pass pattern. Swann would go deep on the right side and then cut in the middle of the field. Bradshaw was going against the percentages. Instead of going for a first down, he was going all the way for a touchdown.

At the snap of the ball, Dallas blitzed from the right side. D. D. Lewis stormed in from his linebacker spot. Sensing the blitz, Bradshaw took one step to his right and ducked under Lewis. That allowed him the extra second he needed to throw the ball; and he needed it, too. Right behind Lewis came Harris. It was a double blitz!

However, Bradshaw got the pass off. Just as he did, Harris hit him with a crushing blow to the head that dropped Bradshaw on the spot. Swann sped downfield, covered tightly by cornerback Mark Washington, who ran step by step with him. At the last split second, Swann put on a burst of speed, reached out and caught Bradshaw's pass on his fingertips on the five-yard line without breaking stride. It was a picture play. Bradshaw's pass went 59 yards in the air, and Swann made a sensational catch to score the touchdown that gave Pittsburgh its second straight world championship, 21-17. The fact is that Staubach hit Ron Howard with a 34-yard touchdown pass a minute later that could have won the game.

Bradshaw never saw the play. He was flat on his back, unconscious. A few minutes later he was revived and helped off the field. His steps were uncertain as he was taken directly to the dressing room. While most of his teammates were enjoying the post-game celebration, Bradshaw sat quietly in the trainer's room. He was attended by a doctor who reported that he suffered a concussion. A half hour later, Bradshaw was allowed to leave the room. When he faced the reporters and television cameras, he was still a bit shaky. He had a headache and appeared tired as he answered one question after the other. He didn't seem to mind although he was uncomfortable.

"I was in the locker room, and the game was just about over when I understood what happened," explained Bradshaw. "I didn't know it was a touchdown until then. I didn't see the catch. I'm still a little hazy about things. I got hit from the blind side, and I heard bells ringing. I wanted to go deep all day, and the play was my call all the way. I barely got the ball off. They were coming on a double blitz. I got hit right here on my left cheek.

"Our strategy was to run the football then mix it. Then I decided to throw more on first down and then throw some more. I had lots of time out there, great protection. I felt we were in control even though we were behind most of the game."

Bradshaw had a good day overall. He completed nine of 19 passes for 209 yards

116

Steeler cornerback J. T. Thomas starts upfield with an intercepted pass behind Dwight White (78) and Glen Edwards (27).

117

and two touchdowns. Not one of his passes was intercepted. His favorite receiver, Swann, grabbed four catches, three of them outstanding ones, for 164 yards and a touchdown. It was his most satisfying day, one that removed the mask of uncertainty about his playing career.

"I've never had a day when I felt so loose," sighed Swann. "No one hit me hard enough to hurt me, just hard enough to want to get up and catch another one. One hundred and sixty-four yards and a touchdown in the Super Bowl is heavy.

"I gave a little thought to not playing if it wasn't advantageous to my health. I would have felt bad emotionally and psychologically if I didn't play. But to get hurt and not play in the future would be worse. I was worried that my timing and concentration were off because I didn't have good practices during the week. But I told myself, 'Hey, this is it. Either play your best or not at all.' That first catch gave me a lot of confidence."

Bradshaw, too. Otherwise he might never have called Swann's play at the end . . .

Super Bowl XI

January 9, 1977
Pasadena Rose Bowl
103,438

Oakland (AFC)	0	16	3	13	—	**32**
Minnesota (NFC)	0	0	7	7	—	**14**

It was a strange setting. The Rose Bowl is hallowed ground. It is the mecca of all the post-season college bowls. The professional cleats of the National Football League have never marked its ground, but this year it was different. The pros and the money they generate were a boon to Pasadena. For the first time ever, a Super Bowl was being played on the plush grass of the Rose Bowl. That alone made Super Bowl XI an historic event long before the kickoff. The pros in the Rose Bowl! It was like Lee meeting Grant at Appomattox. One for the history books.

And yet, this was the first time ever that the Super Bowl would be contested on a neutral field. That alone was parity. Neither the Oakland Raiders nor the Minnesota Vikings nor any of the Super Bowl contestants before them had ever battled in an arena that was not part of professional football. Esthetically, it was a completely neutral atmosphere. Financially, it was just as rewarding. The biggest crowd ever in the history of the Super Bowl was assured as 103,424 tickets were sold.

Yet, uncharacteristically, the contest was billed as a game of famous losers. Super Bowls are for winners, but the Raiders and the Vikings were never considered that. The bottom line in professional football is winning the Super Bowl. Oakland in its only appearance had failed in 1968, but that wasn't the only criterion. In all those years since then, the Raiders had dominated the Western Division of the American Football Conference, appearing each year in the playoffs. But it wasn't until the 1976 season was over that they made it to the Super Bowl.

The Vikings were even more infamous. They had been futile in three Super Bowl appearances—1970, 1974, and 1975. They had dominated the Central Division of the National Football Conference and had also appeared with regularity in the playoffs every year with the exception of 1972. So, they were appearing in the Super Bowl for the fourth time; and no other team in the history of the NFL had ever achieved that distinction.

Sunny California was anything but that the week before the game. It rained every day, making practice sessions for both teams difficult. Yet everyone in the environs of Los Angeles was clinging to the weatherman's promise that it would be sunny and dry on game day.

What both coaches were promising was an open, exciting game. Coach John Madden of the Raiders had an explosive offense that was triggered by quarterback Ken

Raider running back Clarence Davis breaks loose on a key third-down 35-yard run against Vikings in opening period.

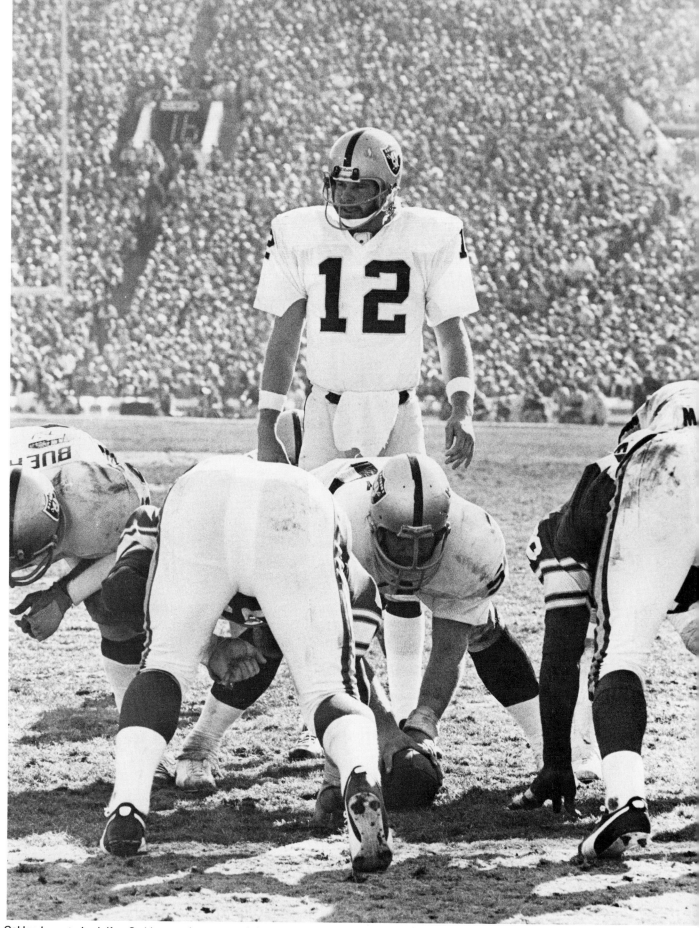

Oakland quarterback Ken Stabler was in command throughout the game in Super Bowl XI.

Stabler. Since he assumed control of the Raiders at the young age of 33, Madden had been the winningest coach in the NFL. Grant, too, had distinguished himself since he took over the Vikings' coaching reins the same year. In eight of those ten years, the Vikings had won the Central Division championship.

The coaches were a study in contrast. Madden was a big, bubbly type who often displayed emotion on the sideline during the game. Grant was the direct opposite. He was lean and quiet and never displayed any feeling. He preferred to mask his emotions behind steely blue eyes and a set of earphones that set him apart on the sidelines. Like coach Tom Landry of the Dallas Cowboys, he was looked upon as being more computer than human.

This time Grant appeared more outgoing. On Friday night he attended the big Super Bowl bash put on by the NFL. He seemed quite relaxed, walking around talking to people.

"It won't be a 14-10 type game," said Grant about the approaching Sunday contest. "This is one of the first times that both Super Bowl teams have good balance. Pittsburgh, as strong as it was on offense, was dominant on defense; and Miami was awfully strong on defense.

"This team has a new dimension. It has emotion now. Maybe it's nothing new. It might have been dormant all the while. But some players thought we needed it. It's the kind of spirit they have to build up themselves. It can't come from the coaches."

One of the players in question was the Vikings' star runner, Chuck Foreman. He was the most versatile back in football and perhaps one of the most frustrated. He had come away empty in two previous Super Bowls. Adding to his frustrations was the fact that he wanted the Vikings to give him a new contract—something he asked for when he discovered he was getting less money than other backs with far less ability. It made him brood inside, and he had to let loose his emotions.

"I decided to initiate some action," began Foreman. "So one day in the locker room before a game, I told everybody: 'I know you're all emotionally high, but you don't show it. Well, show me how you feel.'"

That was only the beginning. A strange

Big tight end Dave Casper of Raiders rambles for yardage after catching a pass.

rift occurred between Foreman and the Vikings' front office on Wednesday before the monumental game. He just about told them to drown in the rain: they hadn't renegotiated his contract, something he had asked them to do before the season began.

"I won't play for the Vikings after this Super Bowl game unless my contract is renegotiated," exclaimed Foreman. "It's probably the wrong time to make this public, but I'm not happy with my contract. I won't play with it again. I have proven myself. I think I'm the best, and I want to be paid like it."

The Vikings' veteran quarterback, Fran Tarkenton, couldn't have agreed more. Like Foreman, he, too, had suffered the frustrations of two Super Bowl losses. He, more than anyone, appreciated Foreman's talents.

"We don't give Foreman the ball to set a record like Buffalo did with O. J.," claimed Tarkenton. "Foreman is the most valuable player on this team. He's in fact the most valuable player in the league."

Since their last Super Bowl defeat, the Vikings had redesigned their offense to take

120

away some pressure from Tarkenton and Foreman. They added Brent McClanahan, a runner with outside speed, and two swift wide receivers in veteran Ahmad Rashad and rookie Sammie White.

"There's an obsession with this team to win this game," remarked Tarkenton. "It started last year in the Dallas game. This team is literally on fire to play this game."

White had had a sensational rookie year in providing the Vikings with a deep pass threat. He had 51 receptions, sixth best in the NFC. He gained 906 yards, more than any receiver, and he averaged 17.8 yards a catch. His leading NFC total of ten touchdowns didn't go unnoticed, either.

What didn't go unnoticed by White was how tough the Raiders' safety George Atkinson played. He had studied films of the telling blow Atkinson inflicted on Pittsburgh's Lynn Swann—which created a season-long controversy.

"It was a real bad cheap shot," exclaimed White. "He should have been thrown out of the game. It was the most flagrant cheap shot I've seen all year. What the Raiders want you to do is to be ready to fight rather than let you play your own game.

"I'm aware that they will probably try to belt me, and I'm going to be mentally prepared. If you have it in the back of your head that they're going to be shooting cheap shots, you probably can survive any of them. But when the ball comes, there ain't nothing else in your mind except catching the ball, total concentration."

Rashad felt much the same way. He knew the feeling well about being an open target in an area where defensive backs like to hit.

"They play a rough style of football," added Rashad, "but the game is rough. Things like that you can't let get to you. I'm sure they can intimidate you if they start doing things like that, but I never think of anybody's territory. When I play, the field is mine."

Oakland cornerback Skip Thomas breaks up a long pass that was intended for Minnesota wide receiver Sammie White.

Since both teams had excellent quarterbacks and receivers, it was felt by some that the final outcome of the game would quite likely be decided in the 15-yard area beyond the line of scrimmage. That was the fertile ground when Tarkenton dumped his short passes to Foreman and Stabler looked for his wide receiver, Fred Biletnikoff, to demonstrate his curl patterns. No one in football performed it better than the cagey Biletnikoff. He was without question Stabler's favorite receiver.

"Everybody thinks that a pass play is prearranged," disclosed Biletnikoff, "but it's not. Kenny calls the pattern, and everybody runs the pattern. He reads the defense, and he goes away from the strong side of the defense. It's not so much practicing how to get open, but how to get away from the defense.

"I don't consider it my duty to catch one key pass a game. But it's like if you have to be at work at 8 o'clock and you keep getting there at 8:15, they're going to let you know sooner or later. You've got to go out there and come up with a catch.

"We don't throw a lot of slants. We don't have to get our people beat up or throw dangerous passes to our receivers. We have the talent to throw a lot of other things."

The other talent was wide receiver Cliff Branch, who could fly, and tight end Dave Casper, who was big enough and strong enough to catch a ball in a crowd. Minnesota could be left vulnerable if they decided to double any of the Raider receivers. Branch was one of the best on sideline patterns, and Casper proved his value on crossing patterns. The three receivers together had caught 29 touchdown passes during the season.

The feisty Atkinson answered White and many of his critics three days before the game. He wasn't about to accept an "intimidating" rap. He cleared the air once and for all.

"I'm an aggressive player," he admitted. "I'm an intimidator. I have to be. I am rough, but I'm not dirty. I play with a lot of emotion, even ferociousness. I'm six feet tall and weigh 185 pounds. I play against a lot of bigger guys. I have to play this way if I want to stay around. I'm just a football player, but they've made me look like a bad guy."

"We hit. I don't deny that. Our secondary is a little more aggressive than most. Because of the kind of defense we play, I can be isolated. The least little thing looks flagrant and gets blown up out of proportion. There weren't any fouls in the Pittsburgh game. There was nothing the media could say. We beat the team the media called awesome, but the media still had to go back to September to find something to write about.

"I'm playing back there with three guys I've been with for several years. We know each other, and we look for each other. You never get the feeling you're out there alone. It's good to know that."

Stabler also harbored some resentment. Despite the fact that the Raiders under his command had won more games than any other team over the same corresponding period, they were labeled as "the team that couldn't win the big one." He, perhaps more than any other player, had a flaming passion to win on Sunday. It was more than just another game to Stabler. It was the bottom line.

The southpaw quarterback had had a fantastic season. He had completed 194 of 291 passes for 2,737 yards and 27 touchdowns. His 66.7 completion percentage was the second highest in NFL history. Only Sammy Baugh, who had a 70.3 percentage in 1945, was higher. But Baugh threw over 100 passes fewer than Stabler. Still, Stabler put individual accomplishments behind him. He knew what it would mean to win the Super Bowl. That was where the season was for him now.

"I'd like to think that it's just like a sandlot game, and all we've got to do is to go out and have some fun," said Stabler early in the week. "But I can't. The game is just too big. It means too much to too many people for me to say it's just another game. It means money and job security.

"When we beat Pittsburgh two weeks ago for the AFC championship, it got the monkey off our back; but that was only temporary. It just shut up the critics for two weeks. Now we've got the monkey on our back again; and after we win the big one here, next year they'll be saying, 'Can the Raiders repeat?' It's something that never ends.

"We've had a lot of injuries on defense, which meant that the offense went out

Veteran Raider cornerback Willie Bown looks back as he runs into the end zone with an intercepted pass.

ball, but I've seen Branch run right by zones. You can get big ones on anybody.

"I'm not a real hard thrower like Terry Bradshaw or Dan Pastorini, guys who have shotguns. My game is accuracy, touch, and anticipation."

The Vikings also had to anticipate another Raider strength, the run. Oakland's top runner, Mark van Eeghen, gained 1,012 yards on 233 carries, an average of 4.3 yards a run. The other dangerous runner was Clarence Davis, who had good outside speed. They were successful because of the excellent blocking they received from guard Gene Upshaw and tackle Art Shell, who were rated the top two players at their positions—thus enabling the Raiders to run quite fluidly over the left side.

The fact that Oakland would be running left presented an interesting challenge for the Vikings. It was perhaps Minnesota's most vulnerable area. The Raiders would be coming at end Jim Marshall, who was 39; outside linebacker Wally Hilgenberg, who was 34; and cornerback Bobby Bryant, who at 170 pounds was the lightest player on the field. The oddsmakers made special note of that as they established the Raiders as four-point favorites.

The last time the Raiders had played in the Super Bowl, they had been big underdogs. In Super Bowl II, the Green Bay Packers had been listed as two-touchdown favorites to defeat Oakland. Veteran runner Pete Banaszak, a starting member of the 1968 squad, remembered how it felt.

"Daryle Lamonica was our quarterback then, and he would go into the huddle and ask our receivers what they thought would go and get no answers.

"I remember coming out of the huddle on the first play and looking at them—Ray Nitschke, Henry Jordan, Herb Adderley, Willie Davis. They were guys I collected bubble gum cards with when I was younger. I grew up near Green Bay.

"On the first play, I was supposed to block Dave Robinson, and Hewritt Dixon carried the ball. I didn't even touch Robinson. Nitschke came over to get Dixon for no gain. I had spike marks all over my back. I thought after that Super Bowl we'd be back the next year. It took nine years. Now it's so much bigger. It's a circus."

Jim Finks, general manager of the

123

knowing it was going to have to score a lot of points. We've fought through it all. We're probably hungrier than we've ever been because we've played through so much adversity.

"We showed that you don't have to establish the run before you can pass. You can pass any time you want to as long as you have good protection. Branch is our home-run guy. Freddie is a great clutch guy as you all know; and Casper is a real smart, strong guy who out-muscles people for the ball. They're very difficult to cover. People say that the zone has taken away the long

Another Raider veteran, running back Pete Banaszak, bowls into the end zone for a touchdown.

Chicago Bears, also looked back. He was the general manager of the Vikings from 1964 to 1973 and had helped to assemble the current champions. He felt that the Vikings were better than the Raiders.

"I'm not convinced that David Rowe, Otis Sistrunk, and John Matuszak strike fear in the hearts of anybody," remarked Finks about the Raiders' three defensive front men. "I am not discounting the fact that they've played very well for most of the year. But I'm not convinced that they are in the same league with Carl Eller, Alan Page, Doug Sutherland, and Jim Marshall. I just don't think they're the same kind of people.

"I believe Minnesota is the better team. From number one to number 43, they have better players. Defensively, Minnesota's linebackers are just as good, their front four are better, and their secondary as a unit is as good, even if they don't have as many individual outstanding athletes.

"Minnesota also has more ways of scoring. I'm convinced that Oakland can't break a play from the line of scrimmage for any distance. Chuck Foreman has that ability, but I can't see where anybody on Oakland has that ability."

George Allen, the resourceful coach of the Washington Redskins, saw it the other way. He is not one to venture an opinion on something he can't control, which is a good way to avoid arguments, but he liked the Raiders' chances.

"It's tough to pick," he cautiously began, "and the game could go either way. This is the best Viking team I've seen since I've been in the league. But if there is any edge this time around, it might be that Oakland has a little better depth in personnel. That counts in a game that figures to be so close.

"Oakland's big threat is the home run. Stabler goes deep, and no team has been able to stop him. The only way is with a great rush or layoff and give away the short stuff underneath. Their defense will get a real test because they haven't played anyone with that time back there. Stabler gets the best protection in football. He has time to find the open man, and their receivers have the speed and knowledge to get open."

The real focus was on the quarterbacks. Each was the heart of his team. Tarkenton made things happen for the Vikings in much the same manner as Stabler did for the Raiders. The one doubt surrounding the game was the condition of Stabler's ribs and Tarkenton's knee. Some skeptics claimed that Stabler's ribs were still sore from the hit he had taken from the Steelers in the AFC championship game two weeks before. Both Stabler and Madden denied it. Tarkenton, who admitted that his knee had bothered him two weeks earlier in the NFC championship game against the Los Angeles Rams, remarked that it was fine now and let it go at that.

As the weatherman had predicted, the fans got a sunny day, although not a warm one. The temperature for the 1 P.M. kickoff was 58 degrees, but the main thing was that rain would not interfere with the players' performance and neutralize their skills. The excellent drainage facilities of the field helped. Despite the week-long rains, the playing surface was dry, although the ground wasn't firm.

Len Dawson, a sportscaster for NBC television, was on the field, checking its condition before game time. Asked his opinion of the outcome, Dawson smiled and remarked, "I think the Raiders will kill them."

There were 100,421 seated behind Daw-

son. It was a record **crowd** to witness a Super Bowl. Somehow or other, 3,003 people didn't believe the weatherman or got lost on the freeway leading to Pasadena. They were classified as no-shows.

Nevertheless, the Raiders won the coin toss and unhesitatingly instructed the referee that they would receive the kickoff. On the first play of the game from the 34-yard line, Davis characteristically ran to his left for a yard. Van Eeghen went the same way and got four yards. Then Stabler zipped a 25-yard pass to Casper for a first down on the Vikings' 36.

Stabler went back to the run. First Davis picked up four yards around the left side. Then he broke through for a 20-yard burst to the Vikings' 12-yard line. In just five plays the Raiders were already threatening to score, but the Vikings held. Errol Mann tried a field goal from the 29-yard line but the ball hit the left goal post.

The Oakland fans moaned. Madden was a bit upset as Stabler walked off the field. He headed straight toward Madden. "Don't worry, Coach. There's plenty more where that came from," Stabler assured him.

Yet, with just over five minutes left in the quarter, Ray Guy had to punt the Raiders out of danger from the 34-yard line. Guy was regarded as easily the premier punter in the NFL. He was the only punter ever to be drafted on the first round of the league's college draft. That was how highly the Raiders thought of Guy in 1973.

It looked so routine for Guy. He took the snap from center and started to punt. Suddenly, linebacker Fred McNeil got through and blocked. The ball bounced all the way to the Oakland three-yard line, where it was recovered by McNeil. In one play the momentum of the game had quickly changed.

It looked as if the Vikings would score first as Tarkenton came back on the field. The first play went quite naturally to Foreman, and he picked up a yard. Then it was McClanahan's turn. He hit the line and fumbled. Underneath the big pile-up, linebacker Willie Hall recovered the ball for the Raiders.

The fumble seemed to take the heart out of the Minnesota defense as they came on the field for the fourth time in the period. Stabler had a difficult field position on the three-yard line. Two running plays netted

125

Defensive linemen Tom Keating (74) and Otis Sistrunk (60) signal they're number one as game comes to an end.

Guard Gene Upshaw (63) holds up sign announcing that Raiders are number one as Oakland coach John Madden smiles.

only three yards. Eliminating the expected pass, Stabler called Davis's number. The speedy Davis shook loose around left end for 35 yards to get the Raiders out of the hole. That was the spark the Raiders needed. When the opening quarter ended, they were on the Minnesota eight-yard line.

It had been a strange first period. Although the Raiders had made seven first downs to Minnesota's one and had gained 174 yards to the Vikings' 26, the game was still scoreless. It seemed incredible that Oakland hadn't scored a single point.

Even though Stabler had moved the Raiders 97 yards in just 12 plays, he couldn't get a touchdown. Instead, the Raiders had to settle for a 24-yard field goal by Mann for a 3-0 lead. It was only a portent of things to come. The next time Oakland got the ball, Stabler got them a touchdown. He took them 64 yards in just ten plays, hitting Casper with a one-yard touchdown pass for a 10-0 lead.

Stabler wasn't through. When he got the ball again, he moved the Raiders 35 yards in only five plays and gained a touchdown when Banaszak went over from the one-yard line. Mann's kick was wide, and the score stayed at 16-0. When the half ended three minutes later, it appeared as if a rout was in the making.

The Raiders had clearly dominated the game. They ran off 48 plays to the Vikings' 22. They made 16 first downs to Minnesota's four and had gained 228 yards while the Vikings could produce only 86. It was a wonder the Raiders weren't ahead by a bigger margin.

Grant tried to rally his team at halftime. He approached his players and broke the silence of the dressing room.

"We can't fold our tent now," he said. "We've been down by 16 points before. We have to come back to score 17 and win. If you can find an easier way to lose, let me know."

The victorious Raiders were well rewarded. Each received a 14-karat gold ring that contained diamonds totaling 2.3 carats.

Still, the Vikings couldn't do anything. With just over five minutes left in the third period, Mann booted a 40-yard field goal to send the Raiders into a 19-0 lead. But the Vikings didn't fold. Just before the quarter ended, Tarkenton took the Vikings 68 yards on 12 plays, the touchdown coming on an eight-yard pass to White. Trailing 19-7, the Vikings still appeared to have a chance.

But Stabler killed their hopes early in the final period. A 48-yard pass to Biletnikoff gave the Raiders a first down on the two-yard line. Banaszak took it in to give the Raiders a 26-7 edge. Moments later, veteran Willie Brown intercepted Tarkenton's pass and ran 75 yards for a touchdown that put the game totally out of reach, 32-7. An unmeaningful eight-yard touchdown pass from reserve quarterback Bob Lee to tight end Stu Voigt ended the scoring. The 32-14 triumph was a rout, as Dawson had predicted.

The win was most satisfying to owner Al Davis. He had rebuilt a weak Raider team after the 1963 season and had coached them in their first Super Bowl game in 1968. (He had also served a brief two-month period in the spring of 1966 as commissioner of the old American Football League before returning to coach the Raiders.) In 1969 he left the coaching ranks and named Madden as head coach of the team.

But for many years it was felt by practically everyone that Davis was still the coach and was merely running things through Madden. It was unfair. Madden did not

receive the full credit he deserved until he won Super Bowl XI. On that day he stood tall. In eight years as coach, he had compiled a record of 83-22-7, a winning percentage of .790. That was better than any other coach in the NFL.

When the Raiders came into the locker room, Madden climbed upon a platform. The players all looked up at him.

"We're number one!" he shouted. "You did a great job. You had a great season. They can't say it any more that we don't win the big one."

Almost an hour later, after he had answered an endless stream of questions, Madden reflected upon the game. He seemed relieved.

"We controlled things out there," he said. "We felt very confident. We have been ever since we beat Pittsburgh. We decided to hang it all out. We wanted to pass when they expected us to run, and we decided to run when they expected us to pass. That's how much confidence I have in this team. On our first drive we did what we wanted to do, and that set the tempo for the game. We waited a helluva long time for this."

So had Biletnikoff. He was named the most valuable player, grabbing four clutch passes for 79 yards. He positioned three touchdowns: once from the two-yard line and twice from the one-yard line. He had played on the team that lost to the Packers, 33-14, in Super Bowl II.

"I don't even want to remember the last one, but I wasn't scared for this one," said Biletnikoff. "I would have liked to score, but winning the game was the big thing. If I can get close enough for somebody else to score, it's all right with me. On that last 35-yard run I was looking for a gas station along the way.

"I really appreciate Stabler. He throws the ball where I can catch it, low and away from people. To me, Kenny Stabler is the best quarterback to play football. He doesn't pop off."

Stabler, too, was relieved.

"This will stop the critics until this time next year," pointed out Stabler. "They said for years we couldn't win the big one. Now I guess we will hear, 'Will the Raiders be able to win it twice?'"

Once is never enough . . .

Super Bowl XII

January 15, 1978
New Orleans Superdome
76,400

Dallas (NFC)	10	3	7	7	—	27
Denver (AFC)	0	0	10	0	—	10

It was like something out of Grimm's fairy tales. Nobody had believed that the Denver Broncos would ever reach Super Bowl XII. The Dallas Cowboys' presence was expected. After all, they had been there before, three other times. But they were easily the class of the National Football Conference. They were heavily favored to win the NFC playoffs and won both their games against the Chicago Bears and the Minnesota Vikings quite easily. And they did so in the methodical, efficient manner of an IBM computer.

The Broncos were something else again. In both of their American Football Conference playoff contests, they had been the underdogs. It was as if they had been cast in that role all season long. Even when they had won their first six games of the season, no one took them seriously enough. When they reached the playoffs, the experts felt that if the Pittsburgh Steelers didn't beat them, then the Oakland Raiders would. But the Broncos didn't believe them and proved how wrong they were. They had carried a new dimension with them throughout the season, a wave of emotionalism that helped to bring them this far. It was a part of professional football that is rarely seen. Their infectious emotion carried to the fans and became Broncomania. By now, the football world recognized it.

Super Bowl XII had somewhat of a circus atmosphere. New Orleans is an all-night town. It's an old, beautiful city with its historic French Quarter and excellent restaurants, a town not wanting to give up the past. In the confinement of the Quarter, the excitement of the game circulated. Tickets were harder to get than for any of the previous Super Bowls. Ticket scalpers were asking for and getting as much as $200 for a $30 ticket. Some 50-yard line seats were

The Dallas defense looks on. From left, end Harvey Martin (79), tackle Randy White (54), tackle Jethro Pugh (75), and linebacker Tom Henderson (56).

128

attracting prices of up to $250. Any time the Cowboys are involved in a big game, ticket hustlers have a shot at a big payday. Texas money is big and loose. The fanatic sentiment for the Broncos assured the gougers a bonanza.

But the Las Vegas betting line wasn't looking at sentiment. They established the Cowboys as five-point favorites. Some betting parlors were giving six toward the week's end. Danny Sheridan, a football analyst for ABC television's *Good Morning, America* program, liked the Broncos with the points. However, he expertly qualified his pick.

"It is imperative that the Broncos not only force mistakes but score first as they are not capable of playing catch-up football against Dallas," said Sheridan, who had correctly picked ten straight Super Bowl games with the points. "Denver has to force four turnovers by the Cowboy running backs. It is very important for the Broncos to achieve this. They have to create turnovers and score first. I can't see them covering the points if they don't accomplish this.

Dallas quarterback Roger Staubach looks downfield as he sets up to pass.

130

They will quickly fall behind, and the game could turn into a rout."

Others offered respected opinions. Allie Sherman for one. The former coach of the New York Giants in their glory days was known as a brilliant offensive innovator. He had strong convictions that the Broncos had to throw the ball for them to win.

"The Broncos have to come out throwing," observed Sherman just three days before the game. "They have to throw on first down and use a lot of play action passes to slow down the rush and freeze the linebackers. There is no way they can run successfully against Dallas's flex defense."

It was the same view shared by Len Dawson, an analyst for NBC television. A former premier quarterback with the Kansas City Chiefs until he had retired in 1975, Dawson had been a leading figure in two Super Bowls himself.

"I'd come out throwing early," Dawson said. "Not the bomb; but I'd throw short, working on their linebackers.

"I'd use my tight end a lot; and in Riley Odoms the Broncos have an outstanding one. And I'd throw to my backs quite a bit,

screens and outlet passes, to pick up five or six yards; and I wouldn't hesitate to do it on the first down. In fact, I'd prefer throwing on first down to pick up four, five, six yards at a clip. If I'm successful this way, then the Cowboys will have to play defense; and they'll be the ones doing the guessing.

"Denver has good receivers with good speed in Haven Moses, Rick Upchurch, and Jack Dolbin. Moses, especially, is a good pattern runner. I'd throw to him deep early because the Dallas secondary will be looking for him to run intermediate patterns. By sending him deep early, it'll keep their secondary honest.

"In throwing deep, I'd do so to the outside. This will prevent their safeties from getting involved in the play. In Charlie Waters and Cliff Harris, Dallas has a pair of great safeties; and it's not smart to challenge them too much.

"On defense, the Cowboys do blitz occasionally. They don't have to blitz much because they get a great deal of penetration from their front four. They have great size up front, Too Tall Jones (6-9), Jethro Pugh (6-6), Harvey Martin (6-5), and Randy White (6-4). They are really big and quick, and they come at you with their hands up, which makes it difficult to throw over them. If you're in a third-and-long situation and they play pass, they come at you all out; and it's murder. It places the quarterback in jeopardy of getting sacked or having to throw the ball before he's ready, which increases the percentage of interceptions.

"The flex is tough to run on. On the ground, I would attack them more straight ahead than sideways. Sweeps don't work against them because they are so big, so quick, and so well disciplined. There is no question that the Denver offensive line is going to have their hands full controlling the Dallas front four and linebackers.

"Denver's strength has been that they don't turn the ball over on offense. That's been demonstrated all season long. It is a big reason why they are in the Super Bowl. The other team has to earn what it gets against the Broncos' defense, and that hasn't been much. But the main thing is that Morton has to avoid turning over the football to the Cowboys. That would be a primary objective. You just can't give the Cowboys too many chances with the football. They have a lot of offense and can put points on the board in a hurry. And if Denver falls behind early, it could be a long night.''

The Dallas flex was a creation of head coach Tom Landry. It was a difficult defense to attack. No other team employed it. As such, it was also a difficult defense to teach; but the Cowboy players had mastered it after several years of executing it. The defense was particularly impregnable against running plays. It presented a picket line effect in that the linebackers and down linemen covered all the running holes. The most successful way to attack it was with straight ahead drive-blocking.

The Cowboys' offense was also solid. Veteran quarterback Roger Staubach had demonstrated his leadership and skill for nine years, making the Dallas offense one of the most explosive in the NFL. He had excellent receivers in wide receivers Drew

Pearson, Golden Richards, and Butch Johnson and in tight end Billy Joe DuPree, and a sensational runner in rookie Tony Dorsett.

Like the Cowboys, Denver's strength was also its defense. They played a contrasting style to that of the Cowboys and most other NFL teams for that matter. Denver stopped its opponents with a 3-4, which utilized three down linemen and four quick, active linebackers. The Broncos blitzed quite often, which presented a lot of pressure to opposing quarterbacks.

Denver's offense was not nearly as powerful as Dallas's. It was best described as being resourceful in that the powerful Denver defense would present the offense with positive field positions from which to operate. They had a new quarterback in Craig Morton, a 13-year veteran who had played the better part of ten years with the Cowboys. Morton also had fine receivers to throw to, provided he could get the time from an "average" offensive line. His best pair was wide receiver Haven Moses and tight end Riley Odoms, who had the speed to go deep. The Broncos also had a threat on the ground in speedster Otis Armstrong.

The game had an extra bit of emotion for Morton. Besides playing against his old team, he was also facing in Staubach the quarterback who took his job away from him. He had been booed by the fans his final two years there and left Dallas in a trade to the New York Giants greatly saddened and disillusioned. He had suffered the same feelings for the better part of two years with the Giants before he was sent to Denver and started a new career at the age of 34. Morton brought stability to the Denver offense and, for the first time, leadership on the field that resulted in Denver's finishing with a 12-2 record.

It was a tribute to Red Miller and the miracle he had created in his first year. He had taken over a team that had mutinied after the 1976 season. The players had refused to play another season for coach John Ralston, despite the fact that the Broncos finished with their best record in history, 9-5. So, Ralston was fired, and Miller replaced him. The Broncos responded not only to his knowledge but to the emotion with which he approached his work.

"You know, a lot of people didn't expect

131

Rookie Denver running back Rob Lytle turns corner as he picks up some yardage against Cowboys.

(Above) Dallas defensive end Harvey Martin grabs Bronco quarterback Norris Weese around the waist.

Running back Scott Laidlaw of the Cowboys picks up yardage before being stopped by Bronco linebacker Joe Rizzo.

us to be here," he said and smiled. "I knew we had something going after training camp. We had a great camp. The players were in great shape, and they had a great mental attitude. I knew we had the makings of a good team.

"How good remained to be seen. I didn't concern myself with any goals. What I instilled in my coaches and players was to take one game at a time and keep going from there. It all began to happen. Pretty soon we were eight and one, then nine and one, then ten and one, then 11 and one, and 12 and one. Then we knew we'd be in the playoffs for the first time.

"But you know something? Nobody ever gave us credit. After each victory, none of the rival coaches ever congratulated us. They'd come up to me after a game and say, 'We played a bad game today.' Or, 'We sure got a lot of work ahead of us.' I didn't care what they said. All I was concerned with was how well we played and looked forward to the next week's game.

"By the end of the season, we made believers out of just about everyone; but it's funny in a way. All along you're doing the job, winning games week after week; and nobody seems to recognize it. Finally, when the season is over and we're here in the Super Bowl, they finally realize it. It's been a great season for us, the greatest in Denver history. Just being here is more than anyone expected."

Everyone seemed to expect that the Cowboys would be in the Super Bowl practically every year. In 11 of the previous 12 years, the Cowboys had qualified for the playoffs. They had never been subjected to a rebuilding program in any one season. Rather, they merely had to find a replacement here and there for any players who retired. It was a reflection on their organization, which was considered just about the best in pro football. Landry had been their only coach in the 18-year history of the franchise.

"I go to training camp every year scared to death," confided Landry. "That keeps me on edge. It makes me careful about evaluating what has happened in the past. When we kept going to the playoffs, people would tell me that the law of averages was going to catch up with me. That scared me, too. It made me work harder, and the result is that the players work harder.

"You've got to pay an awful price to win.

You've got to pay the price to get ready to win. If you're not willing, you lose. But if you think winning is not too important, then you are not willing to pay the price to win. This game is played with the heart.

"The reason I take on the appearance of being unemotional is that I don't believe you can be emotional and concentrate the way you must to be effective. When I see a great play from the sideline, I can't cheer it. As a team we win by concentrating, by thinking. The players don't want to see me rushing around and screaming. They want to believe I know what I'm doing.

"Against Denver's 3-4 defense, you can't isolate on people with individual match-ups. It is a stunting defense, a difficult one to concentrate on any player, any area."

The area around the Superdome was swarming with fans long before game time. For the first time all week the sun had shone brightly, almost eliminating the cold that had gripped the city. Some fans were still seeking to purchase tickets. Strangely enough, the high prices that prevailed earlier in the week remained. That was how much interest there was in Super Bowl XII.

Even Joe Namath was an interested observer. He attended the spectacle with an entourage that included two beautiful women and among others his attorney Jim Walsh and aide Tad Dowd. Nattily dressed and with a deep Florida tan, the handsome Namath was waiting to ride a private elevator deep underneath the stands to his private box.

"This Denver team is somewhat like the Jets in Super Bowl III," a friend remarked.

"Only we were a bigger underdog," pointed out Namath.

"That's true. Besides that, the Broncos don't have somebody like you at quarterback."

"You're very kind," Namath replied, smiling. "Who do you like in the game?"

"On paper, it's all Dallas, but . . ."

"Forget about paper," interrupted Namath. "I'm talking about on the field. No way form won't hold up. Dallas has too much going for them."

Although Namath obviously favored Dallas, the big crowd seemed to be with Denver. That's what Broncomania did. Along with the Jets in 1969 and the Kansas City Chiefs in 1970, the Broncos were perhaps the best loved underdogs in the history

of the Super Bowl. That said a lot because for the past two years, the Broncos were completely ignored by ABC's Monday Night Game. Suddenly, the Broncos were an attraction.

After the noise of the pre-game anticipation subsided, the coin-tossing ceremonies took place at the center of the field. This time the loss of the flip wouldn't mean a big decision about which goal to defend. Since the game was indoors for the first time in history, wind was not a factor. Naturally, when Dallas won the toss, they decided to receive the ball.

On the very first play of the game, Dallas almost committed a costly mistake on its 29-yard line. On a double reverse, Butch Johnson fumbled the ball but managed to recover it on the 20-yard line. It was the type of mistake that the Broncos thrived on all season. This time the ball didn't bounce Denver's way.

After a Dallas punt, the Broncos had the ball in good field position but couldn't do much. Beginning on their own 47-yard line, the Broncos did manage to reach the Cowboys' 33 before Morton was sacked for an 11-yard loss. Then, Bronco fans moaned

133

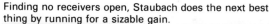
Finding no receivers open, Staubach does the next best thing by running for a sizable gain.

Linebacker Mike Hegman (58) of the Cowboys says it all as Super Bowl XII draws to an end.

On fourth down, Bucky Dilts punted to the Dallas one-yard line. Tony Hill dropped the ball but quickly recovered it from a swarm of onrushing Broncos. The Broncos had just missed a golden opportunity.

The breaks still didn't go their way a short time later. On a second-down play on the 19-yard line, Dorsett fumbled; but center John Fitzgerald recovered for the Cowboys on the 22. Three times in the early minutes of the game the Broncos couldn't get the one break they needed to get on top.

The first break went to Dallas. Pressured by Martin from one side and White from the other, Morton threw a wobbly pass that was intercepted by linebacker Randy Hughes on the Denver 25-yard line. Now the Cowboys were in excellent position to score first.

Staubach didn't waste any time. He positioned the touchdown with a 13-yard pass to DuPree on the 12-yard line. After Bob Newhouse ran to the ten, Dorsett took over. He went over the right side for six, then one, and switched to the left side to score standing up from three yards out. Efren Herrera's kick made it 7-0.

After the kickoff, the alert Dallas defense made another big play. Trying to pass up the middle from his own 42-yard line, Morton's pass was tipped by linebacker Bob Breunig into the hands of Aaron Kyle. The Dallas cornerback ran to the Denver 35-yard line before he was stopped. Six plays later, Herrera booted a 35-yard field goal that sent Dallas's advantage to 10-0 with just over a minute left to play in the first period.

The first time the Cowboys got their hands on the ball in the second quarter, they scored again. On a third-down play from the Denver 19, Staubach scrambled near the sidelines before he threw a pass in the end zone that was picked off by safety Billy Thompson. However, the official ruled that Staubach stepped out of bounds before he threw. Given a break, Herrera then proceeded to kick a 43-yard field goal to extend the Cowboys' margin to 13-0.

Before the first half ended 11 minutes later, the Broncos were victimized by one error after the other. First, Morton was intercepted for the third time when he tried to hit Moses deep on the Broncos' 40-yard line. Then on a Dallas punt, John Schultz lost the ball when it hit his helmet and Dallas recovered. Later, when Morton succeeded in completing a 15-yard pass to his wide receiver, Jack Dolbin, Jack fumbled and the ball was recovered by Hughes. Next, Morton fired a ten-yard pass to Odoms, who fumbled; and once again Hughes grabbed the ball.

Finally, just 17 seconds from the period's end, Morton was intercepted for the fourth time. He tried to hit Odoms, but Mark Washington gathered in the short pass. Morton, who was intercepted only eight times in 14 regular season games, had suffered four in only half a game. The amazing thing was that the score was only 13-0 when the first half was over. That was partly due to the fact that Herrera missed two field goals from the 32- and 44-yard line in between while DuPree fumbled a ball on the Bronco 12-yard line that was recovered by linebacker Tommy Jackson.

Morton didn't look like the same quarterback who had led the Broncos to the Super Bowl. There was something wrong. He didn't appear confident. He kept looking up at Harvey Martin from the huddle, wondering what the big Dallas defensive end would do next. Morton couldn't get the offense moving at all. Dallas's defensive strategy was obvious. They were putting pressure on Morton on every play. Morton couldn't handle it. No quarterback could have for that matter. It was simply because the Denver offensive line was getting beaten in the pits. They weren't giving Morton the time he needed to pass effectively as they had in the playoffs.

Morton couldn't move the ball at all against the Cowboys. The offense was woeful. They could only produce three first downs. Their total yardage was 72 yards, 44 rushing and only 28 passing. Virtually a mistake-free team all season, the Broncos committed *seven* turnovers. Besides Morton's four interceptions, the Broncos lost the ball three times on fumbles. It was miraculous that in allowing a team like Dallas seven turnovers they weren't further behind than 13-0.

That was the only consolation that Miller had in the locker room—along with the fact that his defense did play well. He kept reminding his squad that despite the seven turnovers they were still in the game. He stressed that the second half was a new game, to keep hitting out there, to stay close on the scoreboard, that the breaks would finally come their way.

Then he did something else. After his talk, he called Morton off to one side. It was a private conversation between a coach and his quarterback. He placed his arm on Morton's shoulder and said quietly, "Craig, I'm going to let you start the second half. However, if we can't get something started quickly, I'm going to see what Norris Weese can do. You understand?"

Morton nodded his head. For a moment, he was alone with his thoughts. All he was thinking about was the fact that the Broncos would get the second half kickoff, and he had to get them on the board. He tried to forget about the nightmarish first half. This was the half that counted, the one in which most games are won.

The Broncos felt that they had to get on the scoreboard when they got the second half kickoff. They began a drive from their own 35-yard line and reached the Cowboys'

135

30 before stalling. Miller sent in the reliable 37-year-old veteran Jim Turner to try for a field goal. Turner came through with a 47-yard kick that made the score 13-3.

Midway through the third period the Cowboys struck back. On a third-down-and-ten play, Staubach decided to go deep from the Denver 45-yard line. He told Johnson to run a good pass pattern. As Johnson was running down the sidelines, Staubach let go. Johnson reached the end zone, left the ground, and while flying through the air caught a 45-yard touchdown pass. Dallas shot to a 20-3 lead.

The Broncos had a long way to go. They were not accustomed to playing catch-up football. It was not their style. On the kick-off, Rick Upchurch almost got the touch-down back. He ran a record 67 yards before he was tackled on the Dallas 26-yard line. The run brought the big crowd to its feet.

But Morton almost gave the ball back. His first-down pass was almost intercepted by Too Tall Jones. Morton's errant pass came right into Jones's hands, and he dropped it. Miller then made a bold move. He replaced Morton with reserve quarterback Norris Weese in an attempt to get the Broncos moving. Four plays later, rookie running back Rob Lytle went in from the one-yard line to cut Dallas's margin to 20-10.

When the final period began, the Broncos still had a chance. All season long they had dominated the fourth quarter, outscoring their opponents. However, with about seven minutes left, their hopes faded away. Weese fumbled, and Kyle recovered on the Denver 29. The Cowboys were poised for the kill. On first down, Robert Newhouse started off on what appeared to be a left side sweep. He abruptly stopped and fired a 29-yard pass to Richards in the end zone. Richards made a brilliant catch, looking over his shoulder on a pass thrown directly over his head. The touchdown clinched the victory as Herrera's conversion put the game out of reach, 27-10. Broncomania had a muted end.

Dallas's defense was awesome. The Broncos couldn't contain the oppressive pressure of Harvey Martin, Randy White, and Ed Jones. They came at Denver right at the start and never let up. That was their defensive game plan. They executed it almost to

The look on the face of Denver defensive end Barney Chavous tells the frustration of the Broncos as the curtain comes down on their Cinderella year.

perfection. Never once did the Broncos execute a sustained drive. That's the way defense is played.

"We know we had to pressure Morton," disclosed White in the crowded Dallas interview area underneath the stands. "It was just part of the game plan. We had to pressure Morton and try to upset him. I felt that if we didn't give them turnovers and field position, we would win. Denver is a field position team. We only gave them field position three times, and we stopped them on two of the three instances."

In a game that was devoid of any offensive heroics, White and Martin were named the most valuable players. For students of defensive football, they were truly exciting.

136

"Denver was looking for the blitz," Martin said. "We showed it to them, but we just used good defensive football. We wanted to give Morton something to think about, but it was just four guys rushing the passer.

"It seemed that Morton was looking at me every time he came to the line. I think he was more concerned because he knew we'd be all coming at him. Denver has a lot of enthusiasm, but enthusiasm doesn't win Super Bowl games. Execution does. You could see Denver's enthusiasm draining after the third interception."

The fact that Morton was responsible for a Super Bowl record of four interceptions was simply attributed to the fierce rush that the Cowboys employed the entire game. He would have had an ignominious fifth if Jones hadn't dropped a wobbly Morton pass in the third period. He was so surprised by it that he couldn't react quickly enough.

"I was confident we would win," said Jones. "I just wondered how easy it would be. I had predicted a cakewalk through the playoffs and into the Super Bowl, but only if we played well. I thought we had the game pretty much in control when we settled down.

"We rattled Morton. He'd walk into the huddle looking straight ahead, looking to see if we were playing the run or the pass. He knows something about the flex defense. What we did was to force them into passing situations by stopping them on the first down. The three times I've seen Morton on film, he's had more time to pass than we gave him."

Nobody realized it better than Miller. There just wasn't anything he could do to stop it. His offensive line wasn't one of his team's stronger points, and the Cowboys attacked it.

But the Cowboys had something else going for them that nobody realized, something that everyone had claimed they didn't possess.

"We were more emotional than any of my previous three Super Bowl teams," revealed Landry. "We knew the Broncos had it, and you've got to be emotionally up, too."

And just a bit better . . .

Super Bowl XIII

January 21, 1979
Miami Orange Bowl
78,656

Pittsburgh (AFC)	7	14	0	14	—	35
Dallas (NFC)	7	7	3	14	—	31

Both teams had been there before. They knew what the Super Bowl was all about. The Pittsburgh Steelers and the Dallas Cowboys had indeed met before. Just three years ago in Super Bowl X, the Steelers and Cowboys played perhaps the most exciting Super Bowl game ever. Now they were facing each other again in Super Bowl XIII in the same Orange Bowl in Miami. The early sentiment was that the Steelers would repeat their earlier 21-17 win. Oddsmakers were quoting the Steelers as favorites, anywhere from 3 to 4½ points. But the game had an added meaning. Both Pittsburgh and Dallas had won two Super Bowls in the past. Whoever won Super Bowl XIII would carve some niche of pro football lore by becoming the first team to win three Super Bowls.

The Steelers had finished the 1978 campaign with a 14-2 record, the best in the NFL. Quarterback Terry Bradshaw was the chief reason. The nine-year veteran experienced his best season ever. He completed 56.3 percent of his passes for 2,915 yards and 28 touchdowns to rank second in the NFL behind Dallas' quarterback Roger Staubach, who completed 55.9 percent of his passes for 3,190 yards and 25 touchdowns in leading the Cowboys to a 12-4 record. It was a personally satisfying season for Bradshaw, who, during his career, had been constantly criticized as being a dumb quarterback. It was totally unfair. Everybody knew that Bradshaw tried too hard, inflicting too much pressure on himself to win. But now, in 1978, he had put it all together.

"It's already been a great season," exclaimed Bradshaw. "This is just the dessert. The game plan is in. I'm just here to have fun. I just enjoy the challenge of the game. I'll use whatever works out there, whatever is successful, whether it's the pass or the run. I expect one of us to play wide open,

depending on the early results. I think that it will determine whether the game continues that way. It will probably be played close to the vest starting off and open up as it goes along.

"I'm having a ball. I like to come into a game feeling prepared and relaxed. Then we get into a tough spot and I just think, 'I'll call this little old play here; and if this guy is not open, I'll turn around and hit this guy.' Take Dallas. They'll double-cover Lynn Swann and John Stallworth, but soon one of them will slip past that coverage. Then it's man-to-man, and we got 'em. It's

With guard Sam Davis leading the way, Pittsburgh's star runner Franco Harris rips through big hole in Dallas defense for a dramatic 22-yard touchdown run in the fourth period.

139

not life or death. We're just playing with them."

There was no doubt that Bradshaw was loose. It was a reflection of the whole season. Bradshaw was relaxed and seemed to be enjoying himself despite having to face the brigade of media people. None of his interviews got heavy. In fact, he kept them on the light side which eliminated any tension. He was indeed having fun.

Quite obviously, the theme for Super Bowl XIII was intimidation. It was as if the Steelers were cast in the role of villians. They would even look the part in their black jerseys. Everybody knows the good guys wear white. Simply, the Steelers play hard, basic football which is a contrast to the Cowboys' style of finesse. It is just that the Steelers don't like to engage in the off-field banter that the Cowboys were exhorting from their hotel 30 miles north in Ft. Lauderdale.

Thomas Henderson, the loquacious Dallas linebacker, set the tone. Yet, none of the Steelers were affected by him. Rather, the writers covering the game were actually attracted to Henderson's flippant tongue. And Henderson cleverly positioned the press to gain as much publicity as Joe Namath got exactly 10 years earlier in Super Bowl III. It was no wonder he was called "Hollywood."

"When my mouth is running, my motor is running," exclaimed Henderson. "If I was mute, I couldn't play this game. I put a lot of pressure on myself to see if I can play up to my mouth. I think the Steelers should be favored. The reason is because they've played the most consistent over the season. The first half of the year we didn't play as well as the last half, but I think we're peaking now.

"It's going to be like the Los Angeles game. We'll shut them out on defense, and Hollywood will have the final word again. I said the Rams didn't have any class, and that's why they didn't get to the Super Bowl. The Steelers do have class, but they lack depth. That's their problem. If they lose anybody, they're gonna be in trouble.

"Look at their tight end Randy Grossman. He's a substitute. With Bennie Cunningham out, that little guy's gonna have trouble over there with me. He's the small-

est guy I ever played against. I've handled Russ Francis and Riley Odoms, just to name a few. Grossman's a backup tight end. How much respect can you have for a backup tight end? I mean, he's the guy that comes in when everybody else is dead. He's the last hope.

"I don't care for Jack Lambert, either. Why? Cause he makes more money than I do and cause he don't have no teeth. He's like Dracula. He should at least keep a mouthpiece in there or something. Count Lambert, that's what I call him.

"I'll tell you, they have a real intimidating defense. They're the Pittsburgh Killers. I think the best thing for our defense to do this week is pull out the acetylene equipment, welding gear, and go into the steel mill and disrupt it. I took welding. I know all about metals and steel. They got the Steel Curtain, and we got the Great Wall of China. I think our defense is equal to or stronger than their defense. I think it will be a defensive struggle, but we will prevail."

Unquestionably, the best runner the Steelers had was Franco Harris. Strangely, the Cowboys didn't make any mention of him in all the pre-game euphoria. Maybe they respected him too much. Quite possibly, they realized that they couldn't intimidate Harris with words. With all the excitement that was going on, Harris, nevertheless, was totally relaxed.

"It's a do or die situation," analyzed Harris. "You either win or you lose, and I don't like to be a loser. I always like to come away with something. I always feel we should win, and I go out and try to make that happen. If you don't win, you go home. If we hadn't won the past two games, we wouldn't be in cloudy Florida now.

"I haven't thought too much about the game. I'm just relaxing right now; but when it's time to play, I'll be ready. I'll say this, it's been a good, happy year, one that I have enjoyed playing and have reached a goal we wanted to reach. There's one more big game left.

"It's hard to answer now whether this team is better than the ones of 1974 and 1975. However, I feel that we are closer as a team. I feel that we are enjoying it more, and I hope on Sunday it will get better.

140

Pittsburgh's defensive end L. C. Greenwood halts Cowboys' Robert Newhouse.

"Since this has been Bradshaw's best year, maybe the pressure has been relieved from my shoulders now. I hope so. But it's going to be tough to get past Dallas' front line no matter what happens. I doubt if they'll be taking our running game lightly. It would be nice if they would, but we have so many weapons out there for them to concentrate in any one area of our offense."

Jack Lambert plays football with savage beauty. He is not a person to taunt, as Henderson attempted to do. And he doesn't like any of his teammates being ridiculed. Like the moment in Super Bowl X when Roy Gerela missed a field goal try. Dallas safety Cliff Harris patted him on the helmet and remarked something to the effect that he was the best player Dallas had going for them. Spontaneously, Lambert reacted. He rushed over to Harris, picked him up, and flung him to the ground in a fit of anger. He doesn't like playing against Dallas. Not for who they are, but for the style of football they employ.

"Computerized football is not my kind of football," snarled Lambert. "I'm not a very good computer. Quite possibly, playing in the old days was more fun. I used to love to play Oakland. You knew they were going to run over Art Shell and Gene Upshaw every play and run right at you. That's why I hate to play Dallas. There are so many formations you have to watch for. You have to be under control."

Lambert's sidekick, Jack Ham, was under complete control. He's not one to engage in verbal warfare. He merely shrugged his shoulders and laughed at Henderson's excessive verbiage. Ham is a very quiet person overall.

"What Henderson says doesn't affect me one way or the other," remarked Ham. "From what I see, he feels he plays better the more he puts himself on the spot. That's fine. I don't think any comments in the paper will make any difference. You won't see 45 players come out foaming at the mouth at Tom Henderson. He just makes good copy.

"I've never seen Henderson play except on television once. I don't know how good a linebacker he is. If all that talk pumps him up to play better, fine. I don't think two or three players on this team have mentioned about his comments in the newspapers. That's not going to affect us one way or the other on Sunday. If you need some article to get you pumped up for a big game like the Super Bowl, then you're in sad shape. This is the biggest football game of the year."

Meanwhile, ticket scalpers were pushing Super Bowl tickets at anywhere from $200 to $250. It was quite a considerable markup from the $30 specified on the ticket. That's how much attraction the game held. After all, each team had won two Super Bowls, and one would be the first to win three. The game also represented the first rematch in history. Despite the inflated price, tickets were hard to find.

The teams were evenly matched. Roger Staubach was the NFL's top passer, and Bradshaw was ranked second. That alone gave every promise that this would be the most exciting Super Bowl of all. Basically, both Pittsburgh and Dallas had similar strengths. Each had an explosive offense and an overpowering defense. The Cowboys, with their Flex Defense, led the NFL against the run, yielding just 107.6 yards a game. The Steelers were right behind, topping the AFC by allowing only 110.9 yards. Remarkably, in winning their last seven games, Pittsburgh's famed Steel Curtain didn't allow over 100 yards on the ground in any one game. They were primed.

Most experts felt the Steelers had a slight edge defensively because of linebackers Jack Ham and Jack Lambert. Ham is like a matador. Nobody can drop or come up quicker than he. He is extremely quick and intelligent. There is no middle linebacker in the NFL who has better lateral pursuit than Lambert. Ham and Lambert influence opposing offenses more than any two players around.

Offensively, the Steelers also appeared slightly stronger. Harris, with his big game potential, offset the speedy Tony Dorsett. However, it was the Steelers' excellent wide receivers, Lynn Swann and John Stallworth, who rated an edge over the Cowboys' Drew Pearson and Tony Hill. Whatever, both the Steelers and the Cowboys were stronger than they were when they met each other for the first time three years ago.

The early morning hours of Super Sunday were bleak. A heavy, wind-swept rain brought dismay to early risers. Yet, it was appealing to Bradshaw. He hadn't slept well and, because of all the distractions of noise and phone calls, had his room changed in the middle of the night. Bradshaw wouldn't be upset if it rained all day. He seems to excel while playing in adverse weather.

There's a time-worn statement in Miami that if you don't like the weather just wait a little while and it will change. The 79,641 fans who were holding tickets in the open Orange Bowl certainly hoped so, especially those with $200 tickets. It rained hard all morning. However, a half hour before the 4 o'clock kickoff, the rain stopped. Incredibly, despite the heavy rains, the field was in excellent shape. There were no water spots or muddy underfooting, and 78,656 fans showed up.

George Halas, who started all this professional football mania to begin with in the 1920s, had the honor of flipping the coin. For the occasion, the venerable 81-year-old owner of the Chicago Bears purchased a

Cowboys' Scott Laidlaw tries to penetrate Steelers' defense.

$320 gold piece. And he arrived on the field in style, in the front seat of an antique car. Dallas won the toss and elected to receive. However, a happy Lambert raced off the field, clutching the valuable gold piece.

The excitement of the opening kickoff roared through the stands as Roy Gerela booted the ball to Dallas' Butch Johnson. The swift wide receiver caught the ball on the five-yard line and streaked his way for 23 yards before being dropped on the 28-yard line. When Staubach led the Dallas offense on the field, the Cowboy fans made their presence known.

On the first play of the game, Staubach pitched out to Dorsett who swept wide to his left for a nine-yard gain. Staubach called Dorsett's number again, and the speedy Dorsett burst through the middle for 16 yards to Pittsburgh's 47-yard line. After Robert Newhouse was stopped for no gain, Staubach went back to Dorsett. He took a pitchout, this time on the right side, and sped for 13 yards and another first down on the Steelers' 34. Suddenly, the Cowboys were threatening. Dorsett had carried the ball three times and found holes in the Steel Curtain for 38 yards!

Dallas wanted a quick score. They disdained crisp, straight-ahead football, and reverted to a gimmick play; but it backfired. On an attempted double reverse, wide receiver Drew Pearson fumbled. Defensive end John Banaszak opportunistically pounced on the loose football on the 47-yard line. The snappy Dallas drive was quickly aborted.

Now it was Bradshaw's turn. He quickly hustled on the field. He had good field position to work from. Yet, he didn't want to be too anxious. On the first play, like Staubach, he pitched out. Charlie Waters expected it and dropped Harris for a yard loss. Then Bradshaw tried the middle, and Harris could only get two yards. On third and nine, Bradshaw expected a blitz. He was right. Nevertheless, he quickly tossed a 12-yard pass to Stallworth over the middle. The Steelers had a first down on the Cowboys' 40.

Bradshaw then went back to Stallworth, this time down the left sideline. However, as the rangy wide receiver caught the ball,

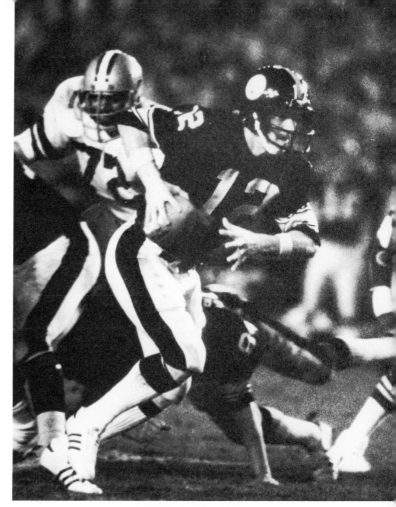

Pittsburgh quarterback Terry Bradshaw looks for running room.

143

he was out of bounds. After Bleier only gained two yards, Bradshaw was again faced with a big third-down play. He delivered. He hooked up with Grossman for 10 yards and a first down on the Dallas 28. The Steelers were in scoring range.

The gutsy Bradshaw didn't wait. He lobbed a soft 28-yard pass to Stallworth in the left corner of the end zone. Stallworth reached up and pulled the ball down for the game's first touchdown. Roy Gerela's kick made it 7-0 with 9:47 remaining.

After the Cowboys reached the Pittsburgh 39 following the kickoff, the Steel Curtain took command. On a second and seven play, Steve Furness broke loose to pin Staubach for a 12-yard loss. Then Dwight White charged through and dropped the Dallas quarterback for a 10-yard loss. The Cowboys, shoved back to their own 39, were forced to punt.

It appeared as if the Steelers would score

again. On a third-down play, Bradshaw sent Harris over the middle and hit him with a 22-yard pass to the Dallas 42. Then Bradshaw connected with Swann for the first down, a 13-yard strike down the right sideline for another first down on the 30. But then Bradshaw made a mistake. He sent Stallworth wide left and stared him down the field. Linebacker D. D. Lewis, seeing Bradshaw's gaze, reacted. He positioned himself in front of Stallworth and picked off Bradshaw's throw.

Near the end of the first quarter, Bradshaw was victimized again. On a third-down play, Bradshaw was sacked for a two-yard loss by Harvey Martin and fumbled. Ed "Too Tall" Jones quickly pounced on the ball on the Steeler 41 with just a minute remaining. Dallas had a chance to strike back.

Newhouse only moved for two yards on first down. Staubach sent Pearson deep into the end zone, but Shell jumped and deflected the possible game-tying touchdown. With only :06 left, Staubach went into the shotgun on third down. He found Hill open on the 26-yard line. Hill ran by Shell down the left sideline, past Mel Blount, who was shielded by Drew Pearson, and into the end zone for the first touchdown

ever scored in the first quarter against Pittsburgh all season. With no time remaining on the clock, Rafael Septien kicked the tying point at 7-7.

After the ensuing kickoff, Bradshaw fell prey to yet a third mistake. Confronted with a third and 10 on his own 48-yard line, Bradshaw dropped back to pass. The Cowboys had a double linebacker blitz on. Henderson locked Bradshaw in his arms and stripped the ball. Mike Hegman picked it up and, before anyone realized what had happened, ran 37 yards for a touchdown. Septien's kick was accurate; and Dallas suddenly led, 14-7.

More importantly, Bradshaw had hurt himself. Unknown to the crowd, he had his shoulder checked on the sidelines after the fumble. Luckily, it was his left shoulder. Although he experienced pain, Bradshaw nevertheless returned to the lineup after the kickoff.

He didn't attempt to pass right away. Instead he gave the ball to Harris twice. Both times he tried the left side and managed a total of five yards. Bradshaw was in an obvious passing situation on third down and five from his own 25.

Bradshaw sent Swann on a deep post, but he attracted too many defenders. He looked

The Steel Curtain—L. C. Greenwood (68), Jack Ham (59), and Ron Johnson (29)—closes in on Tony Dorsett.

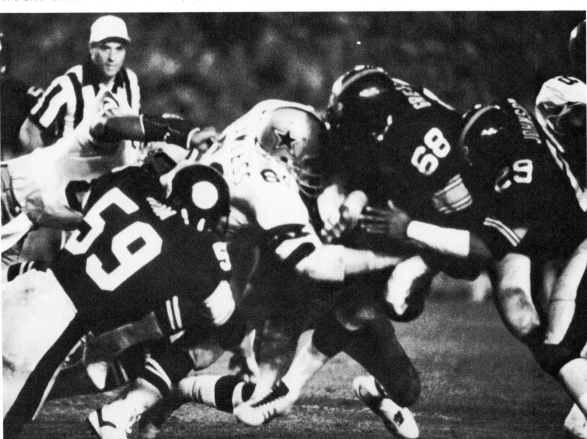

at his secondary receiver and discovered that Stallworth was wide open on the 35. From the time he caught the ball, it was just a matter of how far he would run before he was caught. Stallworth sped past Aaron Kyle and then outran every other defender who was straining to catch him. He ran for 65 yards to complete a 75-yard touchdown play, and Gerela's kick tied the game at 14-14.

With five minutes left in the first half, the Steelers tried to break the deadlock. On third down and eight from the Dallas 23, Hegman blitzed Bradshaw and dropped him for an 11-yard loss. Gerela was sent out to attempt a 51-yard field goal. While Dallas was wary of a fake, Gerela followed through with his attempt. The ball traveled far but just wasn't quite long enough as it hit the crossbar to the moans of the crowd.

Dallas started a drive of its own. In five plays, Staubach led the Cowboys from their own 34 to the Steelers' 32. On first down, Staubach called pass. Mel Blount figured Staubach would throw. He cut in front of Drew Pearson on the 16 and ran 13 yards with an interception.

Bradshaw reasoned he had enough time to get on the board again, especially after Dallas was penalized 15 yards on the interception. He put the ball in play on his own 44. A holding penalty set back the Steelers to the 34. Bradshaw looked up at the clock. There was only 1:44 left. Then he looked down the right sideline and found Swann for a 29-yard pass to the Dallas 37. He went back to Swann on the next play for 21 more yards to the Cowboy 16.

A pass failed. There were 40 seconds left. On second down, Bradshaw went with the run; and Harris broke free for nine yards. Now it was third and one on the seven. Will Bradshaw go for the first down? He had the Cowboys guessing. Bradshaw alertly called a pass-run option to his right. Dallas defended the run. Immediately, Bradshaw reacted. He lofted a high pass to Bleier in the end zone. The doughty back leaped, and with his legs stretched open, clutched the ball between his hands. It was a fine effort by Bleier. Gerela's kick pushed Pittsburgh's margin to 21-14 just before the first half concluded.

Bradshaw had already enjoyed a big game. He had completed 11 of 18 passes,

three for touchdowns, for 253 yards, and was nearing a Super Bowl record in those categories. He had control of the air, like a pilot about to shatter the sound barrier. His critics were mute now. Bradshaw was picking Dallas apart.

The Pittsburgh faithful anxiously awaited the second half kickoff. The Steelers were the receiving team. The fans were figuring that Bradshaw would pick up where he left off in the first half and turn the game into a rout. He certainly demonstrated a hot hand. If Bradshaw could get another quick touchdown, then the Cowboys would definitely be in trouble.

Yet, the first two times the Steelers had possession in the third period they couldn't do anything. They couldn't produce a first down as Bradshaw completed only one of the three passes he attempted. It looked as if the Steelers were playing cautiously. The fact that Stallworth left the game with severe leg cramps might have caused Bradshaw to pull back somewhat.

After a punt midway through the quarter,

Steeler linebacker Robin Cole clamps his arms around Scott Laidlaw.

145

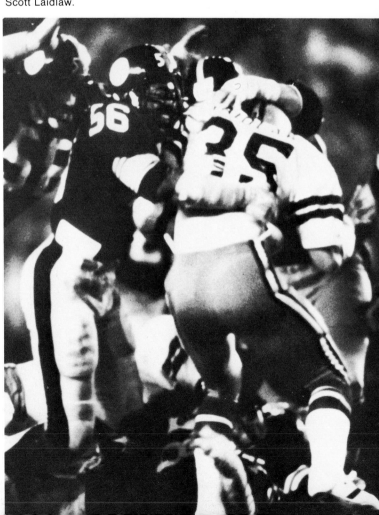

the Cowboys had excellent field position. They had a first down on the Pittsburgh 42. Staubach tried a surprise play. He handed the ball to Dorsett who faked going through the line. Instead, he stopped, turned, and lateraled the ball back to Staubach. Hill sped down the sidelines. Staubach threw deep into the end zone, but rookie cornerback Ron Johnson knocked the ball down.

Dorsett took a pitchout and gained four yards. On third down, Staubach kept the drive alive by hitting Preston Pearson with an eight-yard pass for the first down on the Steelers' 30. Dorsett then got a yard, Scott Laidlaw got seven, and then Dorsett got another five yards and another first down on the 17. The Cowboys were riding in for a score.

Staubach tried to get it all on first down. He sent his tight end, Billy Joe DuPree, down the right sideline but overthrew him. He then sent Dorsett up the middle, and the second-year star burst for seven yards before Shell stopped him on the 10. Dallas had a third and three, and called time out. Staubach went over to the sidelines and conferred with coach Tom Landry. He wanted to be certain of the next play.

The Cowboys lined up with two tight ends. The veteran 38-year-old Jackie Smith was inserted into the lineup. Staubach bent over center. He analyzed the Steeler defense and began to bark his signals. Lambert sensed a pass and blitzed. However, Staubach got his pass off, a soft throw to Smith who was all by himself in the end zone. He reached back, slipped, and the pass hit him on his chest. Smith fell over backwards, and the ball bounced on the ground. A certain touchdown was lost.

Instead, the Cowboys had to settle for a field goal. There was some slight confusion as Septien ran onto the field; some of the Dallas players felt that maybe they should try for a touchdown or at least a first down. But Septien calmly booted a 27-yard field goal to trim Pittsburgh's advantage to 21-17 with 2:30 left in the period.

When Bradshaw hit Stallworth's replacement, Theo Bell, with a 12-yard pass for a first down on the Steeler 44, it appeared as if he had the offense moving again. However, he suffered a couple of bad breaks on his next two passes to Swann. On the first one,

Looking for a receiver, Steelers' Terry Bradshaw rolls out on pass play.

Swann juggled the ball and then dropped it. He came right back to Swann on the same sideline pattern, but the reliable receiver dropped the ball as he was hit by cornerback Benny Barnes. When Bradshaw was blitzed for a three-yard loss on third down, Pittsburgh's drive fizzled as the quarter neared its end.

Still, when the final period began, the Steelers clung to a 21-17 edge. After the Cowboys couldn't mount a scoring threat, they punted deep into Pittsburgh's territory. Bradshaw put the ball in play on his 15. Harris managed only two yards with a pitchout. On second down, linebacker Bob Breunig exerted pressure on Bradshaw and caused him to underthrow Bell on the left side.

Bradshaw was now confronted with an important third-down play. If he didn't convert it, then Craig Colquitt would have to punt from deep in Steeler territory. It would offer the Cowboys an excellent opportunity to secure prime field position. Bradshaw had to execute perfectly on whatever play he called. He did, by one yard. He zipped a nine-yard pass to Grossman that provided a first down on the 26.

The quarterback had a little more room to operate from. He turned to Swann. This time Swann clutched a 13-yard pass for another first down on the 39. Harris picked up five yards to move the ball to the 44. Bradshaw decided to pass on second down. He dispatched Swann down the right side on a post pattern.

However, Barnes kept alongside Swann. It was a foot race. The two bumped. Barnes fell down on the Dallas 23-yard line. As Swann was about to make his cut, he fell, too. He tried vainly to reach out and catch the ball but couldn't. Swann looked up for a referee's flag. He saw field judge Fred Swearingen drop his and signal a tripping penalty on Barnes.

The Cowboys fumed. They argued but to no avail. The Steelers had a first down on the 23. A short pass to Swann gained four yards. Harris leaned forward for two yards, and the Steelers looked at a third and four on the 17. Pittsburgh was assessed a five-yard penalty for taking too much time. That put the ball back to the 22.

It was now third and nine. Bradshaw reasoned that the Cowboys would blitz again as they had done on the penalty down. He called a trap over left tackle. It was Harris' play. It worked perfectly. Harris burst through with the speed of a halfback and ran untouched into the end zone. Gerela's kick gave the Steelers a 28-17 lead with 7:10 left in the game.

Gerela kicked short on the kickoff. Tackle Randy White, who had a fractured left hand that was heavily wrapped, couldn't control the ball on the 24-yard line. It rolled loose to the 18 where Dennis Winston recovered it for the Steelers. Pittsburgh had a golden opportunity.

Bradshaw didn't hesitate. He called

Swann's number deep. Bradshaw uncorked a long pass toward the back line of the end zone. It looked too long for Swann to reach. But the gifted receiver, who has the flair for circus catches, ran hard, jumped off the ground, reached out as far as he could, and pulled the ball down. It was the most dramatic catch of the day. After Gerela added the extra point, Pittsburgh's margin ballooned to 35-17 with only 6:51 showing on the clock.

Yet, Dallas never quit. Staubach, who had been in tough situations before, led the Cowboys back. He drove them 89 yards in just eight plays, hitting DuPree with a seven-yard touchdown pass. Septien's conversion cut Pittsburgh's advantage to 35-24 with only 2:27 remaining from oblivion.

But time was Dallas' enemy now. Still, they pressed, ever hopeful. Their hopes rose when Tony Dungy fumbled Septien's onside kickoff. Rookie Dennis Thurman recovered for Dallas on the Cowboys' 48-yard line. The clock showed 2:23 left.

Immediately Staubach went to the pass. That's all he could do, throw and throw and hope for a quick touchdown. There was an incomplete pass, then a completion and a sack. But Staubach kept throwing, even when he was confronted with a fourth down and 18 on the Steelers' 38. A 25-yard completion to Drew Pearson gave him life. Then, on the four-yard line, he drilled a pass to Butch Johnson in the end zone for a touchdown. Septien's conversion pulled Dallas to within four, at 35-31, but time was the biggest barrier. There were just 22 seconds remaining.

Another on-side kick was evident. The Steelers placed some extra players on the first line. They were ready for the kick. They couldn't afford another mistake now. Septien positioned his short kick. It went toward Bleier. He carefully fell on the ball. It clinched the victory. The Steelers became the first team in the history of the NFL to win three Super Bowls. The night was theirs.

The flotilla of press made it practically impossible to reach the victorious Steeler dressing room. Immediate access was delayed while Commissioner Pete Rozelle made the Super Bowl trophy presentation in front of the television camera to Art

147

Rooney and his sons, Dan and Art, Jr. The dour owner exhibited controlled joy. For 42 years his team had never won anything. Now, in the last five years the Steelers had won three Super Bowls. No other team could equal that.

When the doors were finally opened, the horde of writers sought out Bradshaw. They were directed to a large interview area in another section underneath the stands. Bradshaw, calm and relaxed, stood on a platform leaning against a steel girder. He had one leg propped up against the pillar and held a paper cup in his left hand to relieve his mouth of chewing tobacco wastes.

"Boys, you can't say anything bad about this game," said Bradshaw. "This son of a gun was fun. Both teams played their game. I want all of you guys to say, 'By God, this was an exciting game.' It was just that we were a little flat when the second half began. We weren't coming off the ball real well. I didn't call plays that well, and they got some pressure on us.

"I threw more passes today than any time in my life because I was having success. I don't think I had anything to prove except I never did play well against Dallas. I guess I always tried too hard not to lose to Dallas. I was very conservative. But this year I learned that you don't play well unless you relax and let your abilities go to work for you. I was going to play my game today, play-action passes, mixing it up, just throwin' the ball, baby. I wasn't going to let the Super Bowl dictate to me. I was going with what got us here. Win or lose, I didn't give a hoot."

For the first time in his nine-year career, Bradshaw passed for over 300 yards. He established three Super Bowl records: most

Dallas quarterback Roger Staubach hands ball off to Tony Dorsett.

148

yards passing, 318; most touchdown passes, four; and longest scoring pass, 75 yards to John Stallworth.

"Terry is just fantastic," exclaimed Stallworth. "He did what a quarterback has to do. He's a super quarterback. He read the zones. He deserves whatever comes his way, like the MVP. Nothing we accomplished out there surprised me. We got into the playoffs on our passing. There was no reason not to stick with it."

Stallworth's buddy, Swann, was right alongside. He had on a baseball cap and was ready to open a large magnum of champagne. He was interrupted by the writers, who wanted to know about the pass interference call in the fourth period.

"Definitely pass interference," explained Swann. "As a receiver, all I was interested in doing was watching the ball. I really didn't see Barnes, but he did kick my leg. It felt like he got me twice. I don't think it was intentional, but you never know. All I was looking for was a flag. Franco's run after the penalty was the greatest run I've ever seen.

"You know, Terry had an awful lot to do with us playing so well. He played a great game. His play selection was good, and he was confident and relaxed."

In the solemn Cowboy dressing room, the players dressed quietly. Even Henderson. But reflecting on the loss, coach Tom Landry felt that the key to his team's defeat was the interference penalty called on Barnes.

"I'd say it was the ball game for Pittsburgh," sighed Landry. "Obviously, it was the key play. A tight game became lopsided quickly. When you have an alley-oop pass and Swann jumps all over you, it's hard to call interference. It looked like both went for the ball and collided. I don't think interference should be called unless it was pushing.

"That dropped pass hurt, too. Jackie Smith was so wide open that Roger wanted to be conservative. He threw so soft he couldn't miss it, but he came in short; and Jackie's feet slipped as he went for it. We were running well then and had a chance to turn the momentum our way."

Above the din of the noisy Steeler dressing room, Chuck Noll cut a quiet figure. He's like that. He never displays any visual emotion. He analyzes a victory in the same manner he would a defeat. Somehow, one had the feeling that he had expected to win.

"Our veteran players wanted to win this very badly, boys like Joe Greene, Terry Bradshaw, L. C. Greenwood, Franco Harris, Lynn Swann, John Stallworth, and especially our offensive line," remarked Noll. "The line gave Terry great pass protection against Dallas' great pass rush. I wasn't surprised at our passing success. We think we can do anything we set our mind to. They gave us a lot of man coverage. We didn't think they could cover us man-to-man, and we still don't think so.

"Do I think Terry proved himself? Terry had nothing to prove. After all, he has won three Super Bowls; and nobody else did that. I told the football team as we came off the field, I don't think this team has peaked yet."

That's saying a lot . . .

SCORING

Pittsburgh: 5:13 First Period—Stallworth 28-yard pass from Bradshaw (Gerela kick).

Dallas: 15:00 First Period—Hill 39-yard pass from Staubach (Septien kick).

Dallas: 2:52 Second Period—Hegman 27-yard run on fumble recovery (Septien kick).

Pittsburgh: 4:35 Second Period—Stallworth 75-yard pass from Bradshaw (Gerela kick).

Pittsburgh: 14:34 Second Period—Bleier 7-yard pass from Bradshaw (Gerela kick).

Dallas: 12:24 Third Period—Septien 27-yard field goal.

Pittsburgh: 7:50 Fourth Period—Harris 22-yard run (Gerela kick).

Pittsburgh: 8:09 Fourth Period—Swann 18-yard pass from Bradshaw (Gerela kick).

Dallas: 12:37 Fourth Period—DuPree 7-yard pass from Staubach (Septien kick).

Dallas: 14:38 Fourth Period—Johnson 4-yard pass from Staubach (Septien kick).

149

Super Bowl XIV

Pittsburgh Steelers (AFC)	3	7	7	14	—	31
Los Angeles Rams (NFC)	7	6	6	0	—	19

The heavy rain in and around the Los Angeles area made its ominous presence felt most of the week. The shuddering thought was that perhaps Super Bowl XIV would be contested in the rain on a field of mud. Not since Super Bowl IV in New Orleans had rain threatened to mar the performance and pageantry of the biggest single day in the world of sports. However, by Thursday the rain had subsided, and officials of the game exhaled a collective sigh of relief. The only question now created by the rain was whether the soft field of the immaculate Rose Bowl would serve as an ally to the Pittsburgh Steelers or the Los Angeles Rams.

None of this seemed to concern the oddsmakers. The powerful Steelers were established as 11½-point favorites to defeat the Rams, the largest spread since Super Bowl III when the Baltimore Colts were established as 17½-point favorites to beat the New York Jets. By the end of the week, bookies were looking for more Pittsburgh money to help offset the heavy amount of wagering on the Rams by bettors who were attracted to the 11½ points.

Actually, there weren't many who gave the Rams a chance of upsetting the Steelers. Earlier, *Sports Illustrated* had labeled the game a mismatch, practically saying that the Rams didn't belong on the same field as the Steelers. What was underscored was the fact that Los Angeles had made it to the Super Bowl with more losses than any team in the 14 years the game has been played. They finished the 1979 campaign with an unimpressive 9–7 record, pale in comparison to Pittsburgh's 12–4 mark. The controversy that surrounded the Rams all year hung over their heads like a bad dream that wouldn't go away.

The controversy began long before the season began when the Rams' popular owner, Carroll Rosenbloom, drowned in the rough surf off his Miami Beach home. Early in the season Rosenbloom's son, Steve, was dismissed by his stepmother, Georgia, in a power struggle that threatened to create havoc with team harmony. Like his father, Steve was popular with the Ram players. The shock of his dismissal was reflected in the players' performance most of the year. At one point in the season they were 5–6, and many experts felt they wouldn't even make it to the playoffs, let alone the Super Bowl.

There was more. Quarterback Pat Haden was injured at that point and lost for the rest of the season with a broken wrist. Replacing him at quarterback was a seldom used third-year pro, Vince Ferragamo. Rumors began to circulate that head coach Ray Malavasi would be fired. By then the local press had begun to pan the Rams' performance, and the team played to more empty seats than ever before in the Los Angeles Coliseum. Fan apathy intensified with the realization that the Rams wouldn't be returning to Los Angeles in 1980 but would be moving to Anaheim instead.

The Rams appeared to be wayward orphans. Somehow they managed to stick together, winning four of their last five games to gain the Western Division title for the seventh straight year. Though hardly awesome in the playoffs, they managed to upset Dallas and then defeat Tampa Bay to reach the Super Bowl for the first time ever. Yet, since they were leaving Los Angeles after 34

Pittsburgh quarterback Terry Bradshaw looks over the Los Angeles' defense.

years, their fan support was divided; and they were still looked down upon by most of the media.

The Rams players resented it. In the final week before the game was scheduled, with some 2,500 media personnel in Los Angeles for the pregame hyperbole, the Los Angeles players threatened to boycott the daily press conferences. Even weeks after their 9–0 triumph over Tampa Bay for their first NFC championship ever, the chafing words of *Sports Illustrated*, "a game for losers, played by losers" still upset them. Even Bob

Rubin, a Miami-based sportswriter for the Knight-Ridder News Service, added to the Rams players' discomfort. He wrote: "There are ways to make Super Bowl XIV competitive. Put weights on the Steelers. Make Terry Bradshaw throw left handed. Let the Rams play with 12 men. Then it might be a game."

No team in Super Bowl history took more abuse. The Rams players were seething. Doug France, the Rams' All-Pro offensive tackle, was one of the more vocal dissenters.

"Everyone's written us off, figuring we

wouldn't beat Dallas and Tampa Bay," snapped France the early part of the week. "I thought we'd get more respect after those games, but we haven't. They act like we're not even supposed to be in the Super Bowl. We should cut off all interviews. Even some of the local writers were against us before jumping back on the boat.

"We say, 'To hell with everybody.' We're going to win this for us. That's why our theme song is 'There Ain't No Stoppin' Us Now.' We are going to win it for *US*. We owe it to each other. We had so much trouble this season, we want a Super Bowl win to say thanks to everybody for getting us here."

Offensive guard Dennis Harrah agreed. "Damn straight," he added. "There was talk in the locker room about what we could do to the press. The way they talk, why even play the game? People keep bad-mouthing us, but we have twice the team Denver had when it was in the Super Bowl. It's disturbing to read and hear all those bad

things when we didn't deserve them, but we all agreed we had to suck it up. We'd have to listen to that crap for two more weeks, and then we'd go out and beat them. When we do, they'll say Terry Bradshaw or some-one visited Disneyland and was tripped up by Mickey Mouse and that's why they didn't beat us. They'll think of something to put us down. The people who think the Steelers are going to walk all over us have another thing coming."

Fred Dryer, the Rams' defensive end, was even more vocal. "It's great for fans, bettors, and neurotics to sit around and hypothesize about football games," said Dryer. "But the people who decide the betting line are not in football. I don't know where Jimmy the Greek gets his dope; but I can just see him in the prone position, with the telephone in his ear, getting his info. He doesn't look at movies; he doesn't talk to players. The line doesn't mean anything. There have been many Super Bowls where the line was way out of line. There have been upsets. It's al

Ram quarterback Vince Ferragamo (15) feels pressure of Steeler defense.

ways amazed me how they figure those things."

Even more amazing was the composure displayed by Ferragamo. Although he was in his third year with the Rams, by playing standards he was practically a rookie. In his first two years he threw only 35 passes, hardly qualifying him as experienced. Yet, when Haden went down, Ferragamo stepped in and rallied the team to six victories in its last seven games, which included two pressure playoff ones. He didn't appear affected by all the media attention.

One reason was his intelligence. A pre-medical student at Nebraska, Ferragamo attends medical school in the off-season. He is tall, six-three, has a strong arm, and is handsome enough to be a matinee idol once he establishes himself as the Rams' regular quarterback. He played very little until Haden got hurt. Placed into a pressure situation with the team floundering, Ferragamo showed that he knew how to win and gained confidence with every game he played. He grew overnight.

"I don't like to hurt anybody," explained Ferragamo about his current status as the Rams' starting quarterback. "Pat is my friend, and I certainly didn't want to get the starting job because he got hurt; but I feel good about my situation right now. I couldn't settle for being number two again, not now. I have great respect for Pat, but now I'm the number one guy.

"The Rams called on me to pull them out of a hole, and I took advantage of it. The last seven weeks of the season have had a profound impact on my career. I was never not confident. I always felt I could do the job, even when we were 5–6. I knew we'd come back. The big-play option of threat—that and the defense have given this team a new dimension. We have the best defense in the league. When they hold and when our offensive line starts blowing people out like they did against Tampa Bay, it doesn't matter who's out there, the Steelers, nobody.

"Things will be different next year. Decisions will have to be made in the off-season. I'm ready for Anaheim, and I want to stay with this organization; but there're other things. There's medical school when that time comes. Before, I thought that time might be pretty near, especially when I

wasn't playing; but I feel very good about football right now, better than I ever have."

Certainly the Steelers couldn't feel any better. They were appearing in the Super Bowl for the fouth time in the last six years. In their three other appearances they won every time. No team in the history of professional football had done that. Several teams have won twice—the Green Bay Packers, the Miami Dolphins, and the Dallas Cowboys; but three wins, with a possible fourth facing them, never. Since they were established as overwhelming favorites, the one thing that the Steelers had to guard against was being complacent.

That was a mood that Steeler coach Chuck Noll would never fall victim to. Low-keyed and businesslike in his approach to coaching, Noll shunned all intimations that the Steelers under his reign were on the verge of establishing a dynasty. Noll only concerned himself with the present and looked at his unprecedented third Super Bowl trophy from Super Bowl XIII as last year's antique. He transmitted his philosophy to his players to keep things in perspective and to meet each challenge presented in game after game. He doesn't look back, only at what's ahead. In the last eight years of the eleven Noll has coached the Steelers, Pittsburgh has appeared in the playoffs every time, winning 88 games and losing only 27 in the process. The motivation for Noll and the Steelers this time would be facing a fourth Super Bowl. That removed the danger of complacency.

"It's something that excites me and excites our football team," disclosed Joe Green, the Steelers perennial All-Pro defensive tackle. He was there with Noll at the beginning when the Steelers were 1–13 in 1969 and were the joke of the league. "As you go along you have to create goals, new goals. Football is very repetitive. Blocking and tackling. Some say all the games are the same. So you have to look for new challenges, new mountains to climb. I never thought it would be possible in today's football, but a fourth Super Bowl would put us much further into the history of the National Football League.

"Four out of six, that would be a tremendous feat, especially with the competition today. If we get over that hurdle on Sunday,

153

you can safely say that we're a dynasty. We're not looking past the game by any means. We're disregarding the Rams' record. They had a tremendous season. They overcame considerable injuries; they had all their playoff games on the road; their fans were not good to them; they had front office problems, and their coach was under fire. It's all the direct opposite of what we have in Pittsburgh. I wonder if we could have handled it."

Greene had it all in perspective, alright. So did Dwight White, the nine-year defensive end.

"This Super Bowl is a little different for us," said White. "All we get is, 'We're just awesome.' A lot of people don't expect the Rams to show up. That's a bunch of junk. I'm terribly afraid of the Rams. If I went through the year that they went through and I was still the dark horse, that can inspire a person. We have a lot of respect for our peers, and some of them happen to be the Los Angeles Rams.

"I'm sure the Rams are tired of what's been said and written. They've made it to the Super Bowl, and people are still down on them. That will make them dangerous. They're a better team than a lot of people give them credit for. They are the representatives of the NFC; and that's what we respect, not what the media or Jimmy the Greek says. I'm sure they're going to play their butts off. I think they are playing smart football, and they've got very good technique in everything they do. The Rams are very difficult for us to play because we don't know them like we do the Cleveland Browns or the Houston Oilers or the Dallas Cowboys.

"We want to win Super Bowl XIV; and you can whoop and holler and shout all you want, but you got to do it on the field. Our approach at this one is very calm, mature, calculated, and serious. There's not a lot of rah-rah. We have respect for where we are. We're in the Super Bowl, but we're not going to make a lot of fanfare about it."

Terry Bradshaw, the Steelers' veteran quarterback, took exception to the theory that there would be more pressure on Ferragamo than on himself. At least he was used to the pressure, having played in three Super Bowls; but it was there anyway. He

was the most sought after player at press interviews, and he handled himself well. He knew what to expect.

"There are a lot of people, a lot of interruptions," pointed out Bradshaw. "It's not your normal week. You don't get up in the morning and go to work; you get up and go to a press conference. But almost all of us have been through it before, and we know how to handle it. This is the time of year you have to enjoy yourself and have a good time. You can't come here and be all uptight and nervous. You just don't play well.

"The Rams are an outstanding team. They have a tremendous defense, and they pose a lot of problems. We played them last year; and we lost to them, 10–7, out here.

Pittsburgh wide receiver John Stallworth on way to 73-yard touchdown that gave Steelers 24–19 lead in fourth quarter.

I've looked at those films over and over, and what I see is a real good team. You look at the odds, but then you have to look at our side of the story. We've never beaten these guys; we're playing in their home city, and it's almost at their home field. If I was back in Ruston, Louisiana, I would say the Steelers got it all the way, no sweat; but I'm here, and I know what the Rams are capable of doing."

If anything, the Rams had enjoyed considerable success over the Steelers in the past. Playing the Steelers 12 times since 1946, the Rams won ten games and tied another while losing only once. They are the only team that Noll has not beaten since he became coach of the Steelers, losing three times in 1971, 1975, and 1978. Still another problem was the fact that three former Noll assistants were on the Rams' staff—defensive coordinator Bud Carson, offensive line coach Dan Radakovich, and receiver coach Lionel Taylor. That, too, Noll filed under Motivation.

Still, the game was projected as a battle of Pittsburgh's offense against Los Angeles' defense. The Steelers finished as the NFL number one offensive team in 1979. They led the league in scoring with a team record of 416 points, an average of 391 yards a game. The Steelers gained a total of 6,258 yards, just 31 short of the all-time pro record. They displayed great offensive balance, ranking second in rushing yardage and third in passing in the NFL.

Quite naturally, Bradshaw was the key to the offense. He had his best season statistically in 1979, setting Steeler and personal records for attempts, 472; completions, 259; and yards, 3,724, and ranked second in the NFL with 26 touchdown passes. Bradshaw had the two best wide receivers in pro football to throw to, John Stallworth and Lynn Swann. Stallworth set a Steeler record with 70 receptions. Although Swann's total dropped to 41 because of injuries, his average of 19.7 yards a catch was the highest of his career.

On the ground the Steelers averaged 4.6 yards a run, their highest average since 1972. Leading the way was Franco Harris who rushed for 1,186 yards. It was his seventh 1,000-yard season, tying him with Jim Brown's all-time record. Harris is one of the greatest big game rushers in history. Until Harris arrived in 1972, the Steelers had never made the play-offs. Now they had reached them in each of his eight seasons.

Defensively, the Steelers presented a difficult problem. They ranked first in the AFC, finishing second in both rushing and passing. They were particularly tough to run against. Greene anchored a veteran line, while All-Pro middle linebacker Jack Lambert offered quick support with his great range. In 11 of the 18 games they played, the defense held their opponents to under 100 yards. They were particularly outstanding in their two playoff wins, holding Miami to 25 yards rushing and Houston to 24.

If anything could dictate the final outcome of the game, it was the Rams' defense. They, too, were a veteran unit led by Jack Youngblood at defensive end and Jack Reynolds at middle linebacker. Their overall strength was the ability to put constant pressure on opposing quarterbacks. They exerted enough pressure on Roger Staubach in the opening playoff game against Dallas to force him into their shotgun formation more often than normal. They continued their assault against Tampa Bay in recording a 9–0 shutout in the NFC championship game. The Rams topped the NFC in sacks with 52, and their pressure defense enables their strong secondary to play for the interception.

Offensively, the Rams were forced to revert to a big-play offense because of injuries to key players. Besides Haden, others who were sidelined were running backs John Capelletti and Elvis Peacock and wide receivers Ron Jessie and Willie Miller. Although Ferragamo was young, he possessed a strong throwing arm that made wide receivers Billy Waddy and Preston Dennard deep threats. On the ground the Rams had a big yardage runner in Wendell Tyler, who gained 1,109 yards, and a sturdy one in Cullen Bryant, who added 619 yards.

On paper the Steelers appeared to have a big edge. No other team ever made it to the Super Bowl with as many losses as the Rams. Yet despite the apparent mismatch, tickets to the game were difficult to get. Although the Rose Bowl seats over 100,000 people, ticket scalpers were having their

155

biggest week ever. The price of a ticket was $30, and scalpers were getting as much as $350 at the early part of the week for a seat on the 40–50 yard line. Even end zone seats were going for as much as $150. For an orphaned team, the Rams managed to generate a great amount of interest. Perhaps, as the Rams maintained, they were a team of destiny.

The rain ended on Thursday, enabling the soft grass of the Rose Bowl to dry properly. By game time the field was well manicured, and a bright sun shown down from a cloudless sky on 103,985 fans, a new Super Bowl record for attendance. Where so many fans secured tickets was hard to determine.

When Art Rooney, the venerable 78-year-old owner of the Steelers, approached the midfield for the traditional coin toss, he carried a gold coin given to him by Chicago Bears owner George Halas. The coin was a token of friendship between the league's two oldest owners, who have known each other for almost 50 years. The Rams won the toss and indicated to referee Fred Silva that they wanted to receive the opening kickoff. As rookie kicker Chris Bahr adjusted the ball, the crowd noise swelled in anticipation of the kickoff. Bahr's kick traveled to the Rams' 13-yard line. Jim Jodat found a little running room and reached the 29-yard line before he was brought down.

The Rams began the game with running plays, an area in which the Steelers excelled in countering. The Steelers had finished second in defending the run in the NFL, and Wendell Tyler found out why. Tyler only gained a yard on his first carry and was caught for a four-yard loss his second attempt, both times by the Steelers' active middle linebacker Jack Lambert. On third down Ferragamo's first pass of the game to his other running back, Cullen Bryant, came up five yards short of a first down; and the Rams were forced to punt.

A clipping penalty on the return sent Pittsburgh back to its 21-yard line. Franco Harris began the Steelers' first offensive series with a two-yard run up the middle. On a quick trap, Rocky Bleier burst through an opening in the middle for nine yards and a first down. Harris tried to go over tackle

and gained only a yard. Bleier ran the same play again and this time got eight yards. A minute later Harris provided Pittsburgh its second first down as he ran for two yards behind center Mike Webster's block.

The first five plays that Bradshaw called were on the ground. After Bleier lost a yard on the sixth play, Bradshaw dropped back to pass for the first time. He connected with a 32-yard toss to Harris in the middle for a first down on the Rams' 26-yard line. Steelers fans stood and cheered as Pittsburgh appeared to be on the way to an opening touchdown. In seven plays they had moved 53 yards.

However, the Los Angeles defense stiffened. Bleier was stopped for no gain, and Harris only gained two yards. On third and eight, Bradshaw had to pass. He sent Lynn Swann deep down the right sideline. Behind good protection from his offensive line, Bradshaw threw to Swann in the end zone; but cornerback Pat Thomas read the play perfectly. He stayed close to Swann, reached up, and knocked the ball away. Their touchdown hopes diminished, the Steelers called for a field goal. Bahr delivered from 41 yards out as Pittsburgh moved into a 3–0 lead with only 4:31 left in the period.

On the kickoff the Steelers pulled a surprise. Instead of kicking deep, Bahr tried to catch the Rams offguard by kicking the ball only 10 yards or so, the necessary distance for an onside kick. If the Steelers could recover the free ball, they would take possession at the spot of recovery. The Rams weren't expecting anything and were in their normal kickoff return formation. Bahr, however, got too much foot into the ball and looped it to George Andrews on the Los Angeles' 41-yard line. The reserve linebacker immediately covered the ball, and the Rams had good field position.

Ferragamo quickly tried to get the Rams going. He flipped a quick pass to Tyler that gained six yards. On second down, he handed the ball to Tyler who started around left end. Tyler managed to get outside, broke a couple of tackles, and almost went all the way for a touchdown before he was brought down by safety Donnie Shell on the Steelers' 14-yard line. The play stunned the

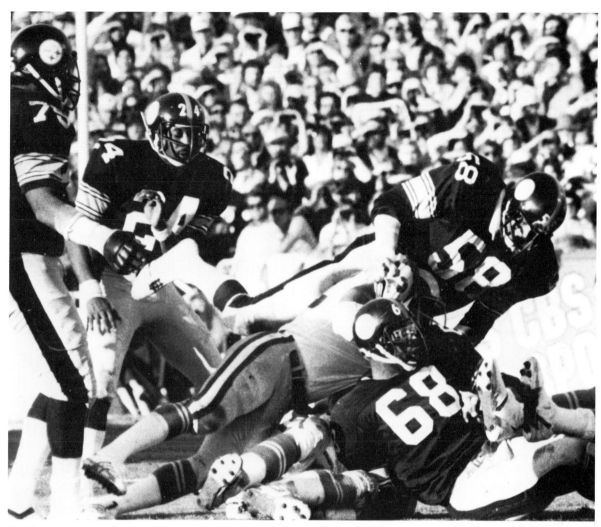

The Steel Curtain, Jack Lambert (58) and L. C. Greenwood (68), smothers a Ram run.

157

Steelers while Rams fans stood and cheered. It was the longest run against the Steelers' defense all year long!

The exciting run gave the Rams a lift. Lawrence McCutcheon carried the ball three times consecutively and gained 12 yards. Los Angeles had a first down on the Pittsburgh two-yard line. Tyler got a yard. He carried again but was stopped. On third down Ferragamo handed the ball to powerful Cullen Bryant; and Bryant scored with 2:34 left in the quarter. Frank Corral added the extra point, and the Rams took a 7–3 lead.

Corral kicked deep to the Steelers' two-yard line, forcing Larry Anderson to drop back. Anderson got past the first wave of Rams tacklers and made it to the Steelers' 47-yard line before he was brought down by

Joe Harris. Bradshaw had excellent field position to work with in the final two minutes of the period. Harris shook loose around right end and gained 12 yards to the Rams' 41. After Bleier got a yard, Bradshaw hit tight end Bennie Cunningham with an eight-yard pass to the 32. Bleier got the ball again and gained two yards and a first down on the 30. On the last play of the period Bradshaw found Swann with a 12-yard pass and still another Steelers first down on the Los Angeles 18. The Steelers were on the move.

On the first play of the second period Bradshaw fired a 13-yard pass to Cunningham on the five-yard line. Harris tried the middle but could only get a yard. Bradshaw looked to pass again but could only find Stallworth on the one-yard line for a three-yard gain before being hit. With the Rams bunched in tight on their goal line defense, Harris rambled around right end with a pitch out and scored standing up. The Steelers moved back into the lead as Bahr's conversion gave them a 10–7 edge.

After the kickoff the Rams put the ball in play on the 19-yard line. Three running plays earned them a first down on the 33. Ferragamo then hit Tyler with a swing pass that gained 11 yards to the 44. After Bryant gained four yards, Ferragamo again went back to the air. He delivered a 16-yard pass to McCutcheon that carried the Rams to the Steelers' 36-yard line. After McCutcheon lost two yards, Ferragamo returned to the pass. For the first time he threw to wide receiver Billy Waddy. Although the pass was incomplete, Shell was called for pass interference. The Rams had a first down on the 18-yard line and threatened to score again.

When Bryant broke loose for eight yards to the 10-yard line, Rams fans began shouting for a touchdown; but Tyler was dropped for a four-yard loss to the 14, and the crowd noise subsided. After Ferragamo missed on a pass to wide receiver Ron Smith in the end zone, Corral came in to try for a 31-yard field goal. His kick was accurate, and the Rams succeeded in tying the game at 10–10 with 7:21 left to play in the first half of an evenly contested game.

Although Anderson ran the kickoff back 38 yards to give the Steelers excellent field position on their own 46-yard line, Pittsburgh was stopped for the first time and was forced to punt. The Rams couldn't do anything either, and they punted out of danger from their 27-yard line. With just 3:14 left in the first half, it appeared that both teams would leave the field deadlocked.

Suddenly the first turnover of the game occurred. On first down on his own 37-yard line, Bradshaw tried to throw a pass to Sidney Thornton who ran a circle pattern out of the backfield. However, strong safety Dave Elmendorf intercepted and got to the Steelers' 39-yard line before he was tackled. With 3:05 left, the Rams had an excellent opportunity to score.

Linebacker Robin Cole got the Steelers out of immediate danger when he sacked Ferragamo for a 10-yard loss to the 49. Ferragamo missed on a pass to Bryant, and the Rams were faced with a third and long situation. The young quarterback came right back to Bryant, and this time the play succeeded for 12 yards. Still, the Rams were short of a first down, facing a fourth and eight situation on the Pittsburgh 37 with just 2:00 showing on the clock.

Ferragamo consulted with head coach Ray Malavasi in front of the Los Angeles bench. Malavasi decided to try for the first down rather than punt. Rams fans cheered as Ferragamo set up to pass. He drilled the ball to Waddy on the 27-yard line, and the Rams had a big first down. Staying with the pass, Ferragamo threw his fourth straight, this time to tight end Terry Nelson for another first down on the 13. The Rams were primed for a touchdown.

Displaying confidence, Ferragamo tried two more passes but failed. Then on third down the Steelers, expecting still another pass, pressured Ferragamo. Right end John Banaszak broke through and dropped the Rams quarterback for a 10-yard loss on the 27-yard line. Corral entered the game with just 25 seconds remaining to try a 45-yard field goal. His kick was accurate; and the surprising Rams trotted into their dressing room at halftime leading the heavily favored Steelers, 13–10.

Pittsburgh didn't look the part of favorites. They managed nine first downs, the same number as the Rams. Los Angeles, executing eight more plays, had a slight edge in total yardage, 130 to 127. However, the Steelers were slapped with four penalties totalling 55 yards while the Rams didn't incur any. Now the question remained if the world champion Steelers could come back in the second half.

The amazing Anderson once again gave Pittsburgh good field position by running the second-half kickoff 37 yards to the Steelers' 39-yard line. Bradshaw worked carefully. Three plays earned a first down. After Harris ran for four yards to the Los Angeles 47, Bradshaw opened up. He threw a long pass to Swann, who leaped up and caught the ball on the two-yard line and fell into the end zone for a touchdown. It was a typical big play strike that the Steelers displayed throughout the season. Bahr's conversion provided Pittsburgh with its biggest lead of the afternoon, 17–13.

The Steelers were now in a position to take control. It appeared that they had stopped the Rams, and the momentum was swinging their way. Los Angeles was in a third and long situation on their 26 after two plays had only produced three yards. Suddenly, Ferragamo brought the large crowd to its feet. He delivered a long 50-yard pass to Waddy on the Steelers' 24-yard line. After just one play the Rams were ready to strike. Ferragamo called the signals confidently. He handed off to McCutcheon, who started wide around right end. Approaching the line of scrimmage, he stopped, looked downfield, and threw a pass to Smith who was all alone in the end zone. On a trick play that caught the Steelers off guard, the Rams regained the lead,

19–17. It remained that way because Carrol's conversion attempt went wide to the left.

Bradshaw had the Steelers moving after the kickoff until he made a mistake. On a third down play from his own 45-yard line, Bradshaw tried to force a pass through the Rams' secondary to wide receiver Jim Smith. Operating as a fifth defensive back, Eddie Brown intercepted the ball and lateralled it to Thomas, who was finally brought down on the 39-yard line.

After forcing the Rams to punt, Bradshaw had the Steelers moving again. Beginning on his own 27-yard line, Bradshaw mixed up his plays well and after seven plays reached the Rams' 16-yard line. However, two running plays failed to gain anything. On third down Bradshaw wanted to pass. Once again he was victimized as Rod Perry intercepted the intended pass for Stallworth on the five-yard line. The third period drew to a conclusion after a 13-yard run by Tyler lifted the Rams out of a hole.

Rams' defense closes in on Steelers' Franco Harris.

159

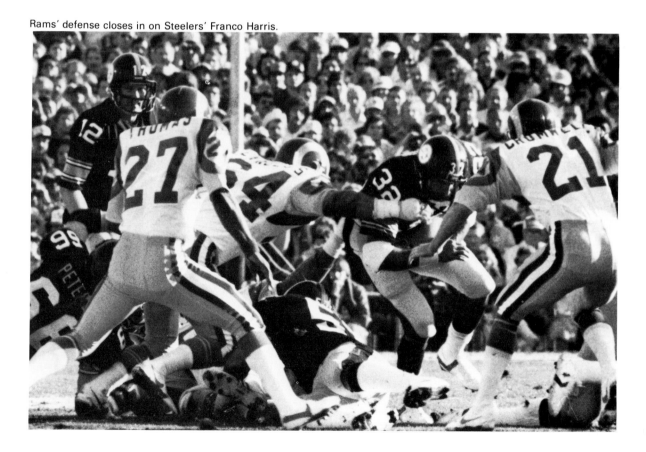

Nevertheless, the Pittsburgh defense stiffened; the Rams were forced to punt from the 23. Ken Clark got off a booming 59-yard punt to put Los Angeles out of further danger. The Steelers had a long way to go as they took over on their own 25-yard line. Two plays later they were on the 27 as Bradshaw was in a third down passing situation. Bradshaw looked over the defense. Instead of throwing short, he elected to go deep. Stallworth started on a hook pattern and then went deep in the middle of the field. Bradshaw threw a long pass that brought the crowd to its feet. Stallworth stretched his arm and made an over-the-shoulder catch on the Rams' 32-yard line. Running at top speed, he raced the rest of the way to complete a 73-yard scoring pass. The exciting play shocked the Rams, and Bahr's conversion moved the Steelers into a 24–19 lead.

Neither the Rams nor the Steelers could produce a first down the next time they had the ball. With just 8:29 remaining to play, the Rams started another offensive series on their own 16-yard line. They had a long way to go for a touchdown, especially since the rugged Steelers defense had stopped them the last three times they had the ball. Los Angeles had to play for a touchdown, because a field goal would leave them short and the clock was a factor now.

Employing the pass, Ferragamo ignited a drive. In just six plays he led the Rams to the Steelers' 32. Four of the plays were passes, and Ferragamo connected on three of them. On first down, Ferragamo dropped back to pass again. He looked for Smith, deep down the middle. He was thinking touchdown. However, Lambert made a deep drop, reached, and intercepted Ferragamo's long pass in front of Smith on the 14-yard line. He clutched the ball in his large hands before he was driven to the turf on the 30-yard line. It was a big play.

With 5:24 left everyone expected Bradshaw to run out the clock. He started with two running plays which only netted three yards. On third down at the 33, the Rams were thinking short pass. Bradshaw did indeed pass but instead went long to Stallworth on the very same play that resulted in a touchdown. Stallworth again made a remarkable over-the-head catch and fell on

the Los Angeles 22-yard line as Steelers fans cheered his efforts. Stallworth had made two consecutive sensational catches.

After Bleier failed to gain a yard, Bradshaw decided to pass once again. He sent Smith deep down the right sideline, but his pass fell incomplete in the end zone as the Pittsburgh receiver and Thomas tumbled to the ground. An official's flag was thrown, and Thomas was charged with interference. The key penalty gave the Steelers the ball on the one-yard line. Pittsburgh was primed for the clinching touchdown.

Bleier tried to get it but was stopped cold. Then Harris tried; he, too, was repulsed by the stubborn Rams defense as 1:52 showed on the clock. Bradshaw gave the ball to Harris again, and this time Harris made it into the end zone for his second touchdown of the game, one that assured the Steelers their fourth Super Bowl victory. Bahr's successful conversion made the final score 31–19, which was important to the Pittsburgh bettors who had given 11½ points.

The Steelers triumph was monumental. Last year they had been the first team to win three Super Bowl titles. Now, they became the first to record four and the first to win back-to-back Super Bowls twice while remaining unbeaten. They were clearly the team of the decade, having won four world championships in six years. The Steelers were compared to the great Green Bay Packer teams of coach Vince Lombardi who had won five NFL championships in the 1960s. In fact, one of the first questions presented to Noll in the happy Steelers dressing room was whether the Steelers team was the greatest team ever.

"I don't think I have to answer that," replied Noll, a low-keyed man who is not one for braggadocio. "The facts speak for themselves. I don't have to say it. The Steelers have proven themselves, but this win feels better than the other three. We had to overcome a lot of injuries, and we came through. They weren't necessarily injuries that kept players out of the lineup but injuries that cut down on efficiency.

"Against the Rams we tried to go deep as we could as often as we could to get the big play, because we knew they would take away the high percentage passes. I told Bradshaw before the game that he was not going to complete the high percentage passes and that he would have to come up with the big play. We expected that they would make it tough to throw short. Fortunately, we got the big play. Swann got one, and Stallworth got two.

"This was a game between two good defensive football teams, but it was characterized by the big play. That's why it was high scoring. The Rams played well. They wanted it badly. They gave us a lot of problems, especially on offense. The difference in the game was our big plays. It was not tough to prepare for Los Angeles. We've been working on what you call 'Deja Vu.'"

Bradshaw by far attracted the largest number of post-game interviewers. He was in a far corner of a large room specifically allocated for important interviews. Since he had thrown three touchdown passes and was named the Most Valuable Player of the game, he had to answer a great many questions. Bradshaw looked tired as he spoke with reporters for well over an hour.

"I'm tired of football," exclaimed Bradshaw. "I've never been so glad that a game's over in my life. Last year I enjoyed it more. This year I didn't enjoy it as much because of the pressure. The intensity and the buildup were so great that I stayed up all night last night.

"I think I played more of a leadership role this game than last year. Last year I just did it. Today I took control of the team. I juiced 'em. I made it a point to get them excited on the sidelines, the offense and the defense. I did it in the second half. That 13–10 score got me juiced up.

"If you ask me, the kicking game was the key to the victory. The punt and kickoff returns were the best I've seen since coming to the Steelers. I didn't think I'd be the MVP. I thought I played better last year. I thought Larry Anderson or Stallworth would be the MVP. They'd both be excellent choices. I couldn't believe Stallworth's first catch. I didn't see Swann's catch because somebody knocked me down. I couldn't believe Stallworth was open for the second catch. Big plays happen on their own. You don't set them up. They just happen."

Actually, the Steelers practiced the big play most of the week; but Bradshaw didn't like the play because he had trouble com-

pleting his passes to Stallworth or Swann. The first time he tried it against the Rams it didn't work, either.

"The play is called '60 percent slot hook and go,'" smiled Stallworth at the other end of the room. "Lynn ran it early in the game, and Terry overthrew him. We wanted to run the ball a little better than we did, but they were shutting it off. We threw the ball more in the second half, and it paid off.

"We knew the way in which they were going to double team us. They move the safety in and out. We knew we could beat them over the middle if we made them think we were going short. I baited the safety, and he jumped on the hook so I went deep. I had double coverage both times. I felt I had the capabilities to come up with the big play. I didn't feel it necessarily had to be me. You never know when it's going to come. You just go all out on every play. You just have to go with the flow.

"During the course of the week in practice we must have tried the play eight times and never completed it. A lot of it had to do with the wet conditions. I love the play, especially after the touchdown. My individual goals were achieved, and our team goals were achieved, so I'm doubly happy."

Although there wasn't any happiness in the Los Angeles dressing room, there wasn't any reason for the players to hang their heads in disgrace. They gave the Steelers their toughest Super Bowl competition. The final outcome of the game was still in doubt five minutes from the end when the score was 24–19. Remember, too, the Rams entered the game as big point underdogs. The Steelers had to work for every point they got; and that, also, is what champions are made of. In retrospect, Super Bowl XIV was the most exciting game of all the games played. No one mentioned the fact that the Rams had now lost seven games. They had played like the NFC champions that they were. They earned their place in the California sun.

"The team did a hell of a job," shouted Rams head coach Ray Malavasi. "They didn't outplay us. We ran on them, and we threw on them. We just didn't get enough big plays, and they did. I thought we were going to win right from the beginning, and I still thought so right up to the end. We

161

Steeler linebackers Robin Cole (56), on ground, and Jack Lambert (58) stop Rams' Cullen Bryant.

still had a chance until that interference call against us. I thought that was a bad call. We almost had them, especially the passes that should have been intercepted. We had a guy right there. On the long touchdown to Stallworth, we had a bust in our coverage. Those two passes to Stallworth turned the game around.

"Pittsburgh is a good team. Bradshaw is an experienced quarterback, and they have good wide receivers; but we stopped their running game. They didn't surprise us; they just executed well."

Not many felt that Ferragamo would execute well. After all, no team has ever won a championship without an experienced quarterback. Ferragamo is young, and until the final six weeks of the season he was a very inexperienced quarterback. However, he did an outstanding job in the face of pressure, completing 15 of 25 passes for 212 yards and only one interception. He learned enough on that one misfire to explain it.

"They were in a deep zone, and we had a play action called," revealed Ferragamo. "I came out of my roll-out, and I had Smith open in the end zone. It was my decision to go to him. Lambert dropped deep like the rest of their linebackers, but he was on a deeper drop than I thought. I didn't see him until the last second.

"We had a solid game plan which was to attack them, but they did a good job of masking their defenses. Maybe I could have dumped off the ball that Lambert intercepted, but I had made the decision to go deep. He made a good play."

After the third period ended with the Rams in front, 19–17, defensive end Fred Dryer felt good standing on the sidelines watching the offense at work. He was talking about that moment to a few listeners.

"We had 'em on the ropes," recalled Dryer. "We knew if we could score again, we'd win. We gave them the opportunity to use their weapons—Bradshaw's ability to throw deep and their receivers' ability to go up for the ball. They're the best team in pro football because they've repeated so many times, but the Rams match up against 'em better and play 'em harder than any other team. I think we proved that this time. We knew it all along, but the world didn't. Now the world knows about it."

They know about the Steelers, too. Four times they had to prove that they were the best. They did, too. Nobody can match that . . .

Super Bowl XV

January 25, 1981
New Orleans Superdome
75,500

Oakland (AFC)	14	0	10	3	—	27
Philadelphia (NFC)	0	3	0	7	—	10

Even the oddsmakers can be wrong. More often than not they are right. It is just that when they establish big odds on a team's never making it to the Super Bowl, it creates even more excitement when they're proven wrong. Bob Martin of Las Vegas is perhaps the leading oddsmaker in the country. Every Monday morning during football season, Martin creates the line for all 14 games that will be played on Sunday and the following Monday night. Before the 1980 season opened in earnest, Martin established the line on every team's chances of meeting in Super Bowl XV.

He wasn't far off on the Philadelphia Eagles. Martin made them a 7–1 choice to reach the Super Bowl. By contrast, he was far out on the Raiders. Martin calculated that Oakland had only a 35–1 chance of winning the American Conference playoffs and advancing to the World Championship in New Orleans. So, when Philadelphia represented the National Conference it didn't come as much of a surprise. It was Oakland that had everyone talking.

None of the professional football experts even picked the Raiders to win the Western Division, let alone compete in the playoffs. The concensus was that the Raiders would finish either fourth or fifth in the five-team division. It came as quite a letdown to Raider followers. In the past 15 years Oakland had never had a losing season.

However, after participating in the playoffs for six consecutive years, 1972–1977, the Raiders could only manage to finish 9–7 the last two years. They were a team in transition. Al Davis, the shrewd owner of the club, made some bold trades after the 1979 season that raised eyebrows throughout the country. In fact, some felt he was panicking.

His first and biggest move was to trade quarterback Ken Stabler to Houston for Dan Pastorini. Stabler had been Oakland's popular quarterback for 10 years and had led the Raiders to an easy 32–14 win over the Minnesota Vikings in Super Bowl XI in 1977. Just weeks after the Stabler deal, Davis sent All-Pro safety Jack Tatum to the Oilers for running back Kenny King, who carried the ball only three times during his rookie season in 1979. Later, he sent veteran linebacker Phil Villapiano to Buffalo for wide receiver Bob Chandler. Yet, Davis wasn't finished. With the season only a month old, he shipped All-Pro tight end Dave Casper to Houston for three draft choices.

When the Raiders got off to a slow start, everyone wrote them off. Pastorini, who was expected to restore "the big bomb" to Oakland's passing attack, was finished for the year with a broken leg. The club was foundering, winning only two of its first five games. It was then that Davis and his coach, Tom Flores, turned to Jim Plunkett to get the Raiders under way. It was a lot to deliver. Plunkett was picked up as a free agent from the neighboring San Francisco 49ers and had tossed only 15 passes in his two years with the Raiders.

In an extraordinary comeback, Plunkett began to take hold. He grew in confidence each week; and when the regular season had ended, Plunkett had led the Raiders to nine victories in 11 games for a final 11–5 record. Oakland finished second in the Western Division behind San Diego and qualified for the championship playoffs as a wild card entry.

Nobody expected Oakland to survive the playoffs. In their opening game they were underdogs against Houston. Yet, they mauled the Oilers, 27–7. The following

164

week they were the underdogs again. On the frozen tundra that was Cleveland Stadium, they upset the Cleveland Browns, 14–12. Despite all this, they weren't given much of a chance in the AFC Championship game against San Diego. They surprised the Chargers and the ranks of the professional football world with an exciting 34–27 victory in which Plunkett played his greatest game of the season.

On the other hand, the Eagles were fresh from a 20–7 triumph over the Dallas Cowboys in the NFC Championship contest. They started the regular campaign impressively, winning 11 of their first 12 games before finishing with a 12–4 record. One of their wins was a tough 10–7 triumph over the Raiders during the 11th week of the season in a well-played defensive struggle.

It didn't come as any surprise when the Eagles were established as three-point favorites to defeat the Raiders. In Ron Jaworski, they had the NFL's leading passer. They also had a big game runner in Wilbert

Montgomery and a big play receiver in Harold Carmichael. Then, too, the Eagles were the top defensive team in the NFL, allowing only 222 points throughout the season.

Rounding out the picture, more high drama had taken place before the game itself than that which surrounded Super Bowl IV in 1970, which was also played in New Orleans. At that time, Kansas City quarterback Len Dawson's name was embarrassingly linked to a gambler from Detroit named Donald Dawson, who was under a national gambling investigation by the FBI. No one knew whether Dawson would be allowed to play in the game against the Minnesota Vikings until later in the week.

Davis was involved in an open war with the National Football League. He and Commissioner Pete Rozelle were not on speaking terms. In fact, Davis had alienated himself from the league's 27 other owners by carrying his threat to move the Raider

Raider defensive backs Lester Hayes (left) and Burgess Owens, bring Philadelphia's Wilbert Montgomery to the ground.

franchise from Oakland to Los Angeles right through the courts. A last-minute attempt at a peaceful solution to the dilemma, 10 days before the Super Bowl, ended in failure in the private chambers of a San Francisco judge.

Writers covering the big event began speculating about whether or not Davis would accept the gleaming silver Vince Lombardi Trophy from Rozelle should the Raiders emerge victorious. The standard line was that the lawyers from both sides would participate in the award ceremonies. Rozelle, who had labeled Davis as an outlaw for his breach of the league's constitution, said that he would indeed present the trophy to the winning team's owner as was his custom over the years, whether it be Philadelphia or Oakland.

Davis would not comment on the matter. Rather, he kept a low profile and avoided any contact with the press. He remained sequestered in the Hilton Hotel, which strangely enough was where Rozelle was also staying. Davis was seen only one night in the city's famous French Quarter. He ate with friends in Jimmy Moran's Riverside Restaurant, practically unnoticed by the other diners that night. Appearing somewhat like the infamous recluse Howard Hughes, Davis remained incommunicado, with a three-day growth of beard on his face. It was in keeping with his image as the mysterious, aloof genius behind the Oakland Raiders.

One Raider who didn't worry about being seen publicly was John Matuszak. Affectionately called "Tooz" by his teammates, the big 6' 8" defensive tackle violated curfew on Wednesday night and was quickly admonished the next day by being fined $1,000. There was some concern whether Oakland's coach Tom Flores would start Matuszak against the Eagles. No one was commenting.

Earlier in the week, a day after the Raiders arrived in New Orleans, Matuszak announced that the Raiders didn't come to New Orleans to party, but to win the Super Bowl. He proclaimed himself the "Enforcer," and said that anybody who broke curfew would have to answer to him. Although Monday was an open night without

any restrictions, the club set an 11 P.M. curfew beginning on Tuesday night.

Matuszak violated the rule with his usual flair. Although he returned to his room by the 11 o'clock deadline, he left again shortly afterward and made the scene at the Absinthe House in the French Quarter, a famous century-old spot frequented by Jean Laffite and other pirates around New Orleans in the 17th century. Matuszak didn't get back to his room until about 4 A.M.

"I didn't go out Monday, and I didn't go out Tuesday," explained Matuszak the next day. "So by Wednesday night I was really feeling the hair. I had to get out. It was my one night out. It was four nights before the game. Now it's out of my system, and all I've got to think about is playing the greatest game I can. Besides, I had to be out to make sure no one else was on the streets after the 11 o'clock curfew. Tooz was cruisin'."

The Eagles received strong support as favorites simply because most experts felt that Plunkett couldn't hold up in a game as big as the Super Bowl. While both teams were about equal defensively, the experts rationalized that Jaworski represented more offensive power than Plunkett. Yet, the easygoing Plunkett didn't seem to be affected by all the negative vibes. He'd felt them all season long.

"I try to take it all in stride," said Plunkett. "I don't want to change anything that got me here, but I also want to maintain my composure. You don't want to get yourself too 'up' for any one game. We've played well this year. We've played a lot of good teams, and we've beaten them. I'm optimistic about Sunday.

"We're going to be as aggressive as we can be. Maybe field position might detract from that a little bit in some cases, but we intend to be aggressive both offensively and defensively. That's the style that got us here. This is something that we all shoot for as professional players. It's eluded me for 10 years. I can hardly wait for Sunday."

Jaworski, too, openly displayed confidence. One reason was that one of his wide receivers, Charlie Smith, was returning to action. Smith, who had broken his jaw, didn't play much in the NFC Champion-

Eagle quarterback Ron Jaworski hands ball to Leroy Harris.

ship game against Dallas two weeks earlier. His replacement, Rodney Parker, had done well. Along with the dangerous Harold Carmichael, Jaworski had excellent receivers to hook up with.

"Conditions are perfect for a wide open game," said Jaworski. "Usually, I'm home waiting for Sunday to get here so I can watch the Super Bowl. I can't tell you how happy I am to be in this situation. It's a tremendously exciting feeling. The coaches get a chance to show their stuff. Even though we're professional athletes, we're still entertainers. Winning against Dallas— that was the game that really pressured us. It's always tougher to play the game that gets you to the Super Bowl than the Super Bowl itself."

On a beautiful Sunday, in sharp contrast to the rain and cold that blanketed New Orleans earlier in the week, the large crowd began arriving early at the Superdome. They saw something they'd never seen before at any football game. A mammoth yellow ribbon was tied around the north end of the saucerlike Superdome. It was there to commemorate the return of the American hostages who'd come home to the United States earlier that day after 452 days of captivity in Iran.

The game was a complete sellout. Those lucky enough to have a ticket paid $40. Those who had to do business with scalpers paid as much as $400. Although the Raiders prefer to wear black, they were dressed in their white jerseys. The Eagles had been designated as the home team and preferred to wear green.

167

Philadelphia would attack first. Oakland's Derrick Jensen incorrectly called heads on the coin toss, and Philadelphia quickly decided to receive the opening kickoff. While the crowd of 75,500 roared in anticipation, Chris Bahr opened the action by booting the ball to the eight-yard line. Billy Campfield caught it and returned it to the 24-yard line. Super Bowl XV had begun.

Jaworski tested the Oakland defense by sending Wilbert Montgomery around left end for eight yards. On the next play, the Eagles achieved a first down when Leroy Harris got three yards. Jaworski then felt it was time to pass. He looked for his tight end, John Spagnola; but Oakland linebacker Rod Martin was looking, too. He picked off the pass and ran it back 17 yards before he was brought down on the Eagle 30.

Oakland had a fine opportunity to capitalize on an early turnover. Plunkett decided to play it safe. He went to the run, first to Mark van Eeghen who got three yards and then to Kenny King who was dropped for a yard loss. On third and eight, Plunkett had to pass. He sent King on a pass pattern out of the backfield but missed him near the goal line. Then he got a break. The Eagles were detected offside. That brought up a third and three. Plunkett handed the ball to Van Eeghen, and he got four yards to the 19. The Raiders got a big first down.

Plunkett went back to the pass. He threw a 14-yard aerial that wide receiver Cliff Branch gathered in on the five-yard line. Plunkett turned to his ground game. Twice he gave the ball to Van Eeghen, first for two yards and then for one. On third down, Plunkett felt it was time to pass. The Eagles pressured him, and Plunkett scrambled around. That allowed time for Branch to get open. Plunkett spotted him in the end zone and softly delivered the ball into his open arms. Chris Bahr added the conversion that gave Oakland a 7–0 lead.

Philadelphia couldn't do anything after they received the kickoff and had to punt.

The Raiders didn't show any offense either, and they kicked the ball back to the Eagles. Starting on their own 37, the Eagles reached the Oakland 45 before they had to punt. The Raiders were deep in their own territory as time was running out.

On first down from the 14-yard line, Plunkett flipped a short pass to Branch that gained four yards. King then picked up two yards to the 20. On third and four, the Eagles played for the pass. They rushed Plunkett who was looking for an open receiver. Plunkett evaded the rush and drilled a pass to King on the Oakland 39-yard line. The speedy halfback grabbed it at his shoulder, slipped by cornerback Herman Edwards and began to run down the left sideline. There wasn't anyone in front of King, and he sped the rest of the way for a touchdown that covered 80 yards. It was a Super Bowl record. More important, it catapulted the Raiders into a 13–0 lead with only 57 seconds left on the clock. Bahr added to it seconds later when his conversion made it 14–0.

When the second period opened, the Ea-

168

Ron Jaworski has time to throw as Oakland's John Matuszak is taken out of play.

Wilbert Montgomery manages to pick up a few yards running up the middle.

gles were in a hole. They never expected to fall behind so quickly. They knew they had a fight on their hands, and they had to come from behind if they expected to win. Starting on their own 26, Jaworski got the Eagles going. He led them to the Oakland 13-yard line before stalling. Tony Franklin then put Philadelphia on the board by kicking a 30-yard field goal that cut Oakland's lead to 14–3.

On the next two series neither the Raiders nor the Eagles could do anything. It was three downs and out as the defenses of both teams asserted themselves. There was 7:23 remaining in the first half when the Raiders got the ball back. Beginning on their own 37-yard line, they got to the Eagle 27 before the Eagles' defense stiffened. At that point, Bahr tried a 45-yard field goal that fell short.

The Eagles flew back. Putting the ball in play on their own 27-yard line, they soared all the way to the Oakland 11 with 1:07 showing on the clock. Jaworski felt it was the opportune time to pass. He tried three passes but was unsuccessful each time.

There were only 54 seconds remaining when Franklin trotted onto the field to attempt a 28-yard field goal. Psychologically, it was important for the Eagles to make it. Not only would it trim Oakland's lead, but it would give the Eagles a lift for the second half. Franklin lined up his kick which was well within his range. However, linebacker Ted Hendricks broke through, stuck up his long arms, and blocked it. A dejected Eagle team headed for the halftime intermission trailing 14–3 and seriously wondering whether they could overcome the Raiders in the second half.

Oakland had performed admirably in the first half. They not only stopped the Eagles from scoring a touchdown, but they also limited Philadelphia's offense. The Eagles could gain a total of only 33 yards on the ground, and Jaworski was able to complete nine of 22 passes for 131 more—hardly enough offense to win a Super Bowl game. Meanwhile, Plunkett, whom many feared would crack under the pressure, completed five of eight passes for 118 yards. Even more significant, he appeared in control. There was strong feeling that the Raiders would become the first wild card team to win a Super Bowl.

The Raiders were set to receive the second-half kickoff. It was an important series. If Oakland could further embellish its lead, Philadelphia's objectives would be that much harder to attain. If the Eagles could turn back the Raiders, then perhaps they could swing the momentum of the game their way.

Oakland began at a disadvantage. A first-down holding penalty pushed the Raiders back to the 14-yard line. After Van Eeghen got eight yards, Plunkett hit King with a 13-yard pass for a first down on the 35. On first down, Plunkett designed a pass play. He connected with Bob Chandler on a crossing pattern for a first down on the Philadelphia 33-yard line. From there, Van Eeghen advanced the ball four yards to the 29. Oakland was threatening. Plunkett

didn't wait to strike. He looked for Branch in the end zone. Just when it seemed that cornerback Roynell Young was going to intercept, Branch cut in front of him in the left corner and plucked the ball out of his hands for a touchdown. When Bahr added the extra point, the Oakland lead zoomed to 21–3. It certainly looked as if it would be Oakland's day.

The Eagles were in serious trouble. They had hoped to stop the Raiders and come back with their own touchdown. Now, they were 18 points behind and battling long odds. To overtake the Raiders they had to score three touchdowns!

Philadelphia had to at least score a touchdown to get back in the game. They had a long way to go. Starting on their own 10-yard line following the kickoff, the Eagles began a drive that carried them to the Oakland 34. On a third down and three play, Jaworski tried to pass for the first down.

Oakland wide receiver Bob Chandler artistically avoids going out of bounds after catching Jim Plunkett's third-period pass.

170

Near the game's end, Oakland's Derrick Jensen looks for an opening in the Eagle's defense.

However, linebacker Rod Martin made his second interception of the game, and turned the Eagles away. Frustration showed on the faces of the Philadelphia players. Their comeback hopes dimmed.

It wasn't long before Plunkett got the Raiders on the move again. Beginning on the Oakland 32-yard line, Plunkett led the Raiders to the Eagle 28. When he missed on a third-down pass to tight end Raymond Chester, Bahr came on to try a 46-yard field goal. His kick was accurate, and it extended Oakland's advantage to 24–3. The Raiders' edge was building. Twice they had the ball in the third quarter, and both times they scored.

The Eagles kept trying. When the third period ended, they had reached the Oakland five-yard line, putting together a drive that began on their own 12-yard line. Still, they faced an uphill climb. They had to score three touchdowns in the final period just to tie the game. It was a lot to ask. No other

team in Super Bowl history had ever scored that many points in one period.

Less than two minutes after the final quarter began, Jaworski gave Eagle fans a flicker of hope. He fired an eight-yard touchdown pass to tight end Keith Krepfle for the Eagles' first touchdown. Franklin added the conversion that trimmed Oakland's lead to 24–10. There was hope that— just maybe—the Eagles could catch up.

The Raiders were determined not to let that happen. They put the kickoff in play deep in their own territory. The Eagles had them with their backs in the shadow of the goal line on the 11-yard line. Oakland couldn't afford a mistake at this point. Relentlessly, the Raiders moved the ball upfield. Plunkett mixed his plays well, producing four first downs in driving the Raiders to the Eagle 17-yard line. They could play for a field goal now, which would just about clinch the game.

Plunkett tried to catch the Eagles by surprise. On third down, he tried to hit Chandler in the end zone; but Edwards broke up the pass. Now Oakland had to go for the field goal; Bahr didn't fail, kicking one from 35 yards out to send the Eagles' faint hopes plummeting to the ground. With just 8:19 left in the game, it was practically impossible for Philadelphia to overcome a 27–10 deficit.

The Eagles got two more chances to score but failed dismally both times. The last time, Martin intercepted Jaworski a third time to set a new Super Bowl record. There was only 2:50 remaining when the Raiders proceeded to run out the clock. Oakland had made Super Bowl history in becoming the first wild-card team to win the world championship.

In the Raiders' dressing room, the wave of excitement was oppressive. It was heightened by the glut of media crews who had crowded their way in to see if Al Davis would receive the championship trophy from NFL Commissioner Pete Rozelle. The Oakland players were also waiting for that moment. Many of them had cameras all set to record what was to them a historic occasion.

Davis kept them all waiting. It was consistent with his style—calculating and enigmatic. There was nothing for Rozelle to do but wait. He stood on a hastily prepared platform with NBC announcer Bryant Gumbel and tensely held the silver Vince Lombardi Trophy. Finally, Davis entered, and the room went wild. His players greeted him with shouts of happiness.

Dressed in Raider gray and white, Davis mounted the platform, He was ready to accept the trophy that Rozelle was holding.

"The Raiders are, of course, the first wild-card team to win a Super Bowl," began Rozelle. "I think it's a tremendous compliment to the organization because you had to win four post-season games. Today, of course, was the big one—the Super Bowl. I think it's a great credit to you for putting this team together, and I think Tom Flores clearly did one of the greatest coaching jobs in recent years—all season, but particularly today. It's a credit to some marvelously dedicated athletes, especially Jim Plunkett and that offensive line today. You've earned it and congratulations."

The joy was evident on Davis's face, al-

though he didn't look directly at Rozelle when he accepted the trophy. He didn't speak with any rancor.

"Thanks very much, Commissioner," replied Davis. "You know, when you look back on the glory of the Oakland Raiders, this was our finest hour. This was the finest hour in the history of the Oakland Raiders. To Tom Flores, the coaches, and the great athletes—you were magnificent out there, you really were. The years will go on. We owe a great tribute to all our alumni all over the country, and to our great fans, and we want to welcome back the hostages to the United States. Take pride and be proud. Your commitment to excellence and your will to win endure forever. You were magnificent."

Plunkett was voted the game's Most Valuable Player. It was a fitting tribute to a most courageous year, a year in which he came off the bench to lead the Raiders into the Super Bowl.

"I'm just happy to be playing after the two-year absence," said Plunkett. "It was probably the worst time of my life. After I was cut by San Francisco, I thought my career was over. I'm very appreciative for the opportunity Al Davis gave me. We're an aggressive team that enjoys playing as well as practicing. There may be something to that—about this city [Oakland] being a player's last stop. I'm not sure how to describe that; but, at heart, this is a team that really works hard."

While the satisfaction was evident on Plunkett's face, deep down, no one could have been more satisfied than guard Gene Upshaw. At the age of 35 he was the oldest Raider and the only one to have played in all three Super Bowl games in which the Raiders appeared. The other games were in 1967 and 1977.

"It was the world against us, and everybody said we didn't have a chance," exclaimed Upshaw. "We knew we had to control the line of scrimmage. It might have looked easy, but it wasn't. They kept reminding us that we're not supposed to win. If we played again next week, we'd be picked to lose."

Defensive tackle John Matuszak agreed. He kept pressure on Jaworski throughout most of the game.

"We have been a comeback team all

172

year," said Matuszak. "We did it the tough way. We had to win our last six games, and that showed a lot of character. I can't say enough about Jim Plunkett. He had a great comeback year."

Nobody could say enough about Tom Flores, either. He never got serious mention for Coach of the Year honors. Yet, he took a team that was picked to finish last in the Western Division and primed them for a Super Bowl victory.

"It's hard to find words to express how I feel," said Flores. "I'm proud of the way that we did it. We were underdogs all year. We went with a quarterback who hadn't played in three years. I can't say enough about Jim Plunkett. He has great competitive spirit and deserves all the credit in the world. Making it to the Super Bowl as a wild card and winning all season under adverse conditions makes it that much more satisfying."

The Eagle players were stunned by the outcome. Not only had they been picked to win, but they were badly outclassed in losing. Once they'd fallen behind, they couldn't bounce back.

"The quick, early turnover hurt us, and then Kenny King came up with the big play," analyzed Eagle coach Dick Vermeil. "They got 14 points on the board real quick. At halftime we talked it over, but we could not get it all together. They picked up our stunts and did a great job of protecting Plunkett."

The renegade Raiders, the underdogs of the season, had captured football's greatest prize and done it brilliantly . . .

Super Bowl XVI

January 24, 1982
Pontiac Silverdome
81,270

San Francisco (NFC)	7	13	0	6	—	26
Cincinnati (AFC)	0	0	7	14	—	21

The cold outside was numbing. The snow had frozen into ice and the dark skies with each passing day were foreboding. It was a Super Bowl unlike any other. The National Football League gave it a catchy title, calling it "Sweet Sixteen." Yet, Super Bowl XVI went far beyond a name. In the first place, it was the first game ever to be played outside a warm weather clime, and the threat of snow in Detroit the last week of January was a strong possibility. It was such a concern that the league decided for the first time to use the National Weather Service to keep a watchful eye on the possibility of snow. And, just in case, they also mapped out a snow emergency plan with state and local authorities.

Indeed, it was a strange setting for a Super Bowl. What was even more unique was the appearance of the competing teams, the San Francisco 49ers and the Cincinnati Bengals. Before the 1981 season began, nobody ever dreamed that the 49ers and the Bengals would face one another in Super Bowl XVI. The year before, both teams finished with 6–10 records. It was certainly not the kind of performance that championship teams are made of. The experts thought so little of both teams that they established odds of 70–1 on Cincinnati and 50–1 on San Francisco that either of them would make it to the Super Bowl before the 1981 season started.

Yet, the very fact that they got there made for an interesting attraction. Both San Francisco and Cincinnati deserved to be there. The 49ers finished with the best record in the entire NFL, 13–3, which was quite a turnaround from the previous year. The Bengals were equally as impressive with a 12–4 record, the finest in the American Football Conference. The experts figured the game to be very close. The betting line out of Las Vegas made the 49ers a one-point favorite. It was the closest spread of any Super Bowl since Washington was established as a one-point favorite over the Miami Dolphins in Super Bowl VI.

The two teams were a contrast in styles, which was a reflection of the head coaches. Bill Walsh, coach of the 49ers, was hailed as an offensive genius with his wide-open style of play. A strong advocate of the passing game, Walsh isn't afraid to throw the ball anywhere on the field. He designed his passing game to effectively produce in the short to medium range. Forrest Gregg, the Bengal coach, is a bit more conservative than Walsh. He primarily favors a strong running game, a veteran quarterback who can throw deep, and a standard 4–3 defense. A majority of NFL coaches who were polled during the week picked the Bengals to win.

There were a number of factors why the coaches preferred Cincinnati. The main reason was quarterback Ken Anderson. The veteran 32-year-old Anderson had a relatively injury-free year and responded by leading the entire NFL in passing. In a game as big as the Super Bowl, coaches all lean to an experienced quarterback. They also felt that Cincinnati, led by 1,000-yard rusher Pete Johnson, had a stronger running game. Nobody on San Francisco came close to Johnson's yardage. In fact, the 49ers biggest threat on offense was quarterback Joe Montana. Although he completed his first full season as the San Francisco quarterback, Montana displayed enough poise to top the NFC in passing.

New York Giant coach Ray Perkins, who had lost twice to San Francisco during the

174

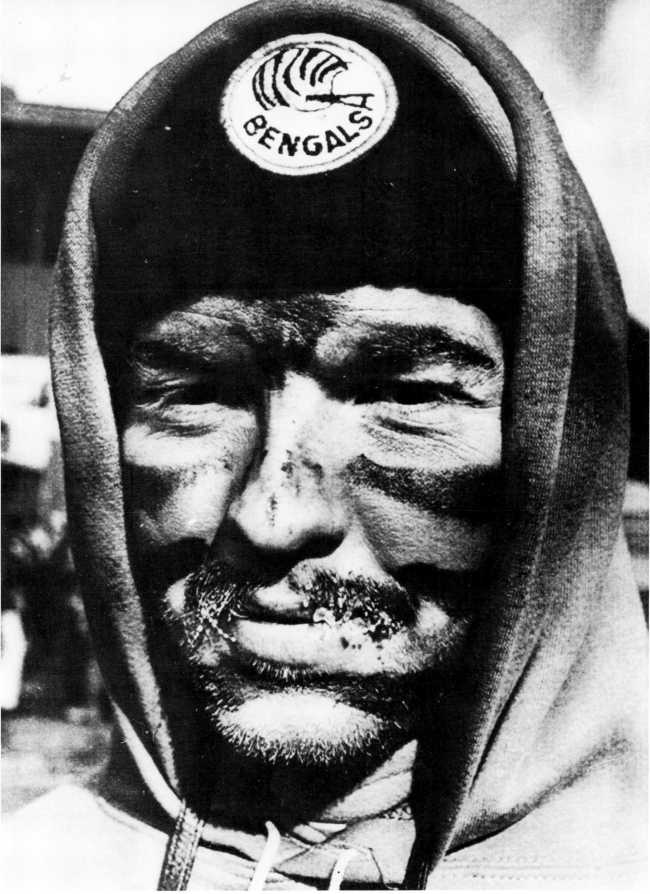

A gutsy Bengal fan seems undaunted by the cold outside Pontiac's Silverdome.

season, the final loss coming in the opening game of the NFC playoffs, nevertheless picked the Bengals to win. In fact, he figured Cincinnati would win by ten points.

"I give the edge to Cincinnati simply because they have the more experienced quarterback," said Perkins. "If you look back over most of the Super Bowls, the teams whose quarterbacks have had the best days are the teams that have won."

Sam Rutigliano, the coach of the Cleveland Browns, was even more expressive in picking Cincinnati. His team was the only one to beat both the Bengals and the 49ers during the regular campaign, doing so each time on the road.

"Dan Ross the tight end and Pete Johnson the fullback are the keys to the Bengal offense, along with Ken Anderson's scrambling ability," pointed out Rutigliano. "They try to get the ball inside to Ross early, and that opens up things deeper. Johnson is very effective as a layoff receiver, and Anderson will go to that right away. You coach your defensive ends to get containment on Anderson, to keep him from scrambling, but when your ends are worried about containment, their pass rush is limited. The rush must come from the inside. Montana is very similar. He'll dodge an outside rush, and both he and Anderson have great patience, waiting for their receiver to get open.

"The danger against San Francisco is to get impatient on defense, to come apart while the 49ers are piling up first downs. You have to concede them first downs, you have to close on their receivers and hold the gains to a minimum, and you have to play a lot of zone underneath and force them into third-and-short situations because the running game is the weakness in their offense."

The game had a deep personal meaning for Walsh. In only three years since taking over a losing program in San Francisco in 1979, Walsh, in his first head coaching job, got the 49ers into the Super Bowl for the first time. Actually, the head coaching position he was hoping for was ironically in Cincinnati. For eight years Walsh had been the offensive coordinator for Cincinnati under Paul Brown. When Brown retired,

Walsh appeared destined to take over. He had worked closely with Anderson and developed him into one of the finest quarterbacks in the league. However, when Walsh was bypassed for Bill Johnson, he became frustrated and left Cincinnati. Still, he had a better knowledge of Anderson than others.

"Anderson's running is the key to the game for us," said Walsh. "We've got to hit Anderson low, because he's very adept at getting underneath tacklers. He's the greatest runner who's ever played at the position. He gives Cincinnati one dimension that other teams just don't have. Anderson is very fast. The only people that can stay with him are defensive backs. He is a great athlete.

"The other problem is to stop Johnson. He has dominated every game they played. My suspicion is that he will be their primary runner. They go out and get a lead and then Pete goes ahead and holds it. The only break we got when we played them earlier was we got ahead early so they couldn't afford to let Pete keep running the ball."

The teams met once during the season the first weekend in December. That, too, was an emotionally filled time for Walsh. He had returned to Cincinnati for the first time since leaving in 1975. The 49ers knew how much the game meant to him and provided him with a 21-3 victory. It was a hard-hitting, closely played game, one in which San Francisco took advantage of six costly Cincinnati turnovers to secure the win. Since the Bengals fell behind early, Johnson didn't get to carry the ball as much as he normally does. He still managed to gain 86 yards in 12 carries, an average of seven yards a run.

"Three things happened to San Francisco last year," said Gregg. "They acquired Fred Dean from San Diego, Jack Reynolds from Los Angeles, and a lot of good defensive backs from the draft. Additionally, their offensive line is more solid than last year. Their secondary isn't inexperienced anymore. They've got 22 games under their belts. They're experienced now.

"The previous game we played against San Francisco isn't a factor this time. We just turned the ball over six times, and penalties were a big factor. But give their defense credit for that. You can't say, 'If we hadn't turned the ball over,' stuff like that. What's an 'if' mean? We've got to come up with our best game yet."

Gregg was right. The big improvement of the 49ers was their defense. First, they shocked everyone by drafting four defensive backs in their first five selections in the college draft that spring. In June they signed veteran linebacker Jack "Hacksaw" Reynolds as a free agent. Then in October, they acquired Fred Dean, a superb pass rusher from the San Diego Chargers. Three of the rookie defensive backs, Ronnie Lott, Eric Wright, and Carlton Williamson, all made the starting lineup with holdover Dwight Hicks and provided San Francisco with perhaps the finest secondary in the league.

Reynolds was a key factor in making the Niners' 3-4 defensive unit operate effectively, and Dean furnished the pass rush they sorely needed. The fact that Reynolds and Dean were experienced veterans provided stability to the young, defensive unit.

Reynolds was only one of two players on either team who had previously appeared in a Super Bowl. The other was his teammate tight end, Charle Young. Both had played in Super Bowl XIV against the Pittsburgh Steelers in 1980. In many ways this particular Super Bowl could be called the "Cinderella Bowl." Nobody expected the 49ers or the Bengals to be there, and practically none of the players had ever experienced the pressure of a Super Bowl. Naturally, it all focused on the quarterbacks. Montana, a youngster who virtually had his first full season as an NFL quarterback in 1981, ap-

Cincinnati got a big break at the beginning of the game when Amos Lawrence fumbled the opening kickoff.

peared calm all week long. So did Anderson. However, that was expected. The 11-year veteran was at his peak, a fact that didn't escape Walsh, when he discussed both quarterbacks.

"Anderson is bigger, stronger, and much more experienced," remarked Walsh. "He is at the peak of his career and in the best health as a pro. He is able to run the ball extremely well and is a great passer. Montana may have the greatest instincts the game has ever seen. He's only in his second year and he'll be at his best five or six years from now. Rolling out, avoiding the rush, and still hitting a primary receiver, he's the best I've ever seen at that.

"I expect one or the other team to score four touchdowns. It won't be a bitter defensive struggle with Anderson and Montana on the field. I suspect both of us will be going for the big play. We usually throw the ball earlier and then try to run. I think a big win is unlikely. Neither team will come apart after the other one makes a big play. We are very well matched. It is unfortunate somebody has to lose. The Super Bowl tends to overemphasize winning and losing. The loser shouldn't have to hide its head."

Injuries weren't a factor for either team. San Francisco was buoyed by the availability of two starters who had been slowed by ailments. Running back Ricky Patton, who had missed playing in the NFC Championship game against Dallas two weeks earlier, was pronounced ready. So was wide receiver Freddie Solomon, who suffered a slight knee sprain in practice earlier in the week. Cincinnati's chances improved with the knowledge that wide receiver and kick return specialist David Verser would be able to play, despite being handicapped by a fractured thumb. Even before these injuries were known, the 49ers had been made slim favorites. Rookie safety Ronnie Lott of the 49ers couldn't understand why.

"Cincinnati probably has more talent than we do," Lott said. "I'm not just saying that to psyche myself up. I'm saying that because it's true. Just look at all the first-round picks they have. And they're all starters. I think they'll throw everything at us. For them to come out and be complacent

with all of their talent, they'd only be hurting themselves. I think they'll come out and throw the book at us.

"I feel they'll try and go deep against us. I think they'll also try to go short, too. Their tight end will play a big part in the game. He gets open a lot. When you have a tight end who can get open like that, it creates a lot of problems for the defense."

Luckily for everyone, there weren't any snow problems on Super Sunday. Although the day was overcast and it threatened to snow, it never did. Still, there were the usual traffic jams that accompany a Super Bowl game, despite the fact that a majority of the fans driving to the Pontiac Silverdome began doing so well in advance of the 4 o'clock kickoff. San Francisco, which won the coin toss, elected to receive, and the excitement of the game began to build.

The fans were brought to their feet immediately. Amos Lawrence couldn't handle Jim Breech's kickoff and fumbled the ball. After a scramble, John Simmons recovered for Cincinnati on the 26-yard line. The Bengals were presented with a great opportunity. Anderson quickly went to work. He fired an eight-yard pass to wide receiver Isaac Curtis on the 18-yard line. On the next play, Cincinnati recorded the game's initial first down when Johnson picked up two yards to the 16. Anderson kept the pressure on by hitting Ross with an 11-yard pass on the five-yard line.

It appeared as if the Bengals would score the game's first touchdown. The San Francisco defense faced its first major challenge. Linebacker Willie Harper stopped Charles Alexander without a gain. Then, defensive end Jim Stuckey nailed Anderson for a six-yard loss on the 11. Anderson had to pass and tried to connect with Curtis near the five-yard line. However, safety Dwight Hicks reacted and intercepted the ball and got the 49ers out of danger by reaching the 32-yard line before being stopped.

Montana opened the 49er offense with a screen pass to Patton that gained six yards. He came right back with another pass to wide receiver Dwight Clark for a first down on the 44-yard line. On second down, he completed his third straight pass, this time

179

Bengal wide receiver Cris Collinsworth fumbled near the goal line after he was hit by 49er defensive back Eric Wright in the second quarter.

to Solomon on the Cincinnati 47. On third and one, the 49ers brought the crowd to its feet with a wild play. Patton started a run to his right and handed the ball to Solomon coming around. Solomon then lateralled the ball to Montana who threw a 14-yard pass to Young for a first down on the 33-yard line.

Turning to the ground game, the 49ers got to the 15 on three running plays. Now they were threatening. Montana then connected with a 14-yard pass to Solomon on the one-yard line. San Francisco fans were now up and cheering. Montana didn't give them a chance to stop. He dove over on the next play for a touchdown. Ray Wersching added the extra point that gave the Niners a 7–0 lead. The drive covered 68 yards in eleven plays and took almost seven minutes. When the first period ended less than six

minutes later, neither team had come close to scoring any more.

The first time the 49ers got the ball in the second quarter, they struck again. They did so commandingly as Montana masterfully directed them on a 92-yard touchdown drive in twelve plays. He did so by coming through with two key third down passes that kept the drive going. The first came back on the San Francisco 11-yard line. Facing a third and seven, Montana connected with Solomon on a 20-yard pass to the 31. When the Niners reached the Cincinnati 43, Montana analyzed a third-and-six play. He threw a 12-yard completion to Clark and a big first down on the 31.

Changing his attack, Montana reverted to the run. Three running attempts advanced the ball to the 19. A personal foul on the Bengals gave the 49ers a first down on the

11-yard line. San Francisco was primed to score again. Montana didn't wait. He sent his big fullback Earl Cooper out on a delayed pass and looped the ball into his arms for a touchdown. Wersching added the conversion that sent San Francisco in front, 14–0.

A happy Earl Cooper spikes the ball after scoring the 49ers' second touchdown in the second period.

Cincinnati couldn't do much, following the kickoff. After getting one first down, they had to punt. There was only 4:11 left in the first half when the 49ers took over on their own 34-yard line. They weren't going to sit on the ball either. Montana came out throwing and hit Clark with a 17-yard pass on the Bengal 49. Two runs by Patton earned a first down on the 39. Then on a key third down play, Montana fired a 10-yard pass to Clark for a first down on the 25. There was now 1:11 showing on the clock, certainly enough time to score. Three quick plays later, the 49ers had reached the 14. Montana then went to the air and hit Solomon with a nine-yard pass on the five-yard line. San Francisco fans were screaming for another touchdown. It never came. Montana's next two passes into the end zone were unsuccessful. They had to settle for a 22-yard field goal by Wersching, which increased the 49ers' lead to 17–0.

There were 15 seconds remaining when Wersching kicked off. Archie Griffin couldn't handle Wersching's squib kick and fumbled. Milt McColl grabbed the loose ball on the four-yard line and the 49ers had another chance to score. There were five seconds left—time for another play or possibly two. An illegal procedure penalty set the Niners back to the nine-yard line. They didn't waste any time sending in Wersching to attempt a 26-yard field goal. He delivered, sending the 49ers into the dressing room with a 20–0 halftime edge.

San Francisco clearly dominated the opening half action. They piled up 208 yards to Cincinnati's 99; they had a big edge in first downs, 15 to seven; and Montana was outplaying Anderson. The young Montana, who appeared cool, hit on 12 of 18 passes for 132 yards and a touchdown. Anderson was eight of 14 for 83 yards and threw an interception at a critical point of the game.

Cincinnati looked like a different team when they got the second half kickoff on the 17-yard line. Alexander got them started with a 13-yard run to the 30. A five-yard penalty on the play earned five more yards. On a third and four from the 41, Anderson fired a 19-yard pass to wide receiver Steve Kreider on the San Francisco 40. After Johnson gained five yards, the Bengals

Quarterback Ken Anderson scored Cincinnati's first touchdown early in the third period.

pulled a trick play of their own. Anderson then completed a 13-yard pass to Curtis. When the 49ers were called for a face mask penalty on the play, the Bengals found themselves on the 11-yard line.

The Bengals needed a touchdown to get back in the game. Two running plays got them to the four-yard line. On third down, Anderson faded to pass. Finding no one open, he ran up the middle for a touchdown. They went 83 yards on nine plays. Breech's conversion cut the deficit to 20–7.

After San Francisco couldn't do anything the second time they had the ball, Cincinnati took over at midfield with 6:53 remaining in the third period. The Bengals had

time and excellent field position to strike again. They didn't get off to a good start. A holding penalty pushed them back to the 41. On second down, Anderson had to throw. He decided to go deep and connected on a 49-yard bomb to wide receiver Cris Collinsworth on the San Francisco 14.

Bengal fans were thinking touchdown. Anderson gave them hope with another big third down play. On third and eleven from the 15-yard line, he hit Ross with a 10-yard pass on the five. Needing only a yard for a first down, Cincinnati went for it. Johnson came through for two yards. The Bengals were only three yards away from a touchdown. Johnson carried again and got to the one-yard line. He tried again and was stopped for no gain. Anderson then tried to hit Alexander with a quick touchdown pass, but linebacker Dan Bunz halted him at the line of scrimmage. The Bengals were down to their final play. Would they go for it or settle for a field goal? They decided to go for the touchdown. The crowd was deafening. Anderson handed the ball to Johnson who charged up the middle. He didn't get anywhere. Led by Reynolds and Bunz, Johnson was repelled as the Silverdome shook with cheers. The San Francisco defense had been magnificent. It denied Cincinnati a big touchdown that could have turned the game around.

When the final period began, the Bengals didn't waste any time in scoring. The first time they gained possession of the ball, they drove for a touchdown. Anderson sparked them on a 53-yard drive that consumed only seven plays. Five of the plays were passes and Anderson connected on four of them. The last one was a four-yard touchdown toss to Ross. Breech kicked the extra point that narrowed San Francisco's margin to 20–14.

The 49ers had to do something. They were offensively inept in the third period, never producing a single first down. There was 9:57 left in the game when they got the ball after the kickoff on the 27-yard line. They didn't begin encouragingly. Montana's first pass was incomplete. Then the 49ers were penalized five yards. Undaunted, Montana came back. He rolled to his right and hit wide receiver Mike Wilson with a 22-yard pass on the 44. The completion seemed to ignite the 49ers. Running the ball seven consecutive times, the Niners got to the Cincinnati 23-yard line. On fourth and five, they decided to send in Wersching for a 40-yard field goal. The thinking was that a field goal at this point was equivalent to a touchdown. Wersching came through with a clutch kick that stretched San Francisco's margin to 23–14.

Cincinnati now needed two scores to win—a touchdown and a field goal. The clock was their enemy. There was 5:14 left when they put Wersching's kickoff in play on the 22-yard line. Immediately, Anderson went to the air. Cornerback Eric Wright, however, was also thinking pass. He intercepted a pass intended for Collinsworth, and Cincinnati's hopes faded along with it. With the ball back on the 22-yard line, all San Francisco had to do was work the clock. Montana did so by calling six straight running plays, finally running out on the six-yard line. With just 1:57 left in the game, Wersching practically clinched San Francisco's victory by booting a 23-yard field goal to give the 49ers a 26–14 bulge.

Cincinnati wouldn't quit, however. Even though only 1:51 remained to play and the Bengals were 74 yards away from a touchdown, Anderson went after it. He threw six consecutive passes and completed every one of them. The final was a three-yard-touchdown flip to Ross for Cincinnati's third and final touchdown. Breech added the point after to make the final score of Super Bowl XVI, 26–21.

The San Francisco dressing room wasn't disorderly with excitement. Rather, there was a controlled atmosphere of jubilation. It seemed to be an extension of the confidence the 49ers had played with all season long. The first telephone call that Walsh received was an important one. It was from President Reagan, who at one time during his movie career played a Notre Dame football player named George Gipp in the film, *The Knute Rockne Story.*

"Hello, Coach Walsh; this is Ronald Reagan," the voice at the other end of the phone said.

"I thought it might be," answered Walsh.

"I just wanted to tell you a couple of Californians want to congratulate you and the entire team. And you might tell Joe Montana and the fellas that they really did win one for the Gipper."

"I think Joe was thinking of the Gipper when he won that one. Thank you very much, I enjoyed shaking your hand the other night and I was hoping I would receive a call from you in about two weeks. I'll tell Joe about the Gipper. Thank you very, very much."

Walsh was indeed happy. Although he isn't an overemotional person, one could sense his joy.

"This is the greatest moment of my life," said Walsh. "This is the ultimate of my ca-

Victorious 49er players carry coach Bill Walsh on their shoulders following 26–21 triumph.

reer. I cannot conceive of a more satisfying moment, to have taken a team and in three years develop it into a Super Bowl champion. It is a rare moment for me to work with such a great group of men and win a championship. This is a group of men who do not have great talent. But they have great inspiration. No one could take us this year. This is the highlight of my life. Anything can happen now.''

Gregg was quite subdued in the Cincinnati dressing room. His players dressed qui-

etly, trying to reflect on why they lost.

"The difference in the game was our four turnovers," Gregg observed. "You don't help a team as good as San Francisco with four turnovers and expect to win. You can't spot a team like the 49ers 20 points. We had an opportunity right off the bat to score. When we didn't, I think the players started thinking about what could have been instead of what was. After that, it looked as if we were trying not to make mistakes.''

Anderson felt much the same way. De-

A happy Bill Walsh playfully hugs Jack "Hacksaw" Reynolds in the 49er dressing room.

spite the defeat, he set a couple of passing records. One was the most completions, 25, and the other was the highest completion percentage, 73.5.

"We had three opportunities to score and that was the key right there," said Anderson. "On the first interception, it was just a poor throw. I thought we could come back. We decided in the second half that we had to get down to business. We started to play then. When we got that second touchdown, I thought we could come back.

"We just made mistakes. You can't play in the Super Bowl and have that many turnovers and expect to win. Hey, I think I'm going to wake up tomorrow. It's not the end of the world. They won it and they get the credit."

Most of the credit went to Montana. He was voted the game's Most Valuable Player. He displayed amazing calm in becoming the youngest quarterback to win a Super Bowl.

"The feeling of winning this game hasn't really sunk in yet," said Montana. "I have a lot of emotion about it right now, but I don't think that it will hit me until maybe when I get showered and dressed. I think we were doing everything we wanted to do. Things were going our way when we jumped off to a good lead and let them play the type of ball we wanted them to. Fortunately, we got ahead far enough.

"The night before the game I rested well. I just ordered room service and took it easy. The two-week delay is one of the toughest things to deal with in getting ready. But it really felt good when we finally got the chance to play the game. I really was surprised I was named the MVP because I didn't think I did that much out there. Probably the whole offensive line should get the award. They did a hell of a job out there today."

That's how low-key Montana is . . .

185

Index

A

Adderley, Herb, 4, 19, 20-21, 123, *illus.* 6
Alexander, Charles, 178, 180
Allen, George, 76, 78-79, 80, 84, 124, *illus.* 78
Alworth, Lance, 3, 72
Anderson, Donny, 17
Anderson, Ken, 174, 176, 178, 180, 181, 182, 183, 185, *illus.* 181
Anderson, Larry, 157, 158, 161
Andrews, George, 156
Andrie, George, 58
Arbanas, Fred, 7
Armstrong, Otis, 131
Arnsparger, Bill, 90, 96, *illus.* 95
Atkinson, George, 121, 122
Atlanta Falcons, 15
Austin, Bill, 12

B

Bahr, Chris, 156, 158, 159, 160, 167, 168, 169, 170, 171
Baker, Ralph, 30
Baltimore Colts, 22-23, 36, 46-59, 60, 65, 150
Banaszak, John, 143, 158
Banaszak, Pete, 16, 123, 124, 127, *illus.* 124
Barnes, Benny,. 146, 147, 149
Bass, Glenn, 3
Bass, Mike, 87
Baugh, Sammy, 122
Bell, Bobby, 37
Bell, Theo, 146, 147
Bengtson, Phil, 12, 13
Beverly, Randy, 30, 53
Biletnikoff, Fred, 20-21, 122, 123, 127
Bird, Roger, 19
Birdwell, Dan, 18
Blair, Matt, 104
Blanda, George, 16, 19, *illus.* 10
Bleier, Rocky, 98, 103, 104, 106, 113, *illus.* 110, 143, 145, 147, 156, 157, 160
Blount, Mel, 144, 145
Boozer, Emerson, 25

Braase, Ordell, 28
Bradshaw, Terry, 98, 101, 103, 104, 106, 112, 113, 114, 115, 116-117, 123, 138-140, 141, 142, 143, 144, 145, 146, 147, 148, 149, 151, 152, 154, 155, 156, 157, 158, 159, 160, 161, 163, *illus.* 102, 111, 143, 146, 151
Bragg, Mike, 86
Branch, Cliff, 122, 123, 168, 170
Breech, Jim, 178, 181, 182
Breunig, Bob, 135, 146
Briscoe, Marlin, 90, 94
Brodie, John, 81
Brown, Bill, 104
Brown, Eddie, 159
Brown, Jim, 155
Brown, Larry (Redskins), 79, 83, 85, *illus.* 79, 81, 83
Brown, Larry, (Steelers), 104, 113
Brown, Paul, 176
Brown, Terry, 104
Brown, Tom, 4
Brown, Willie, 126, *illus.* 123
Brundige, Bill, 87
Bryant, Bobby, 123
Bryant, Cullen, 155, 156, 157, 158, *illus.* 162
Buchanan, Buck, 3, 37
Buffalo Bills, 2
Bulaich, Norm, 48, 57, *illus.* 48
Bunz, Dan, 182
Buoniconti, Nick, 69, 74, 86, 94, *illus.* 68

C

Caffey, Leroy, 4
Capelletti, John, 155
Campfield, Billy, 167
Carmichael, Harold, 165, 167
Carolan, Reg, 3
Carson, Bud, 155
Casper, Dave, 122, 123, 125, 126, 164, *illus.* 120
Chandler, Bob, 164, 170, *illus.* 170, 172
Chandler, Don, 7, 18, 20

187

Chavous, Barney, *illus.* 136
Chester, Raymond, 171
Chicago Bears, 16, 28, 76, 128, 142
Cincinnati Bengals, 174-185
Clark, Dwight, 178, 179, 180
Clark, Ken, 160
Clark, Mike, 57, 72, 73, *illus.* 51
Clark, Monte, 90, 91
Cleveland Browns, 2, 28, 37, 154, 165
Cole, Robin, 158, *illus.* 145, 162
Collier, Joe, 2
Collier, Mike, 116
Collinsworth, 181, *illus.* 179
Colquitt, Craig, 147
Cooper, Earl, 180, *illus.* 180
Corral, Frank, 157, 158
Cox, Fred, 103, 104
Csonka, Larry, 67-68, 72, 73, 74, 83, 84, 85, 86, 87, 91, 92, 94, 96, 104, *illus.* 64, 66, 69, 89, 91
Cunningham, Bennie, 140, 157
Currie, Dan, 7
Curtis, Isaac, 178, 181
Curtis, Mike, 51, 59, *illus.* 27, 29

D

Dale, Carroll, 3, 16, 18
Dallas Cowboys, 2, 10, 46-75, 78, 79, 83, 92, 93, 108-117, 128-137, 138-149, 150, 152, 153, 154, 155, 165, 167
Dallas Texans, 2
Danahy, Jack, 42, 43
Daniels, Clem, 16
Davidson, Ben, 17-18, *illus.* 16
Davis, Al, 14-16, 127, 164, 165, 166, 172
Davis, Clarence, 123, 125, 126, *illus.* 118
Davis, Sam, *illus.* 139
Davis, Willie, 4, 123, *illus.* 6, 19
Dawson, Donald, 40, 43, 165
Dawson, Len, 2, 4, 7, 17, 24, 36, 40-44, 45, 125, 130, 165, *illus.* 8, 34, 36, 39, 40, 42, 44, 45
Dean, Fred, 176, 177
Dee, Johnny, 7
Den Herder, Vern, 94
Dennard, Preston, 155
Denver Broncos, 128-137, 152
Detroit Lions, 48, 49
Dilts, Bucky, 134
Ditka, Mike, 74, *illus.* 71
Dixon, Hewritt, 123, *illus.* 14, 19
Dolbin, Jack, 130, 135
Dorsett, Tony, 131, 134, 142, 143, 146, *illus.* 132, 144, 148
Dowler, Boyd, 3, 7, 9, 16, 19, *illus.* 15
Dryer, Fred, 152, 163
Dubenion, Elbert, 3
Duncan, Jim, 58, 59

Dungy, Tony, 147
DuPree, Billy Joe, 131, 134, 146, 147

E

Edwards, Glen, 113, *illus.* 117
Edwards, Herman, 168, 172
Eischeid, Mike, 18, 103
Eller, Carl, 38, 96-97, 103, 104
Elmendorf, Dave, 158
Evans, Norm, 91, 92
Ewbank, Weeb, 24-25, 28, 32, 33, *illus.* 32

F

Fears, Tom, 12
Fernandez, Manny, 86, 91, *illus.* 72, 81
Ferragamo, Vince, 150, 153, 155, 156, 157, 158, 159, 160, 162, *illus.* 152
Finks, Jim, 123-124
Fitzgerald, John, 112, 134
Fleming, Marv, 16, 18, 87, 90, *illus.* 65
Flores, Tom, 164, 166, 172, 173
Flowers, Richmond, 58
Foley, Tim, *illus.* 93
Foreman, Chuck, 104, 120, 121, 122, 124, 125
France, Doug, 151, 152
Francis, Russ, 140
Franklin, Tony, 169, 171
Fritsch, Toni, 113
Fugett, Jean, 112, 113
Furness, Steve, 143, *illus.* 115

G

Gardin, Ron, 57
Gardner, Larry, 49
Garrett, Mike, 44, *illus.* 3, 37
Garrison, Walt, 49-51, 68, 69, 70, *illus.* 64, 67, 69, 70
Gerela, Roy, 103, 104, 114, 115, 116, 141, 143, 145, 147, *illus.* 114
Gifford, Frank, *illus.* 44
Gilliam, Joe, 101
Gilliam, John, 96, 103, 104, *illus.* 93
Grabowski, Jim, 17
Graham, Art, 3
Grant, Bud, 36-37, 88, 94, 101-102, 103, 120, 126
Grantham, Larry, 49
Green Bay Packers, ix, xiv-21, 25, 29, 38, 76, 78, 79, 87, 91, 123, 127, 153, 160
Greene, Joe, 98, 101, 107, 110, 111, 149, 153, 154, 155

Greenwood, L. C., 98, 107, 111, 112, 114, 149, *illus.* 100, 141, 144, 157
Gregg, Forrest, 21, 174, 176, 183
Griese, Bob, 24, 60, 65-67, 72, 73, 80, 81-82, 83, 84, 85, 86, 87, 90, *illus.* 62, 64, 65
Griffin, Archie, 180
Grossman, Randy, 113, 140, 143, 147
Gumbel, Bryant, 172
Guy, Ray, 125

H

Haden, Pat, 150, 153, 155
Hadl, John, 24
Halas, George, 76, 98, 142, 156
Hall, Willie, 125
Ham, Jack, 141, 142, *illus.* 144
Harper, Willie, 178
Harrah, Dennis, 152
Harris, Cliff, 57, 110-111, 116, 130, 141
Harris, Franco, 98, 100-101, 103, 104, 106, 111, 112, 113, 116, 140, 142, 143, 144, 145, 146, 147, 149, 155, 156, 157, 158, 160, *illus.* 99, 109, 113, 139, 159
Harris, Leroy, 167, *illus.* 167
Harris, Joe, 157
Harrison, Reggie, 115
Havrilak, Sam, 58
Hayes, Bob, 52, *illus.* 50, 74
Hayes, Lester, *illus.* 165
Headrick, Sherrill, 2
Hecker, Norb, 12
Hegman, Mike, 144, 145, *illus.* 134
Henderson, John, *illus.* 41
Henderson, Thomas, 140, 141, 144, 149, *illus.* 128-129
Hendricks, Ted, 51, 55, 169, *illus.* 55
Hennigan, Charlie, 3
Herrera, Efren, 135
Hicks, Dwight, 177, 178
Hilgenberg, Wally, 104, 123
Hill, Calvin, 49, 51, 68, 69, 71, 72, *illus.* 55, 75
Hill, Tony, 134, 142, 144, 146
Hilton, Roy, *illus.* 54
Hinton, Eddie, 57, 59
Holmes, Ernie, 110, 111
Holub, E. J., 2
Hoopes, Mitch, 114, 116
Hornung, Paul, 9, 12, 17, 63
Houston, Jim, 37
Houston Oilers, 154, 155, 164
Howard, Ron, 116
Howley, Chuck, 57, 58, 72, 73, *illus.* 68, 75
Hudson, Jim, 26
Hughes, Randy, 134, 135
Hunt, Lamar, ix, xiv, 2

J

Jackson, Tommy, 135
Jaworski, Ron, 165, 167, 169, 170, 171, 172, *illus.* 167, 168
Jensen, Derrick, 167, *illus.* 171
Jessie, Ron, 155
Jeter, Bob, 4
Jodat, Jim, 156
Johnson, Bill, 176, 180, 181, 182
Johnson, Butch, 131, 133, 136, 137, 143, 147
Johnson, Curley, 30
Johnson, Pete, 174, 176, 178
Johnson, Ron, 84, 146, *illus.* 144
Jones, Ed "Too Tall," 130, 136, 144
Jordan, Henry, 4, 6-7, 123, *illus.* 20
Jordan, Lee Roy, 58, *illus.* 69

K

Kansas City Chiefs, ix, xiv-9, 16, 17, 25, 34-45, 60, 65, 130, 133, 165
Kapp, Joe, 36, 37, 39-40, 45, *illus.* 35
Keating, Tom, 18, *illus.* 17, 121
Kiick, Jim, 67-68, 72, 73, 83, 84, 86, 94, *illus.* 64, 66, 68
Kilmer, Billy, 83-84, 85, 86, *illus.* 80, 82, 83
King, Kenny, 164, 168, 170, 173
Kolen, Mike, *illus.* 70
Kramer, Jerry, 7, 21
Kreider, Steve, 180
Krepfle, Keith, 171
Kuechenberg, Bob, 91
Kyle, Aaron, 135, 136, 145

L

Laidlaw, Scott, 146, *illus.* 142, 145
Lakes, Roland, 49
Lambert, Jack, 155, 156, 160, 163, *illus.* 105, 140, 141, 142, 143, 146, 157, 162
Lamonica, Daryle, 4, 16-17, 18, 19, 20, 21, 24, 123, *illus.* 10, 13, 14, 20
Landry, Tom, 46, 48, 49, 52, 59, 69, 74, 81, 120, 132-133, 146, 149, *illus.* 48
Langer, Jim, 91-92
Lanier, Willie, 37
Larsen, Greg, 38
Lawrence, Amos, 178, *illus.* 177
Layne, Bobby, 26
Lee, Bob, 127
Lewis, D. D., 116, 144, *illus.* 110
Lewis, Frank, 112
Lilly, Bob, 59, 68, *illus.* 63
Litman, Joe, 42-43, 44
Little, Larry, 90, 91, 92

INDEX

Logan, Jerry, 51
Lombardi, Vince, xiv, 2, 5-6, 7, 9, 10, 12-14, 15,
   21, 63, 76, 79, 91, 96, 160, 166, 172, *illus.* 1
Los Angeles Rams, 108, 111, 125, 150, 151, 152,
   153, 154, 155, 156, 157, 158, 159, 160, 161, 163
Lott, Ronnie, 177, 178
Lurtsema, Bob, *illus.* 102
Lynch, Jim, 37
Lytle, Rob, 136, *illus.* 131

M

McCafferty, Don, 54, 59, *illus.* 46
McClanahan, Brent, 121, 125
McClinton, Curtis, 7
McColl, Milt, 180
McCutcheon, Lawrence, 157, 158, 159
McDole, Ron, 76, 78
McGee, Max, ix, 7, 9, 20
McLean, Scooter, 63
McNeil, Fred, 125
McVea, Warren, *illus.* 39
Mackey, John, 30, 55, 57, *illus.* 50
Madden, John, 118, 125, 127, *illus.* 126
Malavasi, Ray, 150, 155, 158, 161
Mandich, Jim, 86, 90, 94
Mann, Errol, 125, 126, 127
Marchibroda, Ted, 79
Marshall, Jim, 38, 103, 123, 124, *illus.* 37
Martin, Bob, 164
Martin, Harvey, 130, 134, 135, 136, 137, 144,
   illus. 128-129
Martin, Rod, 167, 171, 172
Matte, Tom, 30
Matuszak, John, 124, 166, 172, *illus.* 168
Mays, Jerry, *illus.* 35
Mercein, Chuck, 17
Mercer, Mike, 7
Miami Dolphins, 60-97, 153, 155
Michaels, Lou, 25-27, 28, 29, 30
Michaels, Walt, 25
Miller, Bill, 19, 21
Miller, Fred, 28, *illus.* 28
Miller, Red, 131-132, 135, 136, 137
Miller, Willie, 155
Minnesota Vikings, 15, 34-45, 46, 88-107, 108,
   118-127, 128, 164, 165
Mitchell, Tom, 53
Mitchell, Willie, 9
Montana, Joe, 174, 176, 177, 178, 179, 180, 182,
   185
Montgomery, Wilbert, 165, 167, *illus.* 165, 169
Moore, Wayne, 91
Morrall, Earl, 24, 25, 27, 29, 30, 53-54, 58, 59,
   80, 81, 82, *illus.* 26, 54

Morris, Mercury, 73, 83, 85, 91, 92, 94, *illus.* 60,
   91
Morton, Craig, 46, 48-49, 52, 58, 59, 81, 131,
   133, 134, 135, 136, 137, *illus.* 50, 52, 54
Moses, Haven, 130, 131, 135
Mosher, Curt, 50
Mullins, Gerry, *illus.* 99

N

Nairn, Harvey, 31
Namath, Joe, 4, 17, 22-24, 25-27, 28, 29-30, 31-
   32, 33, 133, *illus.* 22-23, 24, 25, 27, 28, 29, 31,
   32, 140
Namath, John, 33, *illus.* 31, 32
Neeley, Ralph, 46, 49
Nelson, Terry, 158
Newhouse, Robert, 114, 134, 136, 143, 144, *illus.*
   115, 141
New Orleans Saints, 15
New York Giants, 101, 130
New York Jets, 22-33, 36, 65, 96, 133, 150
Niland, John, *illus.* 69, 71
Nitschke, Ray, 4, 123
Nolan, Dick, 81
Noll, Chuck, 98, 100, 101, 102, 149, 153, 155,
   160
Nowatzke, Tom, 59, *illus.* 54
Nunley, Frank, 49

O

Oakland Raiders, 10-21, 22, 25, 40, 92, 101, 110,
   118-127, 141, 164, 165, 166, 167, 168, 169, 170,
   171, 172, 173
O'Brien, Jim, 58, 59, *illus.* 56-57
Odoms, Riley, 130, 131, 135, 140
Orr, Jimmy, 53
Osborn, Dave, 45, 103
Otto, Jim, *illus.* 14
Owens, Burgess, *illus.* 165

P

Page, Alan, 38, 100, 103, 124
Parker, Rodney, 166
Pastorini, Dan, 123, 164
Patton, Ricky, 178, 179, 180
Peacock, Elvis, 155
Pearson, Drew, 108, 112, 116, 131, 142, 143, 144,
   145, 147
Pearson, Preston, 112-113, 146
Perkins, Ray, 174
Perry, Rod, 159

190

Philadelphia Eagles, 164-173
Philbin, Gerry, *illus.* 26
Pitts, Elijah, 7, 9, 17
Pittsburgh Steelers, 80, 98-117, 122, 127, 138-149, 150-163
Plunkett, Jim, 164, 165, 166, 167, 168, 169, 170, 171, 172, 173, *illus.* 170
Prudhomme, Remi, 44
Pugh, Jethro, 58, 60, 130, *illus.* 53, 128-129

R

Radakovich, Dan, 155
Ralston, John, 131
Rashad, Ahmad, 121
Rauch, John, 15, 16
Reagan, President Ronald, 182
Reed, Oscar, 94, 96
Reeves, Dan, 59
Renfro, Mel, 57, 58
Rentzel, Lance, 52
Reynolds, Jack, 155, 176, 177, 182
Richards, Golden, 112, 131, 136
Richardson, Willie, 53
Rizzo, Joe, *illus.* 132
Robbie, Joe, 60, 63-64, 65, 88, 89, 108
Robinson, Dave, 4, 12, 19, 123
Robinson, Johnny, 4, 34, 43, 44, *illus.* 41
Rooney, Art, 98, 103, 106, 107, 148, *illus.* 106, 156
Rosenbloom, Carroll, 63, 84-85, 150
Ross, Dan, 176, 178, 181, 182
Rowe, Dave, 124
Rozelle, Pete, 85, 108, 147, 165, 166, 172, *illus.* 106
Rubin, Bob, 151
Rucker, Reggie, *illus.* 49
Russell, Andy, 114
Rutigliano, Sam, 176

S

St. Louis Cardinals, 46
Sample, Johnny, 53
San Diego Chargers, 16, 164, 165
San Francisco 49ers, 46, 71, 81, 164, 174-185
Sauer, George, 30, 32
Schaaf, Jim, 41-42
Schultz, John, 135
Scott, Jake, 87, 90, 96, *illus.* 77, 83
Septien, Rafael, 144, 146, 147
Shell, Art, 123, 141, 144, 146
Shell, Donnie, 156, 158
Sheridan, Danny, 129
Sherman, Allie, 129

Shula, Don, 27, 28, 54, 60, 64-65, 68, 75, 79-82, 84-85, 87, 88, 89-90, *illus.* 78, 84, 85
Silva, Fred, 156
Simpson, O. J., 84
Sistrunk, Oits, 124, *illus.* 125
Smith, Billy Ray, 28
Smith, Bubba, 28
Smith, Charlie, 166
Smith, Jackie, 146, 149
Smith, Jim, 159
Smith, Ron, 158, 159
Snedecker, Jeff, 30, *illus.* 25
Snell, Matt, 25, 30, 96
Solomon, Freddie, 178, 179, 180
Spagnola, John, 167
Spurrier, Steve, 81
Stabler, Ken, 118, 120, 122-123, 124, 125-126, 127, 164, *illus.* 119
Stallworth, John, 112, 139, 142, 143, 144, 145, 149, 155, 157, 159, 160, 161, 162, *illus.* 154
Stanfill, Bill, 90, 94, *illus.* 80
Starr, Bart, ix, xiv-3, 7, 9, 16, 18, 19, 20, *illus.* 5, 17
Staubach, Roger, 46, 60, 71, 72, 74, 75, 81, 93, 108, 112, 113, 114, 115, 131, 134, 135, 136, 138, 142, 143, 144, 145, 146, 147, 155, *illus.* 66, 72, 74, 130, 133, 148
Stenerud, Jan, 39, 44, *illus.* 38
Stram, Hank, ix, xiv, 2, 3, 4, 38-40, 42, 43, *illus.* ix, 42, 43
Stuckey, Jim, 178
Sullivan, Dan, 26, 27
Sutherland, Doug, 103, 124
Swann, Lynn, 110-111, 112, 113, 114, 115, 116, 117, 121, 139, 142, 144, 145, 146, 147, 149, 155, 156, 157, 158, 161, *illus.* 109
Swearingen, Fred, 147

T

Talbert, Diron, 76
Tampa Bay Buccaneers, 150, 151, 152, 153, 155
Tarkenton, Fran, 92-93, 96, 101, 111, 112, 121, 122, 125, 127, *illus.* 100, 105
Tatum, Jack, 164
Taylor, Charley, *illus.* 78, 82
Taylor, Jim, 6, 7, 12, 17
Taylor, Lionel, 155
Taylor, Otis, 3, 44, *illus.* 6
Thomas, Duane, 49, 51-52, 58, 59, 60, 62-63, 68, 69, 71, 72, 75, *illus.* 52, 69, 70, 73, 74
Thomas, J. T., 115, *illus.* 117
Thomas, Pat, 156, 159, 160
Thomas, Skip, *illus.* 121
Thompson, Billy, 135
Thornton, Sydney, 158

191

INDEX

Thurman, Dennis, 147
Thurston, Fuzzy, 7
Turner, Jim, 30, 31, 32, 136
Twilley, Howard, 86
Tyler, Wendel, 155, 156, 157, 158, 159

U

Unitas, Johnny, 24, 26, 28, 32, 52, 53, 57, 58, 59, *illus.* 53, 58
Upchurch, Rick, 130, 136
Upshaw, Gene, 123, 172, *illus.* 13, 126, 141

V

Valley, Wayne, 15
Van Brocklin, Norm, 13
Van Eeghen, Mark, 123, 125, 168, 170
Vermeil, Dick, 173
Verser, David, 178
Villapiano, Phil, 164
Vince Lombardi Trophy, 166, 172
Voight, Stu, 127
Volk, Rick, 51, 59, *illus.* 49

W

Waddy, Billy, 155, 158, 159
Wagner, Mike, 104, 116
Walden, Bobby, 103, 104, 116
Walsh, Bill, 174, 178, 182, *illus.* 183, 184
Ward, Gene, 63
Warfield, Paul, 65, 66, 67, 72, 90, *illus.* 68

Washington, Mark, 116, 135, *illus.* 109
Washington Redskins, 76-87
Waters, Charlie, 130, 143, *illus.* 66, 72
Webster, Mike, 156
Weese, Norris, 135, 136, *illus.* 132
Wells, Warren, *illus.* 12, 13
Werblin, Sonny, 15, 23
Wersching, Ray, 179, 180, 182
West, Charlie, 44
White, Dwight, 98, 111, 114, 143, *illus.* 105, 117, 154
White, Randy, 130, 134, 136, 147, *illus.* 128-129
White, Sammie, 121, 122, 127, *illus.* 121
Widby, Ron, 57
Williams, Howie, *illus.* 15
Williamson, Carlton, 177
Williamson, Fred, 3-4
Wilson, Ben, 17, *illus.* 16
Wilson, George, 5, 63, 64
Wilson, Mike, 182
Winston, Dennis, 147
Winston, Roy, *illus.* 91
Wood, Willie, ix, 4, 7
Woodard, Milt, 2, 29
Wright, Eric, 177, 182, *illus.* 179
Wright, George, *illus.* 58

Y

Yepremiam, Garo, 73, 87, 94
Young, Charlie, 177, 179
Young, Dick, 31
Youngblood, Jack, 155

192